CULTURAL INSIGHTS
FOR CHRISTIAN LEADERS

D1378221

MISSION
in Global Community

SCOTT W. SUNQUIST
AND AMOS YONG,
SERIES EDITORS

The Mission in Global Community series is designed to reach college students and those interested in learning more about responsible mission involvement. Written by faculty and graduates from Fuller Theological Seminary, the series is designed as a global conversation with stories and perspectives from around the world.

CULTURAL INSIGHTS
FOR CHRISTIAN LEADERS

New Directions for Organizations
Serving God's Mission

DOUGLAS McCONNELL

Baker Academic
a division of Baker Publishing Group
Grand Rapids, Michigan

© 2018 by Douglas McConnell

Published by Baker Academic
a division of Baker Publishing Group
PO Box 6287, Grand Rapids, MI 49516-6287
www.bakeracademic.com

Printed in the United States of America

All rights reserved. No part of this publication may be reproduced, stored in a retrieval system, or transmitted in any form or by any means—for example, electronic, photocopy, recording—without the prior written permission of the publisher. The only exception is brief quotations in printed reviews.

Library of Congress Cataloging-in-Publication Data
Names: McConnell, Douglas, 1951– author.
Title: Cultural insights for Christian leaders : new directions for organizations serving God's mission / Douglas McConnell.
Description: Grand Rapids : Baker Publishing Group, 2018. | Series: Mission in global community | Includes index.
Identifiers: LCCN 2017055470 | ISBN 9780801099656 (pbk.)
Subjects: LCSH: Christianity and culture. | Christian leadership. | Missions.
Classification: LCC BR115.C8 M2625 2018 | DDC 261—dc23
LC record available at https://lccn.loc.gov/2017055470

Unless otherwise indicated, Scripture quotations are from the New Revised Standard Version of the Bible, copyright © 1989, by the Division of Christian Education of the National Council of the Churches of Christ in the United States of America. Used by permission. All rights reserved.

Scripture quotations labeled CEB are from the Common English Bible © 2011 Common English Bible. Used by permission.

Scripture quotations labeled NLT are from the Holy Bible, New Living Translation, copyright © 1996, 2004, 2015 by Tyndale House Foundation. Used by permission of Tyndale House Publishers, Inc., Carol Stream, Illinois 60188. All rights reserved.

The use of italics in Bible quotations is added.

In keeping with biblical principles of creation stewardship, Baker Publishing Group advocates the responsible use of our natural resources. As a member of the Green Press Initiative, our company uses recycled paper when possible. The text paper of this book is composed in part of post-consumer waste.

18 19 20 21 22 23 24   7 6 5 4 3 2 1

To the two most influential missionaries in my life,

Paul G. Hiebert and Janna McConnell.

I am forever grateful for your wisdom
and faithfulness to the gospel.

Contents

Series Preface

A mission leader in 1965, not too long ago, could not have foreseen what mission looks like today. In 1965 nations in the non-Western world were gaining their independence after centuries of Western colonialism. Mission societies from Europe and North America were trying to adjust to the new global realities where Muslim nations, once dominated by the West, no longer granted "missionary visas." The largest mission field, China, was closed. Decolonization, it seemed, was bringing a decline to missionary work in Africa and Asia.

On the home front, Western churches were in decline, and the traditional missionary factories—mainline churches in the West—were struggling with their own identities. Membership was then—and remains—in decline, and missionary vocations were following the same pattern. Evangelical and Pentecostal churches began to surpass mainline churches in mission, and then, just when we thought we understood the new missionary patterns, Brazilians began to go to Pakistan and Malaysians began to evangelize Vietnam and Cambodia. Africans (highly educated and strongly Christian) began to move in great numbers to Europe and North America. Countries that had been closed began to see conversions to Christ, without the aid of traditional mission societies. And in the midst of this rapid transformation of missionary work, the alarm rang out that most Christians in the world were now in Asia, Latin America, and Africa rather than in the West.

What does it mean to be involved in mission in this new world where Christianity has been turned upside down in less than a century?

This series is directed at this new global context for mission. Fuller Theological Seminary, particularly through its School of Intercultural Studies (formerly School of World Mission), has been attentive to trends in global mission for over half a century. In fact, much innovation in mission thinking and practice has emanated from Fuller since Donald McGavran moved from Oregon to California—as the first and founding dean of the then School of World Mission—to apply lessons about church growth learned in India to other areas of the world. Since that time many creative mission professors have provided global leadership in mission thinking: Ralph Winter (unreached people groups), Paul Hiebert (anthropology for mission), Charles Kraft (mission and spiritual dynamics), and Dudley Woodberry (Islamics), among others.

This series provides the most recent global scholarship on key themes in mission, written for a general audience of Christians committed to God's mission. Designed to be student, user, and textbook friendly, each volume contains voices from around the world speaking about the theme, and each chapter concludes with discussion questions so the books can be used for group studies. As the fields of mission are changing, shifting, or shrinking, the discussions connect the church and the world, East and West, North and South, the developed and developing worlds, each crossing cultural, political, social, and religious boundaries in its own way and knitting together people living and serving in various communities, both of faith and of other commitments—this is the contemporary landscape of the mission of God. Enjoy the challenges of each volume and find ways to live into God's mission.

Scott W. Sunquist

Amos Yong

Acknowledgments

After thirteen years in the senior administration of Fuller Theological Seminary, I decided that in the next season of life I would like to get back to full-time teaching and the work of scholarship. I am deeply indebted to President Mark Labberton and Dean Scott Sunquist for the sabbatical to make that transition. Their support and encouragement was a blessing beyond what I had hoped for or planned.

I spoke to my colleagues Amos Yong and Scott Sunquist, the editors of the Mission in Global Community series, about the nature of the series in light of my particular desire to reengage with missiological reflection by reading in the fields of anthropology, leadership, and organizational studies. I suggested the approach I would take and was invited to submit a proposal. After a period of rest, I began several months of reading, studying, and writing a proposal. In the six months that followed the acceptance of the proposal, my reading and writing were increasingly productive, which was a pleasant surprise. Amos and Scott were great encouragers and guides. Thanks to both of you!

I am grateful for Paul G. Hiebert's influence as my teacher, mentor for doctoral studies, fellow missiologist, and friend. His influence on my thought and practice is a treasured resource. My colleagues at Fuller Seminary continue to draw from the deep well of Paul Hiebert's knowledge, and we give thanks for the memory of his life among us.

Janna, my wife of forty-seven years, was a wonderful encourager, editor, critic, and cheerleader during the months of research and writing. She has been my missionary inspiration since November 1969, when, through her witness to the love and redemption that come through Jesus Christ, I found life in him. Part of dedicating my life to Christ was accepting Janna's call to missionary service. In these months of sabbatical we often recounted the joys and challenges of the journey, giving thanks for the faithfulness of God. Thank you for your faithful witness and constant support!

I discovered the wonderful resources available in the Orlando area, especially the libraries of the University of Central Florida and Eastern Florida State College at Cocoa, where the lake next to the library has a sign forbidding the feeding of alligators—a caution quite different from those in our David Allan Hubbard Library at Fuller Pasadena. I was able to use the libraries of Reformed Theological Seminary and Asbury Theological Seminary, finding both places a refuge for study and resources.

A very special thanks goes to my colleagues Marcos Orison Almeida, Judy Fitzmaurice, Katharine Thompson, Melody Wachsmuth, Siew Pik Lim, Joanna Sears Lima, John Azumah, and Nam Chen Chan who contributed greatly to this book by providing significant insights through their case studies. Their contributions highlight the dynamic interaction of culture and organizational leadership from the perspective of missiology. We share a common commitment to the mission of God and a common bond as brothers and sisters in Christ.

I want to especially thank Jim Kinney, Brandy Scritchfield, Eric Salo, and the editorial team from Baker for their helpful critique and suggestions; they were gracious in sharing their significant insights with me. My experience with them and everyone at Baker Publishing Group has been encouraging.

Introduction

Leading a Christian organization is a sacred duty. If you accept the position, you must shoulder the responsibility, and that includes being a learner. Learning will never cease to be important in that role. One seasoned veteran charged that as leaders we should "make new mistakes!" I like that approach for a couple of reasons. First, it recognizes our humanity and, therefore, the inevitability of mistakes. The world is moving quickly, and we are trying our best, but that doesn't mean we lead perfectly. Second, we find hope in learning from our mistakes. Although we will make mistakes, we can and must set a course to learn from them and to do it better next time. Does that mean we should feel free to make mistakes? Not necessarily; instead, we should feel free to learn from others and approach the challenges as a community, not a loner. Learning to lead means learning from others, their mistakes and successes. It also means that fear of failure and the overwhelming pace of change should not paralyze us. We lead in humility, as Christians serving the mission of God, and also in faith that God is trustworthy and gracious.

Leaders today face a tremendous challenge in the increasing influence of the cultures that surround our organizations. We cannot simply learn the ways of a particular culture and then move ahead with confidence. Many cultures are at play, not the least of which is the organizational culture of which we are a part. We must become students of culture so as to lead wisely in an era of globalization. Learning is such a privilege; it is too important to squander. The purpose of this book is to explore what we are learning about culture and the implications for Christian leaders of organizations serving God's mission. In gathering my thoughts for this book, I decided to organize it around a central question: *What are we learning about culture that will help shape, catalyze, and propel our organizations missionally?*

An important element of the Mission in Global Community series is the inclusion of missiological reflection from a diversity of international scholars. My approach was to contact eight of my colleagues living in seven different contexts but working on issues of global concern. I asked them to reflect on the general topic from their unique position as leaders who are also scholars influencing their respective organizations.[1] Each sent me a case study, and I have integrated their stories and insights into the substantive discussion of each chapter. Their contributions highlight the dynamic interaction of culture and organizational leadership from the perspective of missiology.

In emphasizing cultural insights for Christian organizational leaders, this book fills an important gap. Over the past three decades, missionary societies and Christian nonprofit organizations have exerted a great deal of energy in studying leadership. Workshops, formal educational programs, and a broad range of written resources have been produced to assist in the task. I have participated in all three approaches, observing the gains and gaps in our learning along the way. It is gratifying to see the gains. However, a big gap remains in our learning about the effects of culture on organizations and leadership, particularly on the organizational mission in relation to God's mission. I address this by reflecting missiologically, moving from areas that we know to areas that we are learning about, principally in the fields of anthropology, leadership, and organizational studies. To be true to the learning process, I ask not only, "What are we learning?" but also, "What should we be learning?"

Missiology and Related Disciplines

Foundational to the approach of this book is a missiological understanding of the mission of God, which we will refer to as thinking missiologically. Missiology is the integrated study of God's mission from the perspective of Scripture (biblical studies), theology, history, and anthropology (social sciences). Missionary anthropologist Paul Hiebert developed a matrix illustrating these four primary disciplines of missiological studies in two dimensions (fig. 1).[2] The vertical axis recognizes that missiology is concerned with

1. John Azumah's contribution, "The Five Faces of Islam," was originally written for Scholar-Leaders *InSights*. I chose to use it because it brings important insights into the conversation on religious worlds.
2. The works of Paul G. Hiebert considered in this volume are as follows: *Anthropological Insights for Missionaries* (Grand Rapids: Baker, 1985); *Anthropological Reflections on Missiological Issues* (Grand Rapids: Baker, 1994); *Transforming Worldviews: An Anthropological*

understanding the gospel as God's divine revelation, as it is communicated in the particularities of human contexts. The horizontal axis considers reality in reference to time, synchronic being a particular point in time (physical, social, cultural, or spiritual) and diachronic viewing the underlying story (biographical or historical).

Figure 1
Missiology and Related Disciplines

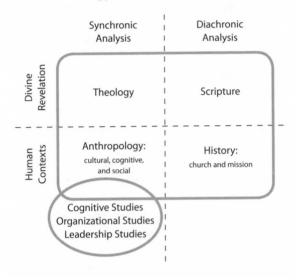

Adapted from Paul G. Hiebert, *The Gospel in Human Contexts: Anthropological Explorations for Contemporary Missions* (Grand Rapids: Baker Academic, 2009), 34.

Our task is to think missiologically about the function of culture in shaping, catalyzing, and propelling organizations and leadership, as illustrated in the lower left quadrant of figure 1. This approach builds on the work of missiologists in contextualizing the gospel in response to the issues raised in different cultures. In considering the contributions of related disciplines, we will pay particular attention to the influence of culture on organizations and leadership as it relates to adapting our organizations to better serve God's mission in the changing contexts of the world.

To do so we will draw primarily on recent studies in the disciplines of cultural and cognitive anthropology, as well as studies in organizations and leadership. Additional input from the work of Christian scholars in the

---

Understanding of How People Change (Grand Rapids: Baker Academic, 2008); and *The Gospel in Human Contexts: Anthropological Explorations for Contemporary Missions* (Grand Rapids: Baker Academic, 2009).

disciplines of psychology, cognitive science, and theology will help us with the missiological considerations. In addressing culture, we will focus first on the organizational culture (internal) and, second, on the societal culture (external) usually associated with the organization's national or geographic location.[3] Beyond the external or dominant culture, many other subcultures exercise influence—even vie for a place—in the contextual landscape; collectively, these will form the third culture of our focus. The fourth domain is religious culture, increasingly an influence on Christian organizations and leaders globally.

One of the most fruitful elements of the study to me personally was taking the time to understand the role of individuals in the process of culture formation. I always approached the subject primarily from the role of the group, leaving me with the question, What about individuals? In the end, every group is composed of individuals who, no matter how much they are products of their cultural contexts, are also unique and created in the image of God. I found the most plausible explanations in the field of cognitive studies, with support from colleagues who share my evangelical Christian faith and my recognition of the significance of the findings. As you think through the separate roles of human nature and culture, my hope is that you will also conclude that these two elements, nature and nurture, are inseparable and, therefore, interdependent. In my case, this realization has given me an even deeper appreciation of the wonder of God's creation.

Chapter Outlines

Chapter 1 addresses the issues of thinking missiologically about our organizational mission in the light of God's mission. It begins by establishing a missiological approach personally and collectively based on the mission of God. It then moves to a missiological understanding of the wonderful mosaic of organizations as they relate to God's mission. Next it introduces leadership from the perspective of missiologists who have considered the role of leaders and followers. The chapter concludes with a case study on institutional leadership from the perspective of a Latin American leader, followed by a review of and reflection on the role of missiology in the tough missional decisions faced by leaders.

3. The choice of organizational and societal cultural categories reflects the common usage in leadership and organizational studies (e.g., for more on the GLOBE study of sixty-two societies focusing on culture, leadership, and organization, see below in chapter 7, under the heading "The GLOBE Project").

Chapter 2 builds on our understanding of culture by introducing the contribution of cognitive studies in explaining human contexts. We will consider new insights emerging in the discussion of human nature and culture as they relate to organizations and the formation of worldview. Studies on the storage and transmission of human knowledge contribute to our insights on how culture relates to individual processes as well as those of groups. Next is a case study on the importance of addressing the needs of the whole person written by an Australian medical doctor and international mission leader. The final section is a review of and reflection on the issues of culture and human nature.

Chapter 3 focuses on members of our organizations as people, human beings who are both physically embodied and culturally embedded. We explore notions of self in recent literature in cognitive studies, providing new possibilities for our care of members, particularly in relating to the people we work among as individuals. The organizational implications of these insights will be highlighted in a case study on children and the mission of God from a founding member of a global network of ministries to children at risk. The chapter concludes by reviewing and reflecting on the notions of self and others from the perspective of organizational leadership.

Chapter 4 explores learning culture from the perspective of imitation and ritual. Introducing the relational process of imitation and the nonverbal means of culture learning provides important insights for leadership development and training programs. This is followed by a case study on ritual from an intercultural leader based in Croatia. Building on the case, the chapter explores the issues of ritual as they relate to organizations and leadership, concluding with a review and reflection of the implications for leaders.

Chapter 5 focuses on the nature of authority. We explore questions of exercising authority, responsibility, and accountability as organizational realities in cultural contexts. Understanding authority raises the concept of trust and how they are two sides of the same coin. Two important contributions from international leaders help to put this into contemporary situations: the first is from the perspective of the president of a theological college in Malaysia, and the second is from an international leader based in Thailand. The chapter concludes with a review and reflection of the critical issues and their implications to intercultural organizations and leaders.

Chapter 6 considers the impact of four major cultures on our organizations and leadership. We begin by identifying religious worlds as a major global force imprinting much of our work as Christian leaders. This is illustrated in a case study looking at Islam as a complex of differing understandings and expressions. The case study is followed by an exploration of societal culture, organizational culture, and subcultures. Thus we consider four worlds that create our intercultural realities. The chapter concludes by reviewing and reflecting on the four worlds around us.

Chapter 7 explores the broader studies of culture and leadership from both a missiological and global perspective. Exploring culture from a systems approach to organizational studies helps to put in context the influences on our organization and leadership. From there a series of global studies on organizational leadership will be introduced as a significant source of new insights and directions. Following the global perspective, a case study in intercultural leadership from a Malaysian leader introduces the concept of interculturality. We then consider the concept of interculturality missiologically, concluding in a review and reflection of the relevant issues applied missionally to Christian organizations.

In chapter 8 we review and reflect on the seven primary concepts of the previous chapters as they relate to the role of leaders of organizations serving God's mission. Writing this chapter offered me an opportunity to think missiologically about the implications of what we are learning from the disciplines of cognitive, organizational, and leadership studies, from the perspective of an organizational leader.

James MacGregor Burns, in reflecting on the rationale for his classic book *Leadership*, bolstered my concern to deal with the theoretical issues of culture in his introduction: "And, when we return from moral and causal questions to ways of practical leadership, we might find that there is nothing more practical than sound theory, if we can fashion it."[4] I do not "fashion theory" in this book, as it is intended for thoughtful practitioners. Yet in offering "cultural insights for Christian leaders," we consider many of the theoretical foundations of the major elements treated in the chapters that follow. Throughout these chapters I also reflect on the theories from the perspective of leaders from different Christian organizations as well as my own experience in leadership.

Many global developments encourage us to press on toward the call of serving God's mission. And as we are all well aware, many developments sadden us even as they beckon leaders to respond in humility and with courage. I hope that in reading this book you will reflect on your own situation and, wherever needed, make appropriate adjustments to ensure that as a leader you are learning new cultural insights to shape, catalyze, and propel your organization toward God's calling to partner in the mission of God.

4. James MacGregor Burns, *Leadership* (New York: Harper Torchbooks, 1978), 5.

1

Thinking Missiologically

Implications for Leadership and Organizations

During a particularly frustrating faculty senate meeting tasked with vetting a proposal for a new international doctoral program in global leadership, an esteemed colleague defended her opposition, exclaiming, "Of course I am committed to God's purposes!" Her opposition came from the observation that new initiatives draw funds and personnel away from the already stretched programs that are core to the mission. A new faculty person in Old Testament concerned for continued funding of his position asked, "Are we sure this will be budget neutral?" After other similar questions, the senate chair, pushing to clarify the issues, responded, "We need to focus here, so let's get back to basics by answering the question, 'What is our mission?'" Sensing the need for a lighter moment, the vice chair led the faculty members in an impromptu recitation of the college mission statement: "To prepare men and women for worldwide service to Christ and his kingdom." After things quieted down, a popular professor, reflecting on the scope of the school's mission, stated the obvious: "Is there anything ruled out by that statement?"

These are tough questions, frequently asked in organizations that are clearly committed to God's purposes. Mission statements, though important expressions of the vision and purpose of the organization, cannot answer every question. That task falls to leaders, who must ensure that a discernment process protects and furthers the organizational mission. In this particular case, the tension was between the established programs, recognized as vital to the core of the mission, and a promising new initiative that would inevitably require and attract more resources. This common problem for leaders of Christian organizations is due in large part to the collision of the ever-changing context of the world around us with the finite resources of our operations. It follows that changes in the context require changes to our organizational practices, including strengthening core practices, adding new initiatives, and discontinuing practices that are no longer effective. The result is that leaders are regularly forced to make hard decisions.

The key question to consider in this chapter is, How should leaders of Christian organizations approach the tough missional decisions about what we should do and how we do it? Taking an interdisciplinary perspective, missiology helps guide us to a better understanding of the world around us. By thinking missiologically, we will learn more about mission and culture that will help us as leaders of Christian organizations in shaping, catalyzing, and propelling our organizations forward missionally. In this chapter we focus on the contribution of missiology to the tough missional decisions, beginning with what it means to think missiologically about God's mission. Next we explore the world of Christian organizations as missional in nature, with unique attributes as part of God's mission. Then we survey some of the contributions Christian thinkers have made to a missiological approach to leading organizations across cultures. The final section of the chapter will introduce a number of related disciplines that contribute to our understanding of culture, leadership, and organization from a missiological perspective.

Missiology Can Help—Thinking Missiologically

Mission begins in the sending heart of the Triune God: Father, Son, and Holy Spirit. The mission is first God's mission, often referred to by the Latin term *missio Dei*, meaning "the mission of God to bring about the redemption of the world."[1] This is the critical starting point. It is through God's unending love that God the Father sent the Son to redeem the world through

1. Scott W. Sunquist, *Understanding Christian Mission: Participation in Suffering and Glory* (Grand Rapids: Baker Academic, 2013), 7. He explains the *missio Dei* as "the basic concern in studying Christian mission . . . based on historical, biblical, and theological material [as] a foundational concept that launches the church from the place of worship and fellowship into the frontiers of God's reign" (xiii).

his death on a cross. God's mission did not stop with the crucifixion and resurrection. The resurrected Christ ascended into heaven, whereby God sent the Holy Spirit to continue the work of redemption and reconciliation in the world. Redemption is God's mission from the beginning to the end. In the words of theologian Veli-Matti Kärkkäinen, "Christian faith proposes a solid, historically based but also history-transcending hope based on the faithfulness of God, who raised from the dead the crucified Son in the power of the Spirit."[2] That mission will continue unabated until the return of Christ. Thus we have hope, and in the words of Revelation 22:20, we say, "Amen. Come, Lord Jesus!"[3]

God's Mission and Our Missions

Beginning with the *missio Dei* as the reason for all mission, we turn to the Bible to build the foundation for missiology. Missiologists tend to view the Bible through the redemptive narrative of God's mission through history, beginning with creation and ending with the eschaton. To focus our attention, consider the following passages as God's mandate for mission, as Christians frequently cite them when illustrating God's redemptive mission.

The Cultural Mandate
God blessed them, and God said to them, "Be fruitful and multiply, and fill the earth and subdue it; and have dominion over the fish of the sea and over the birds of the air and over every living thing that moves upon the earth." (Gen. 1:28)

All the Peoples
Let the peoples praise you, O God;
    let all the peoples praise you.
Let the nations be glad and sing for joy,
    for you judge the peoples with equity
    and guide the nations upon the earth. *Selah*. (Ps. 67:3–4)

The Amazing Love
For God so loved the world that he gave his only Son, so that everyone who believes in him may not perish but may have eternal life. (John 3:16)

The Good News
[Jesus] unrolled the scroll and found the place where it was written:

2. Veli-Matti Kärkkäinen, *A Constructive Theology for the Pluralistic World*, vol. 5, *Hope and Community* (Grand Rapids: Eerdmans, 2017), 78.
3. Unless otherwise noted, Scripture quotations are from the New Revised Standard Version (NRSV) of the Bible, and the use of italics in Bible quotations is added.

"The Spirit of the Lord is upon me,
  because he has anointed me
    to bring good news to the poor.
He has sent me to proclaim release to the captives
  and recovery of sight to the blind,
    to let the oppressed go free,
to proclaim the year of the Lord's favor." (Luke 4:17–19)

The Evangelistic Mandate

And Jesus came and said to them, "All authority in heaven and on earth has been given to me. Go therefore and make disciples of all nations, baptizing them in the name of the Father and of the Son and of the Holy Spirit, and teaching them to obey everything that I have commanded you. And remember, I am with you always, to the end of the age." (Matt. 28:18–20)

The Global Witness

He replied, "It is not for you to know the times or periods that the Father has set by his own authority. But you will receive power when the Holy Spirit has come upon you; and you will be my witnesses in Jerusalem, in all Judea and Samaria, and to the ends of the earth." (Acts 1:7–8)

In these passages, we gain the perspective that the Triune God is working redemptively through history in and through God's own people. God commanded humans to "be fruitful and multiply . . . and have dominion," which we understand as stewardship of all creation. All the peoples of earth are called to praise God. God's amazing love sent Jesus to bring the good news of redemption for all the world. The resurrected Christ in turn sends his disciples into all the world. And as witnesses, believers are indwelt by God the Spirit, who gives power for witness to the "ends of the earth." So many other illustrative passages could be included, notably Genesis 12:1–3; Matthew 22:37–39; John 20:19–23; Acts 4:8–12; Philippians 2:5–11; and Revelation 7:9. The message is, "*Mission is from the heart of God, to each context, and it is carried out in suffering in this world for God's eternal glory.*"[4]

Missiologists approach the entire Bible as the story of God's mission.[5] By building an understanding of mission on the Bible, missiology fosters a wonderful global conversation that further expands and refines our biblical

---

4. Sunquist, *Understanding Christian Mission*, xii (emphasis original). Sunquist's extensive work in the history of mission and world Christianity led him to the thesis that mission is participating with God in suffering and glory, an important perspective for all Christians to ponder.

5. For a biblical overview, see Arthur Glasser, *Announcing the Kingdom: The Story of God's Mission in the Bible* (Grand Rapids: Baker Academic, 2003).

worldview.[6] The global nature of missiology is exemplified in the work of biblical scholars and theologians around the world in further developing mission theology.[7]

Studying the mission of God in history, as well as the Bible, helps us understand that the locus of mission is in particular contexts and continues to be incarnational. God revealed his love for the world in Jesus Christ, coming to a particular place at a particular point in history. As we view the mission movement historically, we see the continuing work of God spread through particular people in particular places: our missions in God's mission. If we define the *missio Dei* as redeeming the world, it follows that "mission is through all of time and into all of creation."[8]

As the heading of this section reminds us, we serve God's mission in the world so that our missions, whatever they may be, are in fact part of God's mission in the present generation, according to God's timing. At the outset, God's mission of redeeming the world instructs our approach by asking how our particular mission is redemptive and how it relates to creation. While we will explore this in depth in the chapters ahead, it is essential that we move beyond the individualistic understanding of our particular mission to the broader, divine mandate of the *missio Dei*, which includes all of our individual and collective missions.

Culture as a Missiological Constant

The importance of historical reflection is exemplified in the work of Andrew Walls, historian of mission and world Christianity. In his book *The Missionary Movement in Christian History*, Walls provides a foundational insight into the cultural diversity of Christianity. "This diversity exists not only in a horizontal form across the contemporary scene, but also in a vertical form across history. Christianity is a generational process, an ongoing dialogue with culture."[9] His critical observation supports our understanding that the

6. Allen Yeh, *Polycentric Missiology: Twenty-First Century Mission from Everyone to Everywhere* (Downers Grove, IL: IVP Academic, 2016).

7. For example, David J. Bosch, *Transforming Mission: Paradigm Shifts in Theology of Mission*, 20th anniversary ed. (Maryknoll, NY: Orbis Books, 2011); Stephen B. Bevans and Roger P. Schroeder, *Constants in Context: A Theology of Mission for Today* (Maryknoll, NY: Orbis Books, 2004); Christopher J. H. Wright, *The Mission of God: Unlocking the Bible's Grand Narrative* (Downers Grove, IL: IVP Academic, 2006); Amos Yong, *The Missiological Spirit: Christian Mission Theology in the Third Millennium Global Context* (Eugene, OR: Cascade, 2014); Charles Van Engen, *Transforming Mission Theology* (Pasadena, CA: William Carey Library, 2017).

8. Sunquist, *Understanding Christian Mission*, 24.

9. Andrew F. Walls, *The Missionary Movement in Christian History: Studies in the Transmission of Faith* (Maryknoll, NY: Orbis Books, 1996), xvii.

role of culture is a historical constant as well as a contemporary reality. This is also true in theology. Theologians throughout the ages have systematically posed questions of ultimate reality and human experience based on their engagement with culture at a particular time. Much is to be gained by engaging in this ongoing intercultural theological reflection because it expands our understanding of God. Three current examples of the great value of this global work are the *Global Dictionary of Theology*, the *Africa Bible Commentary*, and the *Africa Study Bible*.[10]

The "ongoing dialogue" between Christianity and human cultures through the interaction of the Bible, history, and theology highlights the interdisciplinary nature of missiology. In the latter half of the twentieth century, missionaries and mission scholars also began to draw on the work of the social sciences and anthropology.[11] Initially they drew heavily on descriptive linguistics, specifically in support of Bible translation, but it wasn't long before the concept of culture, already well established in anthropological studies, was an important area of study to the much broader missions community.[12]

The initial enthusiasm surrounding the study of culture, particularly from anthropology, raised concerns that missiology was falling captive to a secular explanation of humanity. In 1980 Harvie Conn, a professor of missiology at Westminster Theological Seminary (Philadelphia), was invited to speak on the interaction of anthropology with mission studies at the annual Missiology Lectures at Fuller Theological Seminary. From those lectures, Conn produced an influential work introducing the concept of theology, anthropology, and mission in trialogue.[13] The title itself provides a significant reminder: *Eternal Word and Changing Worlds*. The resolution to the concerns lies in our ability to keep our focus on the *missio Dei* while engaging in the disciplined study

---

10. William Dyrness and Veli-Matti Kärkkäinen, eds., *Global Dictionary of Theology* (Downers Grove, IL: InterVarsity, 2008); Tokunboh Adeyemo, ed., *Africa Bible Commentary: A One-Volume Commentary Written by 70 African Scholars*, updated ed. (Grand Rapids: Zondervan, 2010); John Jusu, ed., *Africa Study Bible* (Carol Stream, IL: Oasis International, 2016).

11. For a helpful survey of anthropology and mission, see Darrell L. Whiteman, "Part II: Anthropology and Mission; The Incarnational Connection," *International Journal of Frontier Missions* 21, no. 2 (Summer 2004): 79–88, http://www.ijfm.org/PDFs_IJFM/21_2_PDFs/79 _Whiteman.pdf.

12. In 1979, Charles Kraft published a groundbreaking work on anthropology and mission, *Christianity in Culture* (Maryknoll, NY: Orbis Books, 1979), which drew critical attention. Building on Kraft's integrative approach, Paul G. Hiebert, *Anthropological Insights for Missionaries* (Grand Rapids: Baker, 1985); Sherwood G. Lingenfelter and Marvin K. Mayers, *Ministering Cross-Culturally* (Grand Rapids: Baker, 1986); and Louis J. Luzbetak, *The Church and Cultures: New Perspectives in Missiological Anthropology* (Maryknoll, NY: Orbis Books, 1989), were well received and widely read by missionaries and missiologists.

13. See Harvie M. Conn, *Eternal Word and Changing Worlds: Theology, Anthropology, and Mission in Trialogue* (Grand Rapids: Zondervan, 1984).

of the cultural worlds of human beings. Even using the plural "worlds" is an important step in the right direction. A broad awareness of the complexities of human existence and the various cultures that humans create is critical to the understanding of mission.

Paul Hiebert, from the perspective of a missionary anthropologist, builds on these concepts by suggesting that the trialogue appropriately recognizes that our biblical worldview is also shaped by the cultures surrounding us—both our particular culture and the cultures of others.[14] Knowing that we are all biased by the cultures that shape our worldview allows for an honest reflection on the significance of the trialogue. Instead of treating the biases as blocks to our understanding, Hiebert calls for engaging in a broader conversation across cultures, knowing that different cultures provide different vantage points for understanding. In summary, his statement on the trialogue recognizes that it will produce profound insights into Scripture, into people, into the kingdom of God, and into the gospel call.[15]

To illustrate the impact of cultural contexts and particular groups of people on an organizational mission, consider the work of Wycliffe Bible Translators (WBT). Founded in 1942 as an organization dedicated to translating the Bible into every language, WBT came to a new understanding of their organizational mission despite what was clearly viewed as success. To quote their website, "Over the following decades, Wycliffe celebrated many milestones—from the first translation completed in 1951, all the way to the 500th translation completed in 2000. Around the same time, Wycliffe adopted a new challenge—a goal of starting a Bible translation project in every language still needing one by 2025."[16] They were clear on their calling as true to the *missio Dei*. Their mission theology was appropriate, as was their understanding of the necessity of engaging cultures and worldviews. But in studying the vast number of cultures remaining, their research revealed that some languages would not require a translation due to the changing demographics, the influence of education in the lingua franca, and other factors. This new cultural reality created an opportunity to say no to certain types of new initiatives, formerly welcomed as missionally significant. In addition, technological advances have reduced the time necessary for the translation process, and in response WBT changed their organizational culture. They

14. Paul G. Hiebert, *Anthropological Reflections on Missiological Issues* (Grand Rapids: Baker, 1994), 10–15. Hiebert was a professor at Fuller Seminary during this period, participating in the planning for Harvie Conn's visit and in hosting him. Hiebert based his reflections on insights from the lecture and the resulting book.

15. Hiebert, *Anthropological Reflections*, 10–15.

16. Wycliffe Bible Translators, "The History of Wycliffe," https://www.wycliffe.org/about.

renewed their missional commitment as an organization by setting a deadline for launching the remaining Bible translations, responding to the changing worlds in which they work.

Missiology sprouted from the soil of biblical, theological, and historical reflection on the world that is the focus of God's amazing love. In pondering the world, missiologists realized that from the perspective of the human contexts that make up God's world, we need to more deeply understand and appreciate humans in relation to one another and to the rest of creation. As a result, they drew on the efforts of the social sciences, particularly anthropology, to study culture and guide the practices of mission, recognizing that culture is a missiological constant. Turning these insights to the tough missional decisions facing an organization requires careful consideration of the cultures influencing the mission and the people whom the organization is called to serve, including the limits of the mission.

Our Personal and Collective Missional Roles

The concept of missional roles is a foundational contribution from missiology not reflected in the trialogue. After years of interacting with the concept of the trialogue, mission theologian Charles Van Engen added the domain of personal experience to recognize the important contribution of human agency in the mission of God.[17] As he explains, "Each person's particular spiritual gifts, natural abilities, experiences, knowledge and personality create a unique mix. God's mission is carried out through the life of particular persons in unique ways that cannot, and should not, be reproduced or repeated (Rom. 12; Eph. 4; 1 Cor. 12)."[18]

In reading the biblical references, we notice that they are in the context of the body, exemplified in Ephesians 4:11–12: "The gifts he gave were that some would be apostles, some prophets, some evangelists, some pastors and teachers, to equip the saints for the work of ministry, for building up the body of Christ." In referring to personal experience, therefore, Van Engen means not only the experience of the individual but also the collective roles of Christ's followers (the body), introducing the organizational experience of those who are committed to serving God's purposes as an important focus of missiology. Each organization is integral to the mission of God, contributing to the overall mission by fulfilling its particular calling or mission. A medical mission, a church-planting mission, a publisher, a development agency, and

17. Charles Van Engen, "Mission, Theology of," in *Global Dictionary of Theology*, ed. William Dyrness and Veli-Matti Kärkkäinen (Downers Grove, IL: InterVarsity, 2008), 550–62.
18. Van Engen, "Mission," 552–53.

a school each contribute uniquely to the whole through their mission. God's mission includes all of our individual and collective missions.

Christian Organizations—Missional in Nature

In discussing organizations as integral to God's mission, we need to differentiate between several terms in common use. The terms "mission," "missions," and "missional" tend to be used interchangeably, making it difficult to keep track. Apart from the context in which each term is used, it also has significant characteristics. The term "mission" in its singular form refers to an individual or organizational mission and to God's mission, or the *missio Dei*, which is the mission of God to redeem the world. For an individual or an organization to have a mission means sensing a call from God to serve in some way as another step in following Christ. From experience, I know that periodically acknowledging the call of God through personal testimonies as part of a corporate meeting powerfully reminds the listeners of God's faithfulness. The same applies to organizational missions: recounting the "tribal stories" together deepens the collective identity. Times of remembering God's calling and our obedience are important rites of intensification, as we will see in chapter 4.

A second term is the plural "missions," used primarily when referring to missionary societies. In a broader sense, however, Christian organizations, including development agencies, Christian schools, Bible colleges, seminaries, and many nonprofits, may also be grouped with missions as organizations committed to the *missio Dei*. Often the origins of these more specialized Christian organizations are a missionary society or denominational mission. For example, Trinity Evangelical Divinity School began as the denominational seminary for the Evangelical Free Church in America, and World Relief was founded for the humanitarian work of the National Association of Evangelicals. The term "parachurch" is also frequently used for faith-based Christian organizations that fulfill many of the practices of God's mission outside ecclesiastical circles, such as relief and social welfare, development, evangelism, counseling, and leadership training ministries, to name a few.

A more recent term often used in relation to local churches is "missional." "Missional churches" refers to the perspective that every church is responsible to actively engage in the fullness of God's mission to the world.[19] This has not

19. Sunquist, *Understanding Christian Mission*, 9. Darrell Guder edited an important collection that further clarifies the vision: *Missional Church: A Vision for the Sending of the Church in North America* (Grand Rapids: Eerdmans, 1998). This understanding is also taken

been the practice of churches in general. In the broader sense, "missional" also refers to a commitment to the redemptive mission of God for all creation so that the organization is defined by its purpose to serve God through its practices or products. For example, World Vision, one of the largest nonprofit organizations in the world, helps millions annually. They work in countries around the world, tackling some of the most significant humanitarian crises. So in defining their organization's mission, they say they are "dangerously softhearted. But just the right kind of dangerous. That's because we're a global Christian humanitarian organization. We partner with children, families, and their communities to reach their full potential by tackling the causes of poverty and injustice."[20]

For our purposes, we should also include those for-profit organizations, businesses, or service agencies that are equally missional in their commitment, normally revealed in their mission statements or in the publicity about their organization. For example, Baker Publishing Group, a for-profit corporation, has a strong missional statement: "We publish high-quality writings that represent historical Christianity and serve the diverse interests and concerns of evangelical readers."[21] Many other for-profit organizations offer important products and services addressing the life needs of people and the broader range of concerns for God's creation. From a missiological perspective, the critical elements are the commitments and practices of the organization in response to the *missio Dei*. I've offered US and international organizations as examples, but many believers in the Majority World have established missional organizations and businesses to address challenges in various contexts around the world.

In the context of organizations in general, the terms "mission statement" or "organizational mission" refer to a concern with setting a common direction so that the purpose and goals of the organization are clearly shared by the entire organization. In Christian organizations, the term will normally identify the particular purpose and the accompanying outcomes of the organization in line with God's redemptive mission. Generally, the more specific the mission statement, the better it is for guiding the work of the members in their context.

Thinking missiologically about organizations also means thinking about the church. How do these missional organizations relate to the church? In

---

up at length in Mark Lau Branson and Juan F. Martínez, *Churches, Cultures, and Leadership: A Practical Theology of Congregations and Ethnicities* (Downers Grove, IL: IVP Academic, 2011).

20. World Vision International, "About Us," accessed May 26, 2017, https://www.worldvision.org/about-us.

21. Baker Publishing Group, "About," accessed May 26, 2017, http://www.bakerpublishinggroup.com/about.

defining Christian mission, Sunquist puts the issue center stage: "Christian mission is the church's participation in the Triune God through the suffering of Christ, who was sent by the Father for the redemption and liberation of the world, by means of the conversion of individuals, and cultures, in the power of the Holy Spirit, to the end that God be glorified in the nations and in all of his creation."[22]

We could consider the question in many ways, but perhaps we should start with the emergence of Christian organizations initially as missionary societies. Missionary societies as we know them today arose in the late eighteenth and early nineteenth centuries as part of an awakening of Protestant churches in Europe and North America. American mission leader Rufus Anderson, writing in 1837, saw these organizations as primarily leading to "the conversion of the world."[23] The multiplication of missionary societies and missional organizations with broader purposes continues unabated into the twenty-first century, changing with the times and contexts; nonprofit or for-profit, specialized or general, they are still committed to the *missio Dei*. Even so, the question of the church in relation to the multiplication of missional organizations remains critical to our understanding.

Two Structures—One Purpose

In 1973 missiologist Ralph Winter addressed the issue of the church and missions directly in a paper exploring the dynamics of organizational structures in the mission of God.[24] Winter adapted the concept of modalities (ecclesial) and sodalities (missional) as a key to understanding the expansion of Christian mission, referring to them as "redemptive structures."[25] "Modalities," as seen in the New Testament, refers to the New Testament church. Characteristically, local churches embraced all those who were redeemed through faith in Jesus Christ: adults and children, male and female, Jew and gentile. The modality included all the faithful in that location. As churches matured, they focused increasingly on clearly defined membership and carefully prescribed beliefs.

22. Sunquist, *Understanding Christian Mission*, 173.
23. Cited in Walls, *Missionary Movement in Christian History*, 241.
24. The original paper was presented to the All Asia Mission Consultation in Seoul, Korea, in 1973.
25. Ralph D. Winter, "The Two Structures of God's Redemptive Mission," in *Perspectives on the World Christian Movement: A Reader*, ed. Ralph D. Winter and Steven C. Hawthorne, 3rd ed. (Pasadena, CA: William Carey Library, 2009), 244–53. As Winter uses the terms, "modality" refers to the church and the accompanying ecclesiastical structures under the auspices of the church or churches, whereas "sodality" refers to the "organized, but non-ecclesiastical initiatives" of Christian mission.

Over time, the churches formed alliances, denominations, formal leadership roles, and theological distinctives. The dynamic of modalities, according to Winter, is centripetal, drawing people into the church.

Sodalities are seen in the missionary bands such as Paul and Barnabas (Acts 11:19–15:41). The key difference is that they require a conscious commitment on the part of the individual to join in the mission of the group (organization) as a second act of obedience. Missionary societies, unlike churches, have open membership that facilitates the work of diverse groups of people in a variety of ministries, both lay and clerical. Free from the more rigid structures of denominations, these voluntary associations recruit members who serve as full-time workers and also volunteers who pray and give financial support, sharing in the unique vision. In many cases, those who respond to the ministries of the organization in locations where the missions serve also affiliate with the organization or the churches associated with it, whether as members, workers, or supporters.

The freedom to act quickly in response to the needs in a given context often results in growth both numerically and in breadth of engagement. This freedom appeals pragmatically to faithful Christians, who are often frustrated by the limitations of ecclesial structures. Generations of dedicated believers have committed themselves to the work and support of Christian organizations, whether missionary societies or the proliferation of other types of organizations. In contrast to modalities, the emphasis of the sodality is centrifugal, sending people out into the world in obedient response to the mission of God. Taken together, modality and sodality as structural dynamics continue to influence the understanding and practice of evangelicals regarding the interrelationship of the church to missional organizations. Winter's goal in identifying the two structures was to emphasize the functional necessity of both structures, not one without the other.[26]

Voluntary Associations—Uniquely Adaptable

One of the most important insights in the study of Christian organizations is Andrew Walls's observation that "there never was a theology of the voluntary society." Walls explains this shocking statement by saying, "The voluntary

---

26. The missional church movement challenges this assertion theologically. It is increasingly evident that missional churches can embrace a multifunctional approach to mission through a variety of approaches. However, in practice, the sodality function built on the vision for outreach often expands beyond the neighborhood of the local church, forcing it to attend to the regulations surrounding the specialized ministry, often resulting in the establishment of a separate organization.

society is one of God's theological jokes, whereby he makes tender mockery of his people when they take themselves too seriously."[27] The implication is that the pragmatic nature of voluntary societies allows them to do what the church cannot or in many cases will not do. This was particularly true in the eighteenth and nineteenth centuries due to the rigidity of Protestant ecclesial structures under Christendom. In contrast, voluntary societies consistently adapted to their context in ways that influenced society well beyond the rigid boundaries of denominational traditions.

The movement outward of the voluntary societies began with missionary societies charged with the Great Commission. They contributed to the spread of the gospel, evangelizing and establishing churches. Other types of Christian organizations arose quickly to address the gaps in the church's ministries and to meet the unique needs (and market niches) of communities and regions. These characteristics of voluntary societies continue through missional churches, mission societies, and Christian organizations, as they multiply and diversify in membership, geography, and activities.[28] And this is a global, not simply a Western, phenomenon.

In reflecting on the reasons for this amazing multiplication of missionary societies and missional organizations, Walls further observes that, "untheological development as it may have been, the voluntary society had immense theological implications."[29] In responding to the mission of God, the characteristic pragmatism of founders and those who join missional organizations is not tied to the formal structures of the church, but rather to the passionate belief that they're responding to God's call directed toward human contexts and the needs and opportunities therein. Creative, unfettered by ecclesial rules and formalities, and mostly driven by the laity, these organizations are an intrinsic part of the mission of the Triune God.

Over the past two centuries, the witness of the gospel through voluntary societies has touched every corner of the earth; with remarkable tenacity, they are indeed witnesses to the ends of the earth. Sunquist, further unpacking the definition of "mission," asserts, "Mission is not centered on the individual, on the mission society, on social movements, on the local church, or even on the church universal. . . . Instead, mission flows out of the divine nature of

27. Walls, *Missionary Movement in Christian History*, 246.

28. For an important assessment of the impact of American "voluntary Christianity" in contrast to European Christendom, see Mark A. Noll, *The New Shape of World Christianity: How American Experience Reflects Global Faith* (Downers Grove, IL: IVP Academic, 2013). Noll makes an interesting link between the shape of the global church and the "remarkable missionary work [that] was accomplished through voluntary means" (12).

29. Walls, *Missionary Movement in Christian History*, 247.

the Holy Trinity as revealed in Scripture."[30] To understand the relationship between these various organizations, the church, and your organization is to acknowledge their functional role and submission to fulfilling the purpose of the Triune God for "the redemption and liberation of the world, by means of the conversion of individuals, and cultures."[31]

Organizational Leadership—Leading across Cultures Missionally

Culture and leadership have been interacting since the early church. The introduction to the letter issued by the Jerusalem Council illustrates the intercultural nature of Christian leadership from the first century: "The brothers, both the apostles and the elders, to the believers of Gentile origin in Antioch and Syria, and Cilicia, greetings" (Acts 15:23). This missiological concern has generated a lot of attention, specifically addressing issues arising in intercultural leadership as it relates to churches, mission societies, and organizations that work interculturally.[32] In line with our question of how leaders of Christian organizations should approach tough missional decisions, we will consider the intercultural and interactional nature of those decisions from the perspective of organizational leaders.[33]

Leading Christianly

Thinking missiologically about leaders begins with acknowledging God's presence and mission. No matter what role is assigned to a given person within the organization, we recognize that God is the leader; we are followers, disciples, and servants.[34] Such a realization is the basis for genuine humility. As Christian leaders, we are entrusted with oversight of the organization or some domain within it, to move it toward the unique mission understood as significant to the broader mission of God. For leaders to live into such

30. Sunquist, *Understanding Christian Mission*, 174.

31. Sunquist, *Understanding Christian Mission*, 173.

32. E.g., James E. Plueddemann, *Leading across Cultures: Effective Ministry and Mission in the Global Church* (Downers Grove, IL: IVP Academic, 2009); Sherwood G. Lingenfelter, *Leading Cross-Culturally: Covenant Relationships for Effective Christian Leadership* (Grand Rapids: Baker Academic, 2008); Branson and Martínez, *Churches, Cultures, and Leadership*.

33. Several terms are used in discussions of culture and leadership. The term "intercultural leadership" (moving between cultures rather than simply crossing cultures) is the most relevant in a global context, and we will discuss it in more depth in chapter 7. The concept of interactional leadership (the relationship of the leader, followers, and situations) is taken from Richard L. Hughes, Robert C. Ginnett, and Gordon J. Curphy, *Leadership: Enhancing the Lessons of Experience*, 7th ed. (New York: McGraw-Hill Irwin, 2012).

34. Plueddemann, *Leading across Cultures*, 55.

an important calling, they must be committed disciples with their focus on following Christ, while leading others toward the goals of the organization collectively. The Bible assures Christian leaders that they are "gifted by the Holy Spirit," emphasizing the work of the Triune God, instilling the leaders "with a passion to bring glory to God."[35]

Leadership as a gift from God does not take away from the responsibility or requirement of diligent effort borne by the leader. The organizational leader's role is to influence others toward the purpose and goals of the organization. Missiologists have identified this in terms of a process of taking initiative; inspiring others; focusing, harmonizing, and enhancing the gifts of others; and building the community in the process.[36] In this process, the leader is interacting with followers in serving God's purpose by working with their gifts (and skills), while recognizing that they are agents of God's mission. The process then is "influencing a specific group of God's people, toward God's purposes for the group."[37] Intrinsic to the process is the belief that the leader can and will discern the organizational mission in intercultural contexts in ways that reflect the organization's commitment to God's mission.

Good leadership is critical to the success of an organizational mission. Likely you share my experience of watching an organization deliberate on the appointment of a leader to an important position such as an international director or president/CEO. Typically, the work of a smaller group of dedicated members in the search process identifies candidates who have demonstrated their ability and giftedness in previous service to a church, institution, or other organization. A prayerful discernment process follows, which identifies the person who best fits the current organizational environment and needs. Generally this process yields a leader whose calling aligns with the organizational mission, and a new era begins in the life of the organization.

A more frequent experience is the troublesome process of identifying and appointing leaders in other positions who have not yet demonstrated their ability and giftedness. Giving individuals an opportunity to learn and serve in leadership is always a challenge, particularly in intercultural contexts. I observe this often in the process of identifying local believers to take on the responsibilities of new ministries and as institutional leaders struggle to find minority candidates to fill strategic positions. This points to the necessity of intentionally developing a diverse group of leaders at various levels in the organization to ensure that our organizations do more than talk about

35. Plueddemann, *Leading across Cultures*, 15.
36. Lingenfelter, *Leading Cross-Culturally*, 21; Plueddemann, *Leading across Cultures*, 55.
37. J. Robert Clinton, *The Making of a Leader* (Colorado Springs: NavPress, 1988), 213.

intercultural leadership. It requires strategic action and a willingness to deal with the inevitable financial and structural impact. Intercultural leadership is not an easy goal, but it is a core missiological goal.

While we will deal with the cultural and organizational aspects of leadership in subsequent chapters, we must not overlook a core theological issue in the process: the role of the Holy Spirit. In recognizing leadership as a gift, Romans 12:6 and 12:8 say, "We have gifts that differ according to the grace given to us . . . the leader, in diligence," to which Plueddemann adds, "We are assured that the Holy Spirit gives this gift wherever and whenever it is needed."[38] Along with other necessary gifts, the gift of leadership requires the community of faithful believers not only to identify the leader but also to faithfully support that person's leadership. Leaders learn to lead in communities that learn to follow. The two are inseparable.

Leaders and Followers as Communities of Trust

Intercultural followers, by definition, come from a variety of backgrounds and cultures, each representing worldview differences that flow through their participation in the group. In some cases, these cultures highly affirm the role of group as a collective responsible for the work; in other cases, they may be very individualistic, thereby showing individual initiative and less interest in the group. The emphasis on building community will be natural for some and unnatural for others, but from the perspective of missiology, the relational community is an integral part of a biblical understanding of our service to God's mission. Leading interculturally carries the expectation that the leader's task is to work with the diverse group of people in ways that inspire them to participate as a community of people, not simply as task-oriented workers. Equally, the followers' response is to be a vital part of the community of trust in order to reach the goals according to the purpose set out in the organizational mission.[39]

Intrinsic to this approach is the assumption that as a follower of Christ, the leader draws on Jesus's life and teaching in a way that provides the resources both spiritually and practically to engage in leading.[40] It also recognizes that the challenge of creating a community of trust with people who come from different cultural traditions means that the work of leading lies in developing the followers' trust in the leader and then their trust in one another as a community, based on the shared vision. In other words,

---

38. Plueddemann, *Leading across Cultures*, 173.
39. Lingenfelter, *Leading Cross-Culturally*, 19.
40. Lingenfelter, *Leading Cross-Culturally*, 16.

the community must focus its "attention to God, to each other and to the world that God loves."[41]

Peter Kuzmic, missiologist and expert in European studies, introduced me to a new dimension in building trust through work with leaders in the Balkans. In the years after the fall of the Iron Curtain, pastors struggled with any efforts to work together across local church or denominational lines. The trauma of war and fear of the strong hand of government left them distrusting others outside their own congregation. Attending a regional conference of the Evangelical Alliance, in which Kuzmic was a featured speaker, I was able to observe the manner in which he drew people together so that they moved toward deeper commitment to Christ and, therefore, to one another. During a plenary session, under a banner stating, "All one in Christ Jesus," Kuzmic called three pastors to the stage representing the peoples of three of the most war-torn countries in the Balkans. After a brief introduction, each of the pastors testified to the healing and sustaining power of Christ in that pastor's life and nation. Their concluding embrace was a vivid reminder of the redemptive power of the gospel in reconciling former enemies.

On a practical level, examples of redemption and reconciliation have great power as part of the narrative of the Christian mission of any organization. The stories offer hope to those we serve through a local church, a Christian institution, a business, or any other organization. It is right to make statements about the missional purpose of our organizations, but when that purpose touches humanity at the point of greatest need, it demonstrates the power of God and brings substance to the missional claims. The witness of communities of trust in a world so divided and in turmoil is a wonderful testimony to God's love in action; it is truly good news. It behooves us as leaders to observe and tell the stories of God's work in and through our lives, bringing credibility to the work and glory to God. Equally important, we must not shy away from testifying to insights gained from weakness as well as strength.

Leading interculturally is essential to the mission of God for the redemption and reconciliation of the world. Thinking missiologically, therefore, requires that we continue to ask biblical, theological, and historical questions while focusing very specifically on the leaders and followers within a given context as trust is built and the mission of God reaches out in redeeming people and cultures. It follows that leading intercultural organizations in a missional direction also requires carefully considering the changing worlds around us with an unwavering commitment to the eternal mission of God.

41. Branson and Martínez, *Churches, Cultures, and Leadership*, 60.

To demonstrate the complexities and challenges these contextual realities pose to organizational leadership, we will consider the case of institutions in Latin America as documented by my friend and colleague Marcos Orison Almeida. I asked Marcos to reflect on the challenges of institutional leadership from his position in Brazil, giving an important global context often overlooked in discussions of organizational missions.

The World of Institutions

Marcos Orison Almeida, Brazil[a]

The universe of institutions in Latin America and in other countries of the Majority World lives in the midst of an inevitable cultural conflict. Part of this conflict has its origin in the formation of the countries, and part results from the influence of globalization. It is fair to state that Western culture strongly shaped the political and economic arenas in Latin America.

After the Second World War, the Western capitalist bloc acted on both of these fronts. Almost all countries suffered the consequences of the dispute between North American capitalists and Soviet communists. The scenario was painted with *coups d'état*, revolutions, military governments, and dictatorships. The economy was structured by multinational companies and banks, leading Majority World countries into a huge international debt. In this sense, the main institutions of society were developed under Western patterns.

Institutional Influences

From a religious perspective, two main movements indicate the way Christian institutions are perceived in Latin America: the Catholic support of Portuguese and Spanish colonization starting in the sixteenth century, and the modern Protestant missionary enterprise after the nineteenth century. In many other Majority World countries, one can notice a very similar phenomenon that resulted in those countries being deeply influenced by European and North American culture.

On the other hand, if we consider the main, basic institutions of society, such as family and some kind of government—religion can also be added—they tend to determine a platform for all other institutions. The cultural models of parenthood, leadership, priesthood, and so on are projected onto those other institutions. Even the patterns of relationship, behavior rituals, and core values are naturally transferred to the institutional structures.

With this background in mind, we observe a very complex environment in Latin American institutions, both religious and secular. Companies, churches, schools, missionary agencies, and so on have inherited their structure and mode of operation from Western culture. However, at the same time, people reinterpret and adapt the functionality of these institutions in light of their own cultural values and habits. Therefore, institutions end up living in a conflictive and often unintelligible environment. The effort to meet the foreign criteria of operation, performance, evaluation, and so on requires greater formation and training of people; this effort also favors certain profiles of personality and professional ability.

For instance, Latin American cultures tend to be more relational, more personal, and less objective. The personal aspect stands out, in comparison to the functional aspect. In work meetings, criticisms are usually interpreted as attacks on the person who presented the idea being debated rather than on the idea itself. This hinders the expression of disagreement or even opinions that are intended to contribute something constructive. Often such a gesture is understood as expressing enmity. Even when it is necessary to evaluate someone's performance, objectivity takes second place, and the level of relationship influences the outcome. When local institutions that have a professional relationship with foreign institutions submit evaluation reports initiated by a Western culture, the reports will in fact contain results influenced by personal relationships. The same happens when people from a Latin American culture are asked to write letters of reference. The personal aspect of relationship does not allow the degree of freedom called for by Western culture in the evaluation of the applicant. As a result, the letter of reference will fall far short of its intended purpose, especially when read by people from a Western culture.

In a similar way and for similar reasons, personal relationships tend to overlap with processes. The rigidity of projects, plans, and actions and the goal of predictability give way to the fluidity typical of what happens in relationships. Therefore, we commonly notice difficulty in complying with plans, schedules, deadlines, and targets. It is not uncommon to see Latin American institutions that have never thought about their development through any kind of structured planning. Institutional life ends up happening in the midst of informality, leaving most of the actions to the last hour, with heavy improvisation and adaptation to everyday contextual situations. The positive side of this phenomenon is a great use of creativity and flexibility in the face of challenges. Considering the political, social, and economic instability of many of these countries, this factor helps people find solutions to their problems.

Institutional Leadership

In reference to leadership, people from Latin American cultures typically express admiration for leaders who are charismatic, autocratic, and self-reliant. Power tends to be centralized, and decisions tend to be made by a single person, with little interaction with or participation of others. Collaboration or teamwork is more common among peers. In the presence of the leader, people tend to withdraw their contribution. Thus, super leaders and super pastors arise, unquestionable in their visions and decisions, making the processes of succession, transfer of responsibility, and continuity of institutional projects very difficult. It's not uncommon for a leader to feel insecure when preparing a successor, because the incumbent fears the successor's importance, and the incumbent's control will diminish when the successor takes over.

Historical heritage, like leadership, can compromise the continuity and sustainability of institutions. Many institutions that were founded and sustained by missionaries for decades suffer during the transition period when responsibility shifts to the local leaders. The reason for the crisis is not only that foreign resources are suddenly cut but also that, because of a history of paternalistic subservience, leaders and communities did not mature. The result is two common problems. First, people come to think resources will always be available without their having to work for them. Second, in many Latin American countries, a culture of exploitation grew out of the process of conquest. Colonizers extracted and removed valuable resources, leaving a minimum for local people. The landlords profited and gathered for themselves and their families, while most of the population existed on the leftovers. Lack of attention to building a society for all and promoting the common welfare weakened the practice of giving, donating, and offering. This scenario directly affects Christian institutions for the relief of the needy that depend almost exclusively on donations, such as orphanages, asylums, and hospitals. The same applies to theological schools, which are not profitable businesses and yet attract mostly poor or low-income candidates.

[a] Marcos Orison Almeida (PhD, Fuller Theological Seminary) is professor of theology at South American Theological Seminary in Londrina, Brazil, and an international leader in theological education based in his home country of Brazil. Almeida is working as a team member with ScholarLeaders International on the vital sustainability initiative among scholar leaders around the world.

Reviewing and Reflecting on the Issues

Almeida's case study from a Latin American perspective sheds a very different light on the contextual issues facing organizations both domestic and international. We referred to the questions asked in the faculty meeting at the beginning of this chapter as "tough questions," and Almeida's reflections emphasize how these questions can be especially difficult when it comes to cultural and historical considerations. Any organization must listen and respond to these issues with wisdom and integrity if its missional commitment is to reflect the mission of God. Another important reason for including this case study is that it emphasizes the need to better understand culture with all its implications in order to better fulfill our individual and organizational missions. We live at a point in history when unchallenged entitlements and privilege can no longer be included in the strategic development of organizational missions. Fellowship with one another and with God as members of Christ's body in the interconnected world of the twenty-first century should be characterized by the truth of 1 John 1:7: "If we walk in the light as he himself is in the light, we have fellowship with one another, and the blood of Jesus his Son cleanses us from all sin."

Reviewing

We began this chapter with the question, How should leaders of Christian organizations approach the tough missional decisions about what we should do and how we do it? Recognizing that our mission, whether individual or collective, finds its purpose in God's mission moves us beyond an individualistic understanding. The unique mission of the organization is the starting place for the tough decisions facing leaders. Given the magnitude of God's redemptive mission in the world, humility should be our default response, since we know that we are depending on the Triune God to lead and guide.

Thinking missiologically, therefore, requires us as followers of Christ to acknowledge our call—not only our individual calling but also the mission of our particular organization—to God's mission of bringing redemption to the world through the presence and power of the Holy Spirit. It is God's mission from beginning to end. We submit to the authority of Scripture as the norm for understanding and critiquing all realities. We must also be aware of the historical and theological implications of the work we do and why we do it. Acknowledging that God works with particular people in particular places, we move forward collectively to take "the whole gospel to the whole world." Building on our missiological understanding, we move to consider the missional nature of Christian organizations.

We applied the concept of missional to organizations with an orientation toward the mission of God in order to make it clear that such an organization is defined by its purpose to serve God through its practices or products. This includes a wide range of Christian organizations, large and small, high profile and low profile, but always characterized by their commitment to serving God. An organization committed to serving God must continually ensure that its practices and products are honoring to God. Thus to think missiologically about organizations is to consider their significant contribution, in all that they are and do, in relation to the mission of God.

Understanding the unique mission of the organization is the starting place for the tough questions such as that of new initiatives versus core commitments. Knowing what we do that fulfills the mission of our organization is vital to deciding between strengthening core initiatives and pursuing new initiatives. The process of discernment begins with the question, What are we called to do? The next step in the process is to consider leaders and followers in relation to the mission of God.

By looking to God for guidance to fulfill the mission, intercultural leaders interact with followers while discerning the processes of decision-making and of action or no action. In turn, followers work together with leaders in building a community of trust so that the organizational culture reflects the beliefs and values in harmony with their Christian commitment to mission. So in faith, we trust and lead.

Tough decisions require tough questions. Here are a few that can be used to focus attention missionally.

1. How does this new initiative or core initiative further our organizational mission?

2. Does it fit with what we are learning about God's mission in relation to our mission?

3. Will the new initiative make a unique and significant difference in the changing world? If so, does it require more of our resources? If not, the missional answer to the new initiative is no.

4. If a core commitment is no longer relevant, then what is the time frame for completing our commitment?

Knowing what we do that fulfills the mission of our organization and how that fits with our commitment to God's mission is vital to deciding between strengthening core initiatives and pursuing new initiatives. In my experience, the process is not a one-time event. It is the discipline of continued renewal of leaders, followers, and organizations. Experience teaches that intercultural leadership of missional organizations is not a job for the faint of heart!

The case study illustrates the complexity of culture we face in the mosaic of human contexts as we respond to the question, What should we do and how do we do it? Contrasting a general description of organizations in the Latin American context with a description of the context in the United States is like contrasting the games of soccer and baseball (appropriately so, given the world-class Brazilian soccer team and American baseball teams).[42] Pushing this a little further, without a clear mission and understanding of the contextual differences highlighted in Almeida's case study, leading an organization that works both in Brazil and the United States can feel like playing soccer with a baseball team or baseball with a soccer team. Although the illustration is humorous, it brings important insights to light. Leaders who are serious about God's mission must accept the degree to which God takes redemption of people and cultures seriously. One of the key issues in making tough organizational decisions is determining what particular abilities, skills, or products our organization offers to the world and how we should approach the missional exercise of our contribution in each context. Needless to say, the quest for cultural understanding is foundational to the process. Almeida responds very candidly to the issues relating to contextualization.

Reflecting

Before moving on, we should personally reflect on the issues before us. If we are to make the tough calls between core practices and new initiatives, we need to consider carefully how our actions fit with what God is doing in the world.

1. How does God's mission affect your organizational mission (or one you are close to)?
2. How do you use the concept of culture in explaining your mission?
3. Do you ever discuss how your interpretation of the Bible is impacted by the organizational culture? Or how, in the local context, observable cultural factors affect how people read the Bible?
4. To what degree are your missional goals impacted by cultural biases?
5. How is your organization struggling with the nature of the eternal gospel in the changing world?

Next, reflect on your organization or one that you are familiar with, such as a seminary or a social ministry. To think missiologically about organizations

---

42. Using a sports analogy to compare the social games of two different cultures is taken from Lingenfelter, *Leading Cross-Culturally*, 57–66.

is both to affirm their significant contribution to the mission of God and to acknowledge that other organizations are also vital to God's mission. These questions will help us do that.

6. Is your organization part of a historical Christian movement or mission, and if so, what have you inherited from the previous generations?
7. How does your organization relate to the church, locally or globally, and to other Christian organizations in the regions where it is working?
8. Are you and your organization faithful to the mission of God, and how do you measure such faithfulness?

The complexities of culture in the mosaic of human contexts are worthy of much deeper reflection. To that end, we move to chapter 2 to consider how culture is made, stored, and transmitted, which, interestingly, will help us better understand human resources.

2

Culture and Human Nature

The Complex Unity of Human Organizations

The email was not extraordinary, considering the normal challenges of leading an international organization. It was another request from the director of personnel to provide assistance for housing in a capital city. Although the policy to limit assistance to only expatriate workers was based on limited financial resources, the Numa family was the exception that made the rule appear arbitrary.[1] From an office in another part of the world, it would be easy enough to grant, since it was a reasonable request. They had just the right mix of professional competency, cultural knowledge, spiritual maturity, and status as children of the church for their strategically important roles. Yet in pondering the exceptional circumstances surrounding this request through the lens of a precedent-setting decision, the general director was facing the complex nature of leading people: they are not just members in a particular category, they are human beings.

Grace Numa, a gifted leader, began serving as chief financial officer for the denomination two years earlier. Her experience in financial management in the corporate world was exactly what was needed. David, her husband and pastor of a growing congregation in the poorest section of the city, shared the

1. The story is based on several of my experiences as a mission director. The names have been changed.

mounting pressure of caring for the endless stream of extended family members migrating to the city. Their combined income was insufficient to provide for the growing clan living with them while trying to find work, not to mention the physical pressure of so many people in their small house. When she accepted the position, Grace reminded the leadership team that the cut in salary and loss of a company house would be a challenge, especially with their extended family situation. In recruiting Grace, the denominational leaders knew that something more than a small flat would be necessary, but the budgetary implications were prohibitive. They depended on their partner organization to help in situations like this, so in finalizing her employment, the denomination provided Grace with a written statement about a good-faith agreement to ensure that her family had adequate housing. Two years later, their good intentions collided with the reality of international partnerships where funds were concerned.

Challenges such as those facing the Numa family are not uncommon in the world of Christian organizations working holistically among poor and migrant populations.[2] The presence of complex personnel issues is inherent in all Christian organizations, international, regional, or local. Organizations require stability and administrative policies that ensure effectiveness in meeting their goals. Requests such as housing assistance based on family or health circumstances are a natural part of life everywhere. Likewise, complications arising in the organizational environment demand responses that do not undermine the work. The dilemma facing the Numa family and the denominational leadership, although extreme for some, is an example of the "hard stuff" facing leaders of complex organizations. Core to dilemmas such as this is the complexity of culture and human nature.

In this chapter we focus on three questions in line with managing the complexities of culture and human nature: (1) What is human and what is cultural? (2) How do individuals store and transmit culture? (3) What difference do these questions make to us as leaders of Christian organizations? An important source of understanding in responding to these questions is found in cultural and cognitive anthropology, particularly the work of cognitive studies as it relates to what it means to be human. Building on the foundation of culture as a missional constant, the chapter begins by reviewing our missiological understanding of the role of culture and worldview. Next we turn to insights from studies of culture and human nature, chiefly studies of the sources of human knowledge and our uniqueness as humans. From there,

---

2. A "holistic" approach in missiology views people as spiritual and physical beings so that both evangelism and social responsibility constitute mission. In Latin America, the concept is known as *misión integral*.

we explore how humans think about culture, focusing on how it is stored and transmitted by individuals. The final section considers the unity of culture and human nature from the perspective of missiology as it relates to our organizational missions.

Approaching Culture

"Culture" is an important term commonly used but not fully understood. It is often used to explain differences that pit people against one another, as in "culture wars." Other times, it is used to refer to diversity within an organization or social context that is "multicultural." It can be an attribute, describing sophistication, as in "she is cultured," or a liability, as in "it's *their* culture." However it is used, as we discussed in chapter 1, the concept of culture is a critical aspect of missiology in general and a source of both confusion and significant insights for organizations and leaders.[3]

Defining Culture

In his book *Anthropological Insights for Missionaries*, Hiebert introduces the concept of culture as "the more or less integrated systems of ideas, feelings, and values and their associated patterns of behavior and products shared by a group of people who organize and regulate what they think, feel, and do."[4] He unpacks the definition by identifying three dimensions of culture: (1) *cognitive*, dealing with knowledge, logic, and wisdom; (2) *affective*, dealing with feelings and aesthetics; and (3) *evaluative*, dealing with values and allegiances. Initially he sets these three dimensions in concentric circles, with the evaluative dimension as the deepest level of worldview. As he worked with the concept over the years, the term "evaluative" changed to "normative," and he clarified this dimension as dealing with beliefs and morality. The concentric circles changed to a directional arrow, indicating the dynamic nature of culture and, therefore, worldview (fig. 2.1).[5] For Hiebert, it is important to

3. An introduction to the anthropological usage of "culture" by Christian scholars is found in Brian M. Howell and Jenell Williams Paris, *Introducing Cultural Anthropology: A Christian Perspective* (Grand Rapids: Baker Academic, 2011), 25–44. A second important conversation surrounding the missiological implications of the use of "culture" is found in Charles H. Kraft, *Anthropology for Christian Witness* (Maryknoll, NY: Orbis Books, 1996), 30–50. To understand many of the challenges present in the concept of culture, see A. Kuper, *Culture: The Anthropologist's Account* (Cambridge, MA: Harvard University Press, 1999).

4. Paul G. Hiebert, *Anthropological Insights for Missionaries* (Grand Rapids: Baker, 1985), 30.

5. Paul G. Hiebert, *The Gospel in Human Contexts: Anthropological Explorations for Contemporary Missions* (Grand Rapids: Baker Academic, 2009), 152. See also Hiebert, *Transforming*

call attention to the missiological implication that the gospel addresses all three dimensions.

Figure 2.1
Dimensions of Culture

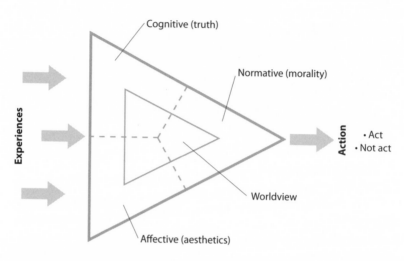

Adapted from Paul G. Hiebert, *The Gospel in Human Contexts: Anthropological Explorations for Contemporary Missions* (Grand Rapids: Baker Academic, 2009), 152.

If we apply Hiebert's model to leadership situations, we see that each culture represented in any given situation has a distinct worldview, which may overlap with others but will also have unique characteristics affecting the way people with that worldview interpret reality, thereby affecting the way they think, feel, and act. In the example of the Numa family, the organization is caught between the practice of accommodating extended family as expected in their collectivist culture—exacerbated by the escalating rural-to-urban migration—and the financial realities of Christian nonprofit organizations. In each case, the cultural interpretation of appropriate action is organized and regulated by the group's understanding of the situation (cognitive), feelings of relational loyalty (affective), and knowledge of the right thing to do (normative).

To make matters even more difficult, the tradition of providing housing assistance and other entitlements for members of the international organization (an old organizational culture) was no longer viable in the current economy. The majority of members believe this is the "right thing to do," while the board

Worldviews: An Anthropological Understanding of How People Change (Grand Rapids: Baker Academic, 2008), 25–28.

and key supporters recognize that they can no longer sustain their financial commitment to providing housing and other physical resources (the new organizational culture). Finally, the desire to localize denominational and institutional leadership is core to their understanding of the organizational mission. Amid the confusion, doubt, shame, and stewardship of financial resources, the Numa family and the leadership team were struggling to know what to do.

In thinking about these complexities of culture, Brian Howell and Jenell Williams Paris provide a synthesis of earlier definitions with the contemporary use of the concept of culture. They define "culture" as "the total way of life of a group of people that is learned, adaptive, shared, and integrated."[6] The term "learned" is particularly important to the thesis of this book, because learning is a continuous process, sometimes emphasized as "lifelong learning." Learning is critical to the health and sustainability of our organizations as we seek to serve the mission of God. We believe that God is active in the world, that culture is dynamic, and therefore, that learning must be an organizational constant.[7] In my own experience as a leader in an international organization, building on the concepts of learning and adapting in order to view problems as opportunities for leaders and followers to learn, significantly impacts the collective practices and the organizational policies.

It follows that culture, as a way of life, must adapt to the ever-changing environment. Adaptation is also a necessary aspect of culture, due in no small part to the exchange between cultures, accelerated by globalization. Typically, we identify culture as shared through language, symbols, practices, and material products (artifacts), with an understanding that cultures do not belong to a single individual. Granted, there are individual idiosyncrasies, but there is no individual culture. Culture is created and transmitted through group interaction. As a result, culture is integrated so each part of the culture relates to other parts. While no culture is perfectly integrated, particularly in times of rapid change or crisis, culture, as Hiebert notes, remains "a more or less integrated system."[8]

Engaging Worldviews

The missiological approach to culture generally focuses on the shared understanding of reality by a people, or their "worldview" (illustrated in fig. 2.1).[9]

---

6. Howell and Paris, *Introducing Cultural Anthropology*, 36.

7. Although the concept of a learning organization was popularized by the research of Peter Senge in 1990, it remains a challenge due to the complexities and pace of change. See Peter M. Senge, *The Fifth Discipline: The Art and Practice of the Learning Organization* (New York: Doubleday, 2006).

8. Hiebert, *Anthropological Insights for Missionaries*, 30.

9. Hiebert, *Gospel in Human Contexts*, 158.

Worldview as an evaluative model brought with it an increasing appreciation of the complexities of human culture, as seen in the case of the Numa family. Using Hiebert's three dimensions—cognitive, affective, and normative—as the core of culture, missiologists were able to identify the effects of systems of religion, law, social organization (including kinship), technology, economics, politics, aesthetics, and so on, on faith and mission in diverse human contexts. The worldview model opened up new worlds of understanding.[10] Missiologists increasingly focused on engaging people at the worldview level, thereby leading them to a deeper understanding of the gospel in context. This process is now known as contextualization.

One of the lingering problems of applying the concept of worldview, however, is the common experience of similarities across worldviews and differences within worldviews, increasingly evident in an age of global connectedness via the internet and cell-phone technology. Initially various explanations were applied to the seeming anomalies of sameness in the midst of differences. Perhaps the most common was simply that idiosyncrasies exist within populations, and mobility, most readily observable through migration, accelerates the transfer of culture and its concomitant worldview change. These remain valid observations of culture change, but they do not account for the wide differences in knowledge and the patterns of thought observed within and across worldviews.

Hiebert acknowledges the role of a cognitive dimension to culture, referring to "the knowledge shared by members of a group or society."[11] Even so, questions remain about how we know and how knowledge is transferred from person to person and culture to culture.[12] Hiebert clarifies his own earlier concepts of cognition as part of his work on critical contextualization.[13] We understand that every sign, such as a spoken word or a sound, exists not only as an identifiable cultural form (sign) but also as a mental image in the minds of individuals. It also exists as an actual physical reality, such as the sound formed and transmitted; thus a triad is created between the sign or form, the mental image, and the reality.[14] In Hiebert's view, recognizing both the objective

10. For a thorough study of the development of worldview, see David K. Naugle, *Worldview: The History of a Concept* (Grand Rapids: Eerdmans, 2002). See also Hiebert, *Transforming Worldviews*; and Charles H. Kraft, *Worldview for Christian Witness* (Pasadena, CA: William Carey Library, 2012).

11. Hiebert, *Anthropological Insights for Missionaries*, 30.

12. Hiebert, *Transforming Worldviews*, 25–28.

13. Critical contextualization refers to the fourfold approach beginning with exegesis of the culture, then turning to exegesis of Scripture and the hermeneutical bridge, followed by critical response, arriving at new contextualized practices. See Hiebert, *Anthropological Reflections*, 88–90.

14. Hiebert, *Gospel in Human Contexts*, 27. This represents the changing views of semiotics in linguistic and cultural anthropology.

and subjective dimensions of culture provides the opportunity to distinguish between human belief systems and reality. It also raises the question of how the mental images are formed and how that relates to culture.

In the contemporary arena of culture studies, the emphasis on human cognition has opened a number of important new areas to consider. These new areas help to explain culture by introducing the relationship of human nature to the issues of human culture. In addition, contemporary culture studies tend to recognize the significance of an individual human being as the point from which to consider culture, without eliminating the importance of group interaction and historical influence.

Humans and Culture

The reason the study of cognition has emerged as a central concern is that the representation of people's knowledge, whether as beliefs, values, or actions, is itself a matter of cognition. Once we claim to know what people "are like" by understanding their worldview, we are in essence doing cognitive anthropology. We are concerned not only with the products of culture but also with the process of making culture and the formation of worldview. This calls for a deeper understanding of the human mind and the physiology of the brain. These are the issues of cognitive anthropology, pointing to questions of culture as acquired and human nature as given. What does it mean to be embodied? How do we understand the mind-brain links? What does it mean to be uniquely human? And how is that interpreted within a specific culture?

As a precursor to the discussion, it is important to offer a disclaimer. The present state of the field of cognitive science, specifically relating to anthropology, is stronger in identifying what things are not like than what they are like.[15] This is inevitable with any new discipline, but particularly one that embraces such an eclectic range of methodologies, including those from both natural and social sciences. Further, I am reviewing the relevant anthropological findings as they relate to leadership and organizational studies. It is beyond the scope of this volume to address the more biological and psychological aspects of cognitive science. The insights gained are intended to contribute to the ongoing conversation in the way of Hiebert's insights, reflections, and explorations.

Fueled by the rapid advances in neuroscience and brain research, cognitive studies are introducing new approaches to understanding culture that

15. Maurice Bloch, *Anthropology and the Cognitive Challenge* (Cambridge: Cambridge University Press, 2012), 9.

have significant implications for our purposes. After years of insisting on an opposition between nature versus culture (nurture), cognitive scientists are increasingly affirming the roles of both genetics and culture. So it is for the sake of integrating our missiological understanding that we turn our attention to the contributions of cognitive anthropology.

Sources of Knowledge

The study of human cognition extends far beyond cultural anthropology, with implications for missiology. Maurice Bloch, a leading anthropologist engaging cognitive science, provides an important distinction of the sources of human knowledge.[16] Bloch asserts that knowledge can come from three sources:

1. It can come from an innate capacity, transmitted genetically from the parents, which either the child already possesses at birth, or which develops later, as he or she matures, much the way boys develop facial hair at adolescence.
2. It can come from the individual learning from the environment as she interacts with it.
3. It can come from learning from other individuals through some process of communication.

[And] for any part of knowledge we may be dealing with a combination of all three.[17]

Generally cultural anthropologists and social scientists have asserted the third source as the favored explanation. This makes sense when one considers the breadth of the concept of culture as "organizing and regulating what we think, feel, and do."[18] For anthropologists, especially those who are influential within missiological studies, Bloch's first source of knowledge is an assault on the foundational understanding of culture. It reduces knowledge and behavior to genetic determinism, whereby biology controls my beliefs, values, and feelings. Further, it requires a careful examination of the process of genetic transmission of knowledge and the resultant behavior using scientific methodologies, uncommon to social science. This is particularly challenging since it questions the legitimacy of the social science methodologies. Concern

---

16. For a very complete and understandable synthesis of the issues raised by cognitive anthropology, see Bloch, *Anthropology and the Cognitive Challenge.*
17. Bloch, *Anthropology and the Cognitive Challenge*, 14.
18. Hiebert, *Anthropological Insights for Missionaries*, 30.

is fueled by the tremendous insights from the Human Genome Project, begun in 1990. As Welsch and Vivanco put it, "'Nature' (biology) appears to be winning out over 'nurture' (environmental and cultural influence)."[19]

The first source also raises a number of other issues, such as the theological concern over the role of sin and free will before a righteous God and our belief in the uniqueness of humans as those created in the image of God.[20] While it is beyond the scope of this book to deal with these concerns in depth, we will consider one particular aspect: the uniqueness of human beings in creation.[21]

For social scientists, a second major concern that fosters resistance is a fear that genetic determinism could once again be adduced to support racist and sexist beliefs. Arguments explaining behavior in terms of biological inheritance have historically supported racist beliefs, with a plethora of negative sociopolitical implications.[22] Christian missionaries have also been among those charged with such deterministic, racist attitudes on the basis that they have been hostage to the colonialist attitudes of the nations that they have come from. This represents a major concern in missiology, raising important questions about the role of missions from the West. Such concerns should be considered seriously, the questioners should be respected, and the response should be clear.[23] Thankfully, both contemporary anthropologists and missiologists have reacted strongly against racist and colonial attitudes.

19. Robert L. Welsch and Luis A. Vivanco, *Cultural Anthropology: Asking Questions about Humanity* (Oxford: Oxford University Press, 2015), 56.

20. For an in-depth discussion of the issue of sin and freedom in this context, see Joel B. Green, *Body, Soul, and Human Life: The Nature of Humanity in the Bible* (Grand Rapids: Baker Academic, 2008), 72–105.

21. The development of cognitive science and neuroscience, particularly within the study of psychology, is a source of new insights as well as challenges not only in anthropology but also in biblical and philosophical theology. In addition to Green, *Body, Soul, and Human Life*, three particularly important additions to the discourse are Warren S. Brown, Nancey Murphy, and H. Newton Malony, eds., *Whatever Happened to the Soul? Scientific and Theological Portraits of Human Nature* (Minneapolis: Augsburg Fortress, 1998); Joel B. Green, ed., *What about the Soul? Neuroscience and Christian Anthropology* (Nashville: Abingdon, 2004); and Warren S. Brown and Brad D. Strawn, *The Physical Nature of Christian Life: Neuroscience, Psychology, and the Church* (Cambridge: Cambridge University Press, 2012).

22. Mayor Mitch Landrieu of New Orleans gave an eloquent example of the problem in a highly publicized speech on race in May 2017 in relation to statues commemorating Confederate leaders. See Peter Applebome, "New Orleans Mayor's Message on Race," *New York Times*, May 24, 2017, https://www.nytimes.com/2017/05/24/us/mitch-landrieu-speech-new-orleans.html?mcubz=1&_r=0.

23. For more discussion from anthropology, see Bloch, *Anthropology and the Cognitive Challenge*, 15–19; George W. Stocking Jr., *Victorian Anthropology* (New York: Free Press, 1987). From the perspective of postcolonial missiology, see Jehu J. Hanciles, *Beyond Christendom: Globalization, African Migration and the Transformation of the West* (Maryknoll, NY: Orbis Books, 2008).

The long-standing debate relates to whether it is human nature or human development that shapes us as human beings; put simply, Is it nature or nurture? "Nurture" here refers to the development of the human being from birth to maturity as fully enculturated within the social unit. The answer seems obvious: both. But in order to fully appreciate what we are learning about culture, we must look more deeply at the interdependence of culture and human nature. A preliminary response to the question of what difference this makes to us as leaders of Christian organizations is that the insights from cognitive studies help us to differentiate between how we are alike as humans and how we differ. This has implications for how our organizational culture is formed and passed on, how we approach orientation and training, and how we regard abilities and liabilities within our members or those we serve, to name a few.

Culture and Human Uniqueness

Cognitive science has centered on the biology of the brain as a key to understanding human cognition. Significant research includes studies identifying patterns of communication among marine mammals and brain studies on nonhuman primates, indicating the ability of these animals to operate not only from instinct but also through communication. The relationship of these studies to human behavior and thought is yielding new discoveries that have significant implications for brain physiology.[24] For our purposes, it also points to the importance of human nature in shaping our understanding, and it raises the question of what makes us uniquely human.

The term "culture" refers exclusively to the nongenetic transmission of knowledge. Other factors, however, primarily genetic and environmental, also impact the transmission of knowledge. The nature-versus-culture controversy, which concerns the role of these other factors, arose from the development of cognitive studies.[25] Cognitive scientists have argued that human societies are made by natural selection favoring the more viable offspring, with the

24. For an introductory discussion, see Welsch and Vivanco, *Cultural Anthropology*, 55–60. For a more thorough study of the mind, see Bradd Shore, *Culture in Mind: Cognition, Culture, and the Problem of Meaning* (New York: Oxford University Press, 1996). The importance of these studies to further consideration of human nature from a Christian perspective is treated in Malcolm Jeeves, "Mind Reading and Soul Searching in the Twenty-First Century: The Scientific Evidence," in Green, *What about the Soul?*, 13–30.

25. Two earlier works illustrating the opposing views are E. O. Wilson, *Sociobiology: The New Synthesis* (Cambridge, MA: Harvard University Press, 1975); and Marshall Sahlins, *The Use and Abuse of Biology: An Anthropological Critique of Sociobiology* (Ann Arbor: University of Michigan Press, 1977).

result that society is a system whose features are determined biologically, similar to physical features of a human body (e.g., eye color or facial hair). This argument asserts that cultural universals common to human beings exist apart from the historical process of culture.[26] The appeal of human universals is particularly relevant for leadership and organizations, because if such universals are real, then—in shaping administrative and structural approaches—leaders can to some extent predict that people will behave according to predictable patterns.[27]

Most social scientists (and philosophers) argue against the validity of cultural universals, despite its appeal. Instead they assert the view that humans are malleable and that culture is autonomous—a view that dates back to the late nineteenth century.[28] An important example in arguing against cultural universals is that the extremely broad variation in kinship systems demonstrates that cultures do not conform to heredity or gene reproduction.[29] The example of the Numa family highlights the inherent cultural differences in approaches to kinship responsibilities that are central to the anthropological argument—that is, the argument that people acquire knowledge chiefly from communication with other people in their cultural setting. This argument emphasizes not the individual, but rather the group, thus allowing for significant change and development over time as part of the historical process of that culture. The relational implications also intersect with the organizational culture. For example, in the Numa family's culture, the organization's members assume they have universal access to certain resources of the organization. In contrast, the cultural values of the international nonprofit organization are different from the local culture, placing a high priority on fiduciary and human-resource considerations, governed by a principle that any given policy must be sustainable in the light of current realities. This supports the anthropological argument because it is an example of the fact that different cultures can have differing beliefs and values (both familial and organizational), which raises serious concerns regarding the concept of cultural universals.

26. Steven Pinker, *The Blank Slate: The Modern Denial of Human Nature* (New York: Viking Penguin, 2002).

27. This topic is taken up at length below in chapter 7 under the heading "The GLOBE Project."

28. This concept can be traced back to 1895 in the work of Émile Durkheim, *The Rules of the Sociological Method* (Glencoe, IL: Free Press, 1962). It was asserted strongly in A. L. Kroeber, "The Superorganic," *American Anthropologist* 19, no. 2 (April–July 1917): 163–213. A thorough treatment of the critique of the concept is found in Pinker, *Blank Slate*.

29. Jesse J. Prinz, *Beyond Human Nature: How Culture and Experience Shape the Human Mind* (New York: Norton, 2012).

Storing and Transmitting Culture

While the nature-versus-culture controversy polarized scholars, it also highlighted the need for greater understanding of the mechanisms governing the transmission of knowledge. Bloch points out that human beings are very similar (biologically), with observable predispositions for certain biological features and behaviors, and also very different (culturally), with each individual and group being unique.[30] Out of the debate intermediate positions arose, providing two important new categories of explanation: cultural representations and mental schemas.

Cultural Representations

Understanding culture involves more than observing the movement of individuals (actors) or the changes people make to the environment (artifacts); it requires representing the observations.[31] These representations may be in the mind of the observer, known as "mental representations," such as beliefs, intentions, preferences, or memories. They may also be material representations such as physical objects, sounds (e.g., language or music), or colors (e.g., a picture or painting); these are known as "public representations" because they exist in a material way outside the observer.

To illustrate the concept of representations, consider a house one sees while out for a walk. The house is immediately recognized in the mind of the person walking. It requires no language for identification; after all, it is a house. On the other hand, that it physically exists on a street means that it will be represented in conversations, on a street map, and perhaps even in a photograph in the office of the owner, each a public representation. As these public representations are repeated throughout the community, they create a mental representation in the minds of the community members. These widely shared representations of the house are known as "cultural representations," a third type of representation. In other words, the house as observed by the walker is a "mental representation" of the actual physical house, which is a "public representation" that, in turn, is known throughout the community as a house, a "cultural representation."[32]

---

30. Bloch, *Anthropology and the Cognitive Challenge*, 49, 70, 74.

31. An important work on the synthesis of culture and nature is Dan Sperber, *Explaining Culture: A Naturalistic Approach* (Oxford: Blackwell, 1996), from which I draw the concept of representations.

32. Sperber's approach is similar to the one developed by Hiebert (*Gospel in Human Contexts*) in developing his concept of critical contextualization. The triad of sign, form, and reality is not exactly equivalent, since Sperber is dealing with the formation of mental representations and their transmission between people as part of the formation of culture.

Cognitive anthropologist Dan Sperber makes a strong case for the view that the human population has countless mental representations. Far fewer are passed on to other people as public representations, thereby creating their mental representations. In the end, only a very small percentage of the universe of mental representations are communicated repeatedly, becoming cultural representations.[33] From a naturalistic approach, therefore, Sperber affirms the brain's ability to select certain representations to make sense of a given situation.[34] Understanding representations in this way also recognizes the role of psychology in explaining individual factors in the process of selecting representations. Identifying this level of cognition introduces another degree of the "more or less integrated systems" that help us define culture.[35]

To illustrate how representations function, let's take the symbol of a cross (a public representation). For a Christian, this is a powerful mental representation, filled with meaning by virtue of the Christian community's frequent exposure to cultural representations of the cross. It is not a mental representation of an instrument of death, but a mental representation of Christ's victory over death (1 Cor. 15:1–5). Thus the Christian worldview, by frequency of use, selects this symbol as a cultural representation (cognitive). But it also has a visceral power for the individual, who may, for example, hold up a cross for protection when confronting their deepest fears or wear a necklace with a cross as a symbol of faith (affective). Finally, Christian teaching imbues the cross with theological significance far beyond the physical symbol (normative). With this in mind, here is a word to leaders: choose your organizational symbols carefully; they are powerful and, as we know from history, may deviate from their original purpose (e.g., a burning cross or a cross as decoration, such as bling).

We know that culture exists among a group of people because it is shared. Viewing culture from the perspective of a group, individuals are active via their public representations (communicated or shared) but not via their mental representations, apart from the actions that result. However, Sperber notes that

33. Sperber, *Explaining Culture*, 25. Sperber also makes the case for an "epidemiology of representations," whereby representations are transformed, with each transmission limiting the stability. Therefore, "cultural representation in particular is made up of many versions, mental and public ones" (26).

34. Sperber also raises the issue of genetic predisposition as a factor in the selection process. An example is autism and its effects on social behavior. For a helpful commentary on genetic predisposition, see Simon G. Gregory, "Commentary: Genetic Predisposition of Behavioral Response," in *PNAS* 111, no. 5 (February 4, 2014): 1672–73, http://www.pnas.org/content/111/5/1672.full?sid=a917c9a4-04f3-4826-97fb-0c0427bcc735.

35. A more thorough discussion of the implications of a systems approach is included in chapter 7.

mental representation can influence the formation of culture through inaction. In that sense, some representations are only in the minds of individuals, therefore are not part of the shared culture. Others are shared widely, making them part of the culture. It is this significant point that brings the process of transmission of culture into focus.

Sperber's point is also significant to us as leaders, since we normally think of culture change as a purposeful action of introducing new perspectives or responding to shifts in society. In the case of inaction, cultural representations may atrophy due to disuse or even misuse. Using the cross illustration, if an individual stops attending a church service, the symbol becomes inactive as a mental representation in the individual. But more to the point, if the cross disappears from the preaching, the sanctuary, and the hymnody, it loses its significance as a Christian symbol, and the process of atrophy is initiated.

Cultural representations are the result of many interactions of both mental and public representations. Public representation is not a simple process of passing on what one has observed or learned. Rather, it is a process that reacts to what was observed and represents it in likeness, while also transforming it in the process. Thus mental representations are not replicated from an individual mind to the minds of others; rather, they are transformed in the process of transmission. Even though transformation implies resemblance, it results from a cognitive process unique to both the individuals that construct the representation and those who receive it.

To illustrate, consider a conversation in the hallway following a lengthy organizational meeting you attended with your colleagues. As you discuss what happened in the meeting, you often differ with each other significantly as to what happened. In some cases, things are mentioned that you simply missed or that were not important to you, while in other cases an individual seems to misrepresent a situation, particularly when their representation happens to coincide with their "pet peeve" or threatens their position. So if you were to ask the participants individually about their opinion of that organization's culture, one individual may characterize it as open and supportive while another may see it as rigid and unsupportive. Leaders must make sure that content is recorded so as to reflect with integrity the intention of the party that produced the content, particularly considering the ease of global information transfer. In many cases, the presentations themselves (PowerPoint, written report, or video-recorded presentation), rather than the more traditional forms of minutes, are preferable. Remember, highly developed communication is a uniquely human characteristic separating us from the rest of creation.

In this example, the limited number of opinions makes it difficult to identify with any certainty the culture of the organization. This points to an important fact in the transmission of cultural representations: it requires not only large-scale exposure, including frequency of repetition, but also as much uniformity as possible, to ensure inclusion in the culture. The latter is referred to as "replication," although we do not mean exact copies; this was reflected in the definition of culture as "more or less integrated." Therefore, we mean that through the process of transmission, the group learns as well as shares the cultural representations, inevitably making adaptations as an intrinsic element of transmission. The capacity to process the sheer volume of these representations as a function of the human brain is in itself a remarkable attribute of human beings, further adding to the complex reality and uniqueness of both human nature and culture.

Understanding the conscious mental representations and how individuals transform these ideas as part of the public transmission of cultural information opens up an important new dimension in our analysis of culture. The next area for consideration builds on cultural representations by moving us into the realm of the mental organization of knowledge.

Mental Schemas

An area with significant insights for how people approach work concerns "knowing how" rather than "knowing that."[36] Cognitive anthropologists and psychologists approach the organization of knowledge by recognizing the presence of abstract structures in human thought, known as modules. These mental structures effectively organize our understanding and facilitate the practical action associated in response "without mobilizing mental images or any knowledge conveyed in declarative statements."[37] These abstract structures, based on modular theory, are referred to as "schemas."[38] The term gained favor across the social sciences, so that it now refers to a diversity of mechanisms used for processing information, experience, and simple routine tasks.

Again the example of the house affords an illustration. A house, common to human experience, is not cognitively stored as a blueprint or list of features

36. The classificatory concepts used in acquiring and organizing knowledge (schemas) are drawn from Philippe Descola, *Beyond Nature and Culture*, trans. Janet Lloyd (Chicago: University of Chicago Press, 2013), 98–107.

37. Descola, *Beyond Nature and Culture*, 102.

38. Modular theory originated in the work of linguist Noam Chomsky. The idea is that a certain part of the mind is dedicated to language. Building on this, cognitive scientists postulated that other modules located in the brain are dedicated to specific domains. The concept of a mental schema is related to modular theory. See Bloch, *Anthropology and the Cognitive Challenge*, 60–67.

such as walls, roof, windows, doors, foundation, and so on. If it were, before recognizing any structure as a house we would have to run through a process akin to a building inspection. On the contrary, we are able to recognize a structure as a type of house instantly, even if it is a Mongolian gher, a Maasai kraal, or a beachfront condominium. Our schematic representation draws together a "vague and unformulated collection of attributes" linked together and representing a typical house.[39]

When we're considering schemas, it is helpful to distinguish between the cognitive schemas as they relate to our common human experience. The existence of universal cognitive schemas as genetically transmitted is not widely accepted, due mainly to the limitations of the research, conducted primarily in Western, industrialized societies. While the existence of universal schemas has significant pragmatic implications, in the same way cultural universals do, at present they remain uncertain. Instead it is the acquired schemas that are significant for our understanding of culture, accounting for both diversity of customs and differences in human behavior.[40]

Acquired schemas are generally idiosyncratic, facilitating individual routines or practices such as daily tasks. Because they are learned, they develop over time, making it possible to organize and effectively perform tasks at a subconscious level without articulating them. An example is the variety of tasks one achieves while getting ready for work or while one is deep in thought considering the day's work. Such practical actions drawn from acquired schemas are the foundation for multitasking. Before jumping to conclusions about the value of such schemas, one must quickly admit that some types of multitasking based on nonverbal actions associated with acquired schemas are not appropriate, for example, texting while driving or writing emails while supposedly participating in a staff meeting.

Schemas that most affect our organizations and leadership fall under the category of collective schemas. These schemas are the stuff of which shared cultural representations are constructed. It is best to think of collective schemas as "how to" manuals for tasks such as recording and storing donor information, operating machines (driving or typing), preparing displays and events, or performing the basics in just about any task. An interesting example is the research done on London cabbies relating to their remarkable grasp of city streets (a type of mental Google Maps).[41] Collective schemas are common

---

39. Descola, *Beyond Nature and Culture*, 99.
40. Descola, *Beyond Nature and Culture*, 102.
41. A popular account is found in Mark Brown, "How Driving a Taxi Changes London Cabbies' Brains," *Wired UK*, December 9, 2011, https://www.wired.com/2011/12/london-taxi-driver-memory/.

in all types of organizations, raising questions about training and leadership development.[42]

Theory suggests that experiences acquired in a social environment as collective schemas are internalized as psychic, sensorimotor, and emotional dispositions. As a result, French anthropologist Philippe Descola identifies three types of skills—regarding perception, expression, and interpretation—that are made possible through collective schemas:

1. To structure the flow of perception in a selective fashion, granting preeminence in signification to particular traits and processes that can be observed in the environment [for example, granting individual actions preeminence illustrated by a police officer in an intersection directing traffic, in contrast to the crowds standing at the corner waiting for the light to change before crossing the street].

2. To organize both practical activity and the expression of thoughts and emotions in accordance with relatively standardized scenarios [for example, the difference between the kind of expression that is acceptable when one is talking with a friend while waiting in line for a roller coaster and the screams of fear that are acceptable while one rides the roller coaster].

3. To provide a framework for typical interpretations of patterns of behavior and events—interpretations that are acceptable and can be communicated within a community in which the habits of life that they convey are regarded as normal [for example, following the liturgy of a service using the Book of Common Prayer or the hand signals from a coach during a game].[43]

As one would expect, collective schemas may be explainable by an individual or group, even if the details are initially difficult to articulate. For example, the preparation of handbooks or operating manuals is normally assigned to people who know the best practices of given tasks from years of practical experience. By doing the hard work of reflecting on actual practice, these workers share knowledge drawn from acquired schemas to create a collective schema. This highlights the important reality that cultural representations are not necessarily transmitted as precepts or clearly articulated instruction. Rather, they are simply assimilated over time by participation in the cultural context or by the repetition of particular practices in a work situation. At the same time, this observation also highlights the importance of tangible external products, such as handbooks, as a way of standardizing knowledge

42. Schemas will be covered in greater detail in chapter 4.
43. Descola, *Beyond Nature and Culture*, 103.

as cultural representations. This standardization relates to Descola's first point, that preeminence can be given to particular processes, in this case as recorded in the handbook.

Other collective schemas may be nonreflective, in the sense that they cannot be articulated in response to questions or reflective exercises. In practice, nonreflective schemas, while still shared collectively within a context, tend to resist objectification. For example, a new cross-cultural worker is often at a loss to know the most important steps to follow in learning to fit into the new culture, such as the rules of hospitality. The worker might be aided by language study, which represents an acquired reflective schema and involves learning vocabulary that makes sense of actions and expectations. But even with a common language, the use of words, expressions, and practices varies widely.

I remember that when I was a new teacher in rural Queensland, my family was invited to an evening at the home of another teacher. The invitation included supper, so we didn't eat before arriving at 7 p.m. At 9:30 p.m., our Australian host announced it was suppertime by asking if we would like cheerios with tomato sauce and a beer. For an American, "cheerios" conjures up images of a bowl of breakfast cereal covered in milk to be served with a cup of coffee, not tomato sauce and a beer. Our polite response was, "Sure!" Much to our relief, she returned with a plate of small sausages, toothpicks, a bowl of ketchup, and bottles of beer. We all have stories like this, but seldom do we analyze them as to their cultural significance. In this case, we learned that "supper" is a late night snack, while "tea" is the evening meal. These concepts are part of a collective schema. But more importantly, the rules of hospitality tend to be a nonreflective mental schema and an interesting case of the difficulty in identifying cultural universals.

An outsider may observe nonreflective schemas, but they still defy explanation, residing instead as attitudes, aesthetics, or bodily techniques—in this case, leaving the new intercultural workers wondering why people find a particular action satisfying, such as sleeping on a hard surface using a solid wooden block for a headrest or wearing a particular type of headdress or other adornment. A quick way to be alerted to the vagaries of nonreflective schemas is the blank look on a new worker's face during a demonstration or when the response to the question of why one does something a certain way is an embarrassed, "It's complicated!"

We have been dealing with these concepts in general terms to this point, so it is a good time to illustrate the encounter of culture and human nature in the mission of Christian organizations. This case study illustrates two central issues. The first is the practical issue of the degree to which our human physicality (nature) encounters our beliefs (culture) in the mission of God. The second is the theological issue of what it means to be human, particularly in body and soul (physical and spiritual).[44] In practice, we who are involved in missions find this dichotomy in our view of ministries, such as preaching, church planting, or evangelism on the one side and medical, educational, or community development on the other. Despite the attention to holistic ministry among evangelicals since Lausanne II in Manila, we are still challenged to truly experience the wholeness that reflects our being as those created by God.[45]

Often we confront the issues of culture and human nature at informal levels of interaction as mental schemas, both collective and nonreflective, rather than in the formal documents of a Christian organization. In practice, these schemas elude the outsider and yet are often a source of frustration and conflict. I asked my friend and longtime colleague Judy Fitzmaurice to provide the case study that follows by reflecting on the topic of mission to the whole person, specifically medical work.

The Place of Mission "to the Body"

Judy Fitzmaurice, Sydney, Australia[a]

When my husband and I arrived as young doctors in Papua New Guinea (PNG) to serve as part of a mission organization that was involved in diverse activities—church work, agriculture, education, literacy, Bible translations, medical care, health-worker training, and so on—one of my senior colleagues casually remarked to me that, with a bit of further study at a Bible college and moving out of medical practice, we might be able to return as "real missionaries" and not simply "support workers." I was surprised and distressed to be perceived as standing on the other side of an imagined dichotomy. Is there really a dichotomy between practitioners of ministry to the body and

44. See footnote 21 in this chapter for resources dealing with the theological and cognitive issues of what it means to be human.

45. Examples of the debate are seen in Ralph Winter, "The Meaning of Mission: Understanding This Term is Crucial to the Completion of the Missionary Task," *Mission Frontiers* (March–April 1998): 15. See also the call to reassert the priority of evangelism in David J. Hesselgrave, "Redefining Holism," *Evangelical Missions Quarterly* 35 (1999): 278–84; and Bryant Myers's support of holism, "In Response . . . Another Look at 'Holistic Mission,'" *Evangelical Missions Quarterly* 35 (1999): 285–87. The strong support for holism in Michael A. Rynkiewich, "What about the Dust? Missiological Musings on Anthropology," in Green, *What about the Soul?*, 133–44, builds on the contributions of cognitive studies.

practitioners of words for the soul? Does one emphasis bring with it a higher status than the other?

Care for the sick is historically an integral and distinctive expression of communities of Christian believers since the early church. All healing was attributed to God's grace, whether it came through the use of primitive medicinal herbs, through nursing care, through prayers, or through the miraculous. God's sovereign power extended into "this world." Christians were known for hospitality and compassionate care of the sick and the poor in the first hospitals.

An Easy Dichotomy

Today we seem to have a war between those who say the gospel is only truly proclaimed in "words" and those who say it is proclaimed in "words and deeds." To the former, "ministry to the body" can seem of distant and secondary importance. Those advocating for prioritization of the perceived ultimate good, in the context of scarce Christian resources, make earnest theological appeals suggesting anything less than a single-minded focus on "Word-based ministry" will dilute our obedience to the Great Commission, with grave eternal results.

These ideas do not arise in a vacuum. The prevailing cultural narrative in the Western church separates the spiritual or sacred from the material or secular. This view of life arose out of the Enlightenment in the seventeenth and eighteenth centuries, when interest in Greek philosophers revived. It was further fueled by the rise of empirical science. The sacred sphere is perceived to be private, personal, and stewarded by religious professionals. The secular sphere is the "real world"—the marketplace of commerce, science, technology, and medicine, ruled by experts. This worldview has led to an awkward dissociation of "ministry to the body" from "ministry to the soul."

It is time to take stock. Secular materialist thinking has influenced our views, our actions, and our inactions. We are at risk of downgrading the relevance of God to his world by saying he is not interested in the care of bodies, the ethics of experimental bioscience, the justice of health-care system inequities, or the stewardship of the earth.

We may have unintentionally embraced an easy dichotomy that lets us get on with life in the marketplace without reference to God, rather than following in the steps of Jesus, who used his discernment to judge when to preach and when to heal, according to the needs of those before him.

My family left medical careers in Sydney, Australia, and planted ourselves in a remote part of PNG for twelve years. We chose this road at the urging of Jesus to respond to his Great Commission, relocating to a place of great physical and spiritual need, where we could apply our medical skills and bear living witness among a people who needed the gospel of Jesus.

Caring for the Whole Person

The physical presence of Christian health care meant that when a child got severe malaria, when a mother was giving birth and things went very wrong, or when a man fell from a tree and was bleeding from a compound fracture, there was a place to go for help. There were people who could offer skilled care. As a result, there was hope.

God requires that we *do* justice and love mercy. Doing justice and showing loving-kindness demands our presence in places of injustice. This sleeves-rolled-up love in action has exemplified the witness of the church over centuries.

It is not only in the developing world that doctors are increasingly seeing the need for ministry to the body to include awareness of a patient's personal faith as an important influence in their response to illness. Doctors are now taught "spiritual history-taking" in medical school. As we emerge from postmodernism to a relativistic society, we are recognizing that we are more than a machine. Whole-person, patient-centered care demands that physicians seek to discover not only the answer to "What is the matter with the patient?"—that is, the objective truth—but also the answer to "What matters to this patient?"—that is, the subjective truth. This is the science and the art of medicine.

Christian doctors and health-care workers are now well placed to be models of sensitive spiritual care that seeks to be aware of the existential concerns of the patient as part of identifying "what matters to the patient." Ministry to the body is becoming more holistic even at our most respected university medical schools.

The work of mission to the body is one where the truth of God is fully revealed and understood in both word and deed. Deeds of compassion engender interest and enhance receptivity to gospel words. By going *to* the sick and doing good *among them* we give shape to what the love of God means. Words explain the deeds and reveal the way of salvation. Both words and deeds are needed.

[a] Judy Fitzmaurice (MBBS Hons., University of Sydney) is a medical doctor who works in medical education at a university in Sydney and is an international missions and governance leader from Australia. Her field of expertise is medical missions and intercultural health care.

Reviewing and Reflecting on the Issues

The work of Fitzmaurice exemplifies the ongoing challenge of what is known as "radical dualism": believing the "soul" is distinctly separate from the "body," with the essence of the person being the "soul." While not a daily topic of conversation in mission circles, this dualism continues to be a struggle when it comes to the mission of many Christian organizations. The problem is how to engage with the needs, physical and spiritual, of the people being served: for the church planters, how to handle poverty and hunger; for the development workers, how to relate to local churches; and for the businesspeople, how to control costs in order to price items affordably.

It is encouraging to see the efforts of scholar practitioners in trying to move away from the dualism by engaging in practices that demonstrate genuine biblical holism. Fitzmaurice continues to live out her calling through leadership in her missionary society, taking an active role in preparing medical missionaries and in medical teaching that affords her the opportunity to bring a nuanced understanding of nature and culture, particularly in exploring the realm of spirituality in health care.

By way of reviewing the implications of our approach to culture and the nature-culture conversation, we will apply the new insights from this chapter to the case study.

Reviewing

We identified two primary issues in the case study, one practical and one theological. Let's first consider the practical issue: the degree to which our human physicality (nature) encounters our theology (culture) in the mission of God. Remember that, normally, we confront issues of culture and human nature at informal levels of interaction, such as the conversation between the young doctor and the senior missionary. This sets the dichotomy in the form of mutually exclusive categories, where A is a "real missionary" and B is a "support worker"; you can be either A or B, but there is no way to be both. While the confrontation of dualistic theology and holistic missiology is central to the problem, it is also a problem of conflicting worldviews and underlying schemas of practice. As a leader, one bears the task of raising the conversation to the level of dialogue in the hope of learning from the differences while adapting the organizational practice missionally; in leadership studies this dynamic is known as "the tyranny of the 'or' and the genius of the 'and.'"[46]

In light of what we learned about the various dimensions of culture (cognitive, normative, and affective), we see that the differences in worldviews are not primarily in the cognitive dimension, since both parties will describe their

---

46. An instructive discussion of "the tyranny of the or" appears in James C. Collins and Jerry I. Porras, *Built to Last: Successful Habits of Visionary Companies* (New York: Harper Business, 1994), 43–46.

commitment in terms of the Great Commission. Fitzmaurice put it this way: "We chose . . . to respond to his Great Commission." One could argue that their theological understanding is a cognitive process based in a shared source of truth (Scripture).[47] The worldview clash, in contrast, was primarily at the level of interpreting the moral nature of caring for the physical well-being of people. All agreed that health was important, but for the "real missionaries," eternal life was normative. For the doctors and health-care workers, care for the sick was normative, seen as a moral imperative. From experience, conflicts in worldview in the affective and normative dimensions are best handled not as a debate or confrontation, but rather by way of personal narrative.[48] Testimonies (stories) based on shared experiences are powerful in reconciling worldview conflicts interculturally.

Another factor at play in the discussion regarding the value of physical versus spiritual care is what schemas are being employed by those representing each side of the debate. It is interesting to consider the schemas of practice from the perspective of church workers and health-care workers. Health-care workers tend to work in shifts, mostly in the same general location, perhaps even the same offices or laboratories. Their routines are embedded in their minds from the disciplines of study and practice. The resulting schema tends to make much of their behavior a type of muscle memory, requiring a high degree of physical skill. In contrast, the schemas of practice for a church worker are varied, based on the frequency of similar behaviors and practices. For example, the frequency of preaching depends on the number of services, normally ranging from one to five times per week. Other ministries, such as leading worship, teaching, chaplaincy, and counseling all have routines that also relate to schemas of practice. However, in the end, the variety of tasks, frequency of contacts, and expectation of preparation make it difficult to make a strong correlation.

Now that we've looked into how culture is created and shared, we can think more creatively about how to create a common culture within an organization. For the leader, problems associated with two (or more) classes of members in any organization are significant. There are important reasons for differentiating based on knowledge, skills, and individual roles. However, divisions leading to feelings of marginalization or low self-esteem undermine the witness of the organization. A fruitful intervention strategy is introducing a practice that

47. For a deeper discussion of the theological and missiological concerns surrounding holistic mission and contextualization, see Stephen B. Bevans, *Models of Contextual Theology* (Maryknoll, NY: Orbis Books, 1992); and Francis Anekwe Oborji, *Concepts of Mission: The Evolution of Contemporary Missiology* (Maryknoll, NY: Orbis Books, 2006).

48. The role of narrative will be covered in depth in chapter 3.

becomes a collective schema. A common approach is to prepare devotionals to be shared among the members, either in groups or individually, with regular times of fellowship that include sharing experiences and new insights. This may seem too obvious; however, good theory and theology stand behind it. The physical benefits of discipline through routine allow for deeper formation of mental schemas that bring a sense of stability and consistent behavior. From the perspective of culture, discipline creates shared patterns of behavior and encourages the creation of shared products or artifacts (songs, prayers, devotionals)—in a word, a common culture. These patterns of behavior include spiritual disciplines vital to our lives as followers of Jesus.

The remarkable ability of human beings to communicate knowledge and to be in a partnering relationship with God marks the uniqueness of humans among creatures of the earth. This reality of both human embodiedness and embeddedness in the human family opens up a much deeper and broader view of what it means to be human. As we relate to these new domains of understanding, leaders who are committed to shaping, catalyzing, and propelling their organizations missionally will find fresh insights to explore.

Reflecting

Reflecting is an opportunity to assess our beliefs and practices along the lines of culture and human nature. The process will inevitably raise concerns that should be addressed as part of the learning process. For some it will raise awareness of great gains made over the years, for others it may reveal a new area to consider, and for still others it may herald the loss of long-cherished beliefs and practices. Serious reflection in the form of assessment should not be a negative exercise. Rather, it should help us identify where our beliefs are true and our practices are strong, which we should encourage. Conversely, some beliefs are culturally biased or inaccurate representations of human nature, calling for deeper understanding and reflection. The same applies to practices that are no longer appropriate or sustainable and therefore in need of serious consideration resulting in more appropriate responses. Remember, organizational as well as individual assessment is developmental, so focus on what you are learning and how to best use that to the glory of God. Along the way, remind yourself of the ways that you are learning and growing in service of Christ.

Now let's reflect on what we know about culture and worldview. Consider the following questions by way of applying the concepts.

1. How do you refer to culture in conversation? What examples can you recall of references to culture in key documents or public statements?

2. What is your initial response to the problem facing the Numa family and their housing needs?

3. What are some of the ideas, feelings, and values that arise in your thinking as you consider their request? If you lack experience in this particular matter, note that it is parallel to the situation for several of the leaders facing the Numa request, so offer your thoughts with confidence as equally worthy of consideration.

4. Do cultural conflicts in your organization (or one that you are close to) obstruct the collective ability to meet missional goals? Do actions and conversations impede witness to the gospel?

Moving from the culture of the group to the individual, consider the implications of mental schemas on our practical actions and those of our colleagues in response to the world around us. These questions may guide your reflections:

5. What are examples of the predominant worldview in your organization in the three dimensions: cognitive, affective, and normative?

6. Identify a mental schema that operates in your organization, perhaps one that you have personally encountered. How might that schema be addressed to shape the results toward new or more missionally appropriate practices?

7. Are there practices that should characterize your organization but are currently limited to a few members or employees? How might you turn those nonreflective schemas into acquired schemas to enhance your mission?

Having reflected on the implications of cognitive studies for our understanding of culture, we now turn our attention to the issues of relationships. As we do, it behooves us to keep in mind our testimony that mission begins and ends with God. We serve the *missio Dei* as those in a partnering relationship with God.

3

Caring about Members and Others as People

Notions of Self and Others

A good way to learn more about the people you lead is to pick a place where people naturally gather, sit across from someone, and listen. The lunchroom, for example, is a laboratory of organizational culture. Conversations tend to be unstructured, focusing on the interests of the people at the table. As long as the organization faces no imminent threats, such as budget cuts leading to layoffs, most leaders can join a group without destroying the mood. The important thing to remember is you are there to listen. People who study culture learned long ago that open-ended questions are a good way to start learning. They allow for a free flow of thought and provide good listeners with a focus for follow-up questions. If it helps, think of your coworkers as friendly teachers rather than vital informants, particularly if you plan to let them know what you are doing. It might help to remember that people's stories are one of their most prized possessions.

An important area of focus for leaders is how members think about themselves as people. Picking up on the idea of stories, do individuals share their own story with others? If so, what are the turning points, the people or events that made a difference? And how do the circumstances individuals present fit into the story? Stories are extremely important notions of personhood and critical to understanding how individuals relate to others. Of course, it is essential that leaders pursue individual stories in a manner that respects the dignity and rights of the person. Social sciences refer to such respect in the context of human subject research, in which two basic tenets are "informed consent" and "confidentiality." It isn't hard to respect these requirements if the motivation is to love others as Christ commands. A formal way to describe this is to think of it as an extension of member care or, more formally, as part of the activities of the human resources department. The goal is to care about people—your members (followers) and those you serve—as people, that is, in ways that are in line with the relational dimensions of leadership.

This chapter provides important background to understand the notions of self, family, and other, taken from what we are learning about human nature and culture, to aid in the process of caring about members and those you serve as people. The guiding question for this chapter is, "Who are we as people, and what difference does it make to our mission?" We begin by affirming that human beings are an integral part of creation, physically embodied persons interacting with the world in which we are embedded, and most importantly in a partnering relationship with God.[1] The first section introduces the notions of "self" from the perspective of cognitive anthropology, focusing on the interdependence of culture and cognition. The second section considers the effects of early childhood, family, and caregivers from the perspective of human development as shaped by the critical relational processes initiated at birth and continuing to adulthood. The third section is a case study of the work of Viva, a networking organization that resources caregivers for children at risk. The final section reviews and reflects on the issues from these perspectives *that will help us in shaping, catalyzing, and propelling our organizations missionally.*

Members Are People First: Notions of Self

At the outset of any discussion of the "self," we encounter the plethora of terms used in the social and cognitive sciences. We find terms such as "self," "the I," "agent," "subject," "person," "individual," "dividuals," and "identity," each

---

1. The theoretical significance of the terms "embodied" and "embedded" is described in detail in Warren S. Brown and Brad D. Strawn, *The Physical Nature of Christian Life: Neuroscience, Psychology, and the Church* (Cambridge: Cambridge University Press, 2012), 28–47. The concept of "partnering relationship with God" is used in the context of what it means to be human in Joel B. Green, *Body, Soul, and Human Life: The Nature of Humanity in the Bible* (Grand Rapids: Baker Academic, 2008), 38.

of which may be found in the literature on the topic.[2] The core of the differences among views of the self appears to be related to human commonalities (emphasized by universalists) and human distinctives (emphasized by culturalists). Bloch's solution to this conflict is to group all of the terms referring to the self as the "blob."[3] In my study of the concept, I found Bloch's use of "blob" particularly difficult to explain, since the word is so infrequently and imprecisely used. However, I equally agree that it is important to try to reconcile the array of terms. For our purposes, we will use the term "self," while recognizing that "blob" does keep the wide range of included terms in view.

We must also clarify the widely shared view that there is a major division between "self" as seen in individualist cultures and "self" in the understanding of collectivist cultures, or between "the individualist West and the social relational rest." Distinctions of this type are found as early as 1893 in Émile Durkheim's work on organic and mechanical solidarity, when he identified relationships (solidarity) arising from doing similar activities in undifferentiated societies (mechanical) and those whose roles were different yet interdependent as human beings in modern or Western societies (organic).[4] A variation of this distinction features in missiological reflection by Hiebert in the form of organic and mechanical analogies, comparing living beings (organic) and inanimate objects (mechanical) as "pictures of the nature and operations of the larger world" (analogies).[5] Driving the search to divide the concept of "self" is the relative value cultures place on interiority (inward focus) and individuality on the one hand and on social relationships and group membership on the other.[6] To illustrate, it is not uncommon in cultures outside the West to find little reference to the individual and to find, instead, references to issues of belonging to a group, a place, or the land. While it is difficult to avoid the challenges inherent in this dualism (individual/group), as already evidenced by the nature/culture controversy, recognizing some major differences is of use when we're approaching the notion of self.

2. Maurice Bloch, *Anthropology and the Cognitive Challenge* (Cambridge: Cambridge University Press, 2012), 119–20. In this reference, Bloch laments the problem of so many different terms and the variations of meaning, "When I attempt such combinations I have to admit that I am completely lost . . . [by] the indistinct galaxy." A well-known example is Geertz's discussion of the Balinese "person" in Clifford Geertz, *The Interpretation of Cultures: Selected Essays by Clifford Geertz* (New York: Basic Books, 1973), 364–89.

3. Bloch, *Anthropology and the Cognitive Challenge*, 120.

4. Émile Durkheim, *The Division of Labor in Society* (New York: Free Press, 1997), 31–87.

5. This first appeared in an influential article by Paul G. Hiebert, "The Flaw of the Excluded Middle," *Missiology: An International Review* 10, no. 1 (January 1982): 35–47.

6. This comparison is critical to the social-game model in Sherwood G. Lingenfelter, *Leading Cross-Culturally: Covenant Relationships for Effective Christian Leadership* (Grand Rapids: Baker Academic, 2008), 58–66.

Levels of Self

Understanding the concept of self in cognitive anthropology requires clearly distinguishing between levels we regularly observe.[7] This includes recognizing the interdependence of human nature and culture revealed in the levels. At the most basic level, the "core" is shared by all animate creatures and does not differentiate between cultures or species. Common to the core are "(1) a sense of ownership and location of one's body, [and] (2) a sense that one is author of one's own actions."[8] These two elements feature as an awareness of life noticeable in common daily actions. For example, a lizard was on the pathway as I returned from a walk; I slowed to avoid stepping on it as the lizard accelerated to avoid the same event.

Using the term "sense" for all creatures, such as the lizard and me, is risky because it raises the question of willful action (volition), which is not intended by using "sense." Instead, it refers to reaction, as when a creature responds to a stimulus such as danger or food. Remember that cognition is a tremendously complex neurological process. "Sense" does not imply reflexive awareness or what we referred to as a reflective schema. Rather, it is an awareness that is part of the individual creature's responsive nature. This level is referred to as the "core self."

The level above the core is known as the "minimal self," which "involves a sense of continuity in time."[9] A continuity of time is significant to any longer-term memory of self and others, as seen in recognition of one's own image in a mirror or identifying familiar persons in a crowd. Research has also demonstrated this level in other social species, particularly nonhuman primates. For our purposes, we understand continuity of time as facilitating a person's sense of "being" enabling the awareness of both a past and a future, as is evident in one's imagination or future planning.

Again, to say that the minimal self considers the degree of risk in a situation is to imply too much; it does not require reflexive awareness, although it does involve retaining memories of events (known as episodic memories). To illustrate, striking one's finger while trying to drive in a nail creates a heightened degree of caution the next time around. On a broader level, being reprimanded in a meeting by a supervisor may or may not involve reflection on the causal conditions, but it will very likely create an emotional response as one remembers the who, what, where, and when of the episode.

---

7. This section draws on the synthesis of various notions of self, relating the current state of the conversation found in Bloch, *Anthropology and the Cognitive Challenge*, 117–42.

8. Bloch, *Anthropology and the Cognitive Challenge*, 126.

9. Bloch, *Anthropology and the Cognitive Challenge*, 127.

The higher and uniquely human level of self is known as the "narrative self."[10] Bloch uses the term "narrative" to imply a close link between the "narrative self" and the "autobiographical memory."[11] In this way the narrative self is individuals' active thought processes, volition, and understanding of themselves in relation to the world around them. It is their story in the context of relationship to other humans: family, friends, coworkers, and so on. The link between story and memory signifies that even though we can distinguish the levels in theory, realistically they are a continuum and blend into one "self," as seen in figure 3.1.[12] Bloch summarizes the notion of self: "All these levels interact continuously . . . [so that] we are psychologically and physically one at all levels."[13]

Figure 3.1
The Self

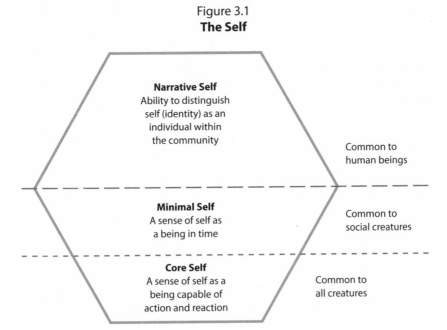

Adapted from Maurice Bloch, *Anthropology and the Cognitive Challenge* (Cambridge: Cambridge University Press, 2012), 124–34.

The narrative self is the level at which we consciously encounter one another as people, in contrast to the encounter of a crowd on a subway, which

10. The term "narrative," while used by a number of notable scholars, should be used with caution since it may be interpreted as referring primarily to autobiographies or other elaborate narratives created by certain people as part of the social discourse, particularly in the arts.

11. Bloch, *Anthropology and the Cognitive Challenge*, 128.

12. Bloch, *Anthropology and the Cognitive Challenge*, 128.

13. Bloch, *Anthropology and the Cognitive Challenge*, 137.

is primarily at the core and minimal-self levels. An example comes to mind of something a Chinese leader once told me about the crowded subways in her home city of Beijing. She said that it is not uncommon for a transit employee to push people into the subway car. She jokingly said, "We get on as people and get off as a photograph!" The point is that an encounter such as this happens to a person at the basic level of core self (sense of body and location) and minimal self (a sense of time), with the person knowing that he or she is in a crowd with a particular destination yet without any personal details.

In practice, some people are inclined to develop elaborate narratives that they tell and retell, while others simply live their lives with less self-focus. Philosopher Galen Strawson's work on the narrative self helps put this into perspective.[14] Instead of identifying cultural differences as accounting for these variations in individual narrative selves, as anthropologists most commonly do, he looked at self-narratives more generally. In considering the narrative self, he identified two types of people: those who were less inclined to create self-narratives, doing so only when it is required (creating episodic narratives), and those who create extensive narratives, even making such creation an art form (creating diachronic narratives), for example, through biographies, sitcoms, or YouTube videos. Strawson's work identifying different degrees of talking about self, broadly represented by the two types of people, while helpful, in the end relates more to rhetorical styles and personality than to substantive differences in the notion of self. So what is the relationship between self and others?

Social Selves

To speak of the levels of self—core, minimal, and narrative—is to focus solely on the internal and private factors of an individual's awareness of their own being in itself and in its relation to the external world. Relating this to concerns about culture points us toward the external and public interaction of individuals. The intersection of individuals and culture is referred to as the "social selves." To identify social selves is to recognize that interaction of all types between people is inseparable from the individuals' levels of self. To illustrate, sitting on a commuter train, one may be chatting with another passenger while oblivious to others until someone nearby begins to sneeze, at which time those chatting begin to worry about catching a cold.

Linking this to leaders, we can say that individual members of an organization will normally consider themselves in terms of the unique contribution

14. Galen Strawson, "The Self and the SESMET," in *Models of the Self*, ed. Shaun Gallagher and Jonathan Shear (Thorverton, UK: Imprint Academic, 1999), 99–135.

they make through their work (lived narrative) and the ways in which the organization provides for their needs as a member or employee (the self). When those same individual members consider the organization, they are more likely to think in terms of the collective contribution as well as the organizational mission, seeing their coworkers as comembers, relating at the level of social selves.

The continuity extends from self to others because humans are social beings. In that way, the physical being, which is genetically formed, is also formed by continuous social exchange, as a dynamic and continuous process. Individuals have the capacity to be shaped by their interactions with others, while also shaping others in the process. The importance of social interaction in shaping our concept of self begins in childhood and continues throughout one's life. The concept of reciprocity refers to the social exchange and illustrates the transformation that takes place as a result of continuous social exchange. In chapter 4 we will consider the implications for culture learning and orientation.

To take it one step further, the social exchange is not only between those within the current social networks of the individuals but also with those of previous generations, so that history and culture are part of the process of forming the self. This helps explain why social and work patterns as well as beliefs and explanations set by the founding generation are so hard to change apart from external forces that render some practices redundant. This insight also supports the significance of preserving the organizational "memory" (or legacy) so as to ensure continuity of the vision and mission. The overall result is that both the individual self and the social self are "moulded and modified" by the process of formation.[15]

Through encounters with the physical, social, and cultural world, the developing self is shaping and being shaped by the interaction. As we apply these insights to our organizational context, we need to carefully assess how we are (or are not) facilitating these significant processes as part of our commitment to equip our members for service to the organizational mission and the mission of God. To illustrate a practical outcome, the change in work patterns brought about by computers introduced the concept of ergonomics, creating a whole new approach to workspace. Another implication is the significance of fostering healthy interaction between individuals—either virtually, through software designed for collaborative work, or by face-to-face

---

15. Bloch, *Anthropology and the Cognitive Challenge*, 139. A significant implication of the formation of the self is that there are no generic humans. Equally significant are the effects of genetic predispositions in providing certain capacities that allow for the processing of experiences and social interaction. The relevance of these findings undermines the extremes of biological determinism and humans as a blank slate.

conversations—to facilitate the continued social, cultural, and missional development of the organization.

Psychologists Brown and Strawn, in summarizing how we become the "complex interactive persons we are," point to the "open and self-organizing nature of human kind."[16] This understanding of human development includes the process of an infant's dynamic brain and body interacting with others in the social environment to develop an increasingly complex mental system in a process referred to as "meaning making."[17] This more nuanced understanding of human development further reinforces our assertion that culture and human nature are interdependent and that culture is a "more or less" integrated and adaptive system.

Individuals and Culture: Metarepresentations

An important next step in moving from self to culture is to consider how individuals influence the transmission of culture. We are aware of those creative people who pen great works of literature, compose songs, design buildings, or perform countless other acts of creativity, but surely there is more to the process than simply producing artifacts that become cultural icons. What is involved in moving from the individual mind to the cultural knowledge shared by the entire group of people? From the perspective of cognitive anthropology, the answer lies in the cognitive abilities that undergird the interaction between self and the social selves within the group. That is, it lies not simply in having access to individual narratives and autobiographical memory, but in actually having consciousness and language in order to interpret and transmit cultural representations.

At this point we need to recall the concept of representations, which we have identified as mental, public, and cultural. Human cognitive systems are able to construct and process mental representations, as well as produce and interpret public representations.[18] Moving from thought to communication requires the capacity to handle multiple representations with the potential to create even more complex representations. Cognitive science identifies these as "metarepresentations," defined as mental representations formed from other representations, or new concepts formed by combining specific concepts; thus scientists refer to the ability to form such representations as a metarepresentational ability (see fig. 3.2). Another way to explain it is as the ability to think

---

16. Brown and Strawn, *Physical Nature of Christian Life*, 53.
17. Brown and Strawn, *Physical Nature of Christian Life*, 54.
18. Dan Sperber, introduction to *Metarepresentations: A Multidisciplinary Perspective*, ed. Dan Sperber (Oxford: Oxford University Press, 2000), 3.

more about what we are thinking and to build more comprehensive thoughts as we think about the subject or issue. To illustrate, to think missiologically is to approach a problem or idea that is of concern by trying to understand it (thinking more about it) and then by integrating ideas from the biblical, theological, historical, and cultural domains to generate responses that will further God's mission.

Figure 3.2
Self and Culture

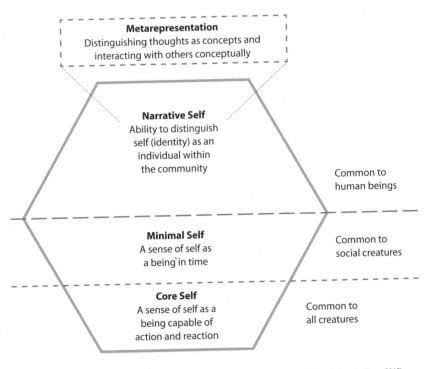

Adapted from Maurice Bloch, *Anthropology and the Cognitive Challenge* (Cambridge: Cambridge University Press, 2012), 124–34.

The domain of metarepresentations, according to Sperber, "is the set of all representations of which the organism is capable of inferring or otherwise apprehending the existence and content."[19] A practical aspect of metarepresentations is the ability to understand and create new ways of looking at a cultural representation that help explain or modify aspects of its

19. Dan Sperber, *Explaining Culture: A Naturalistic Approach* (Oxford: Blackwell, 1996), 147.

meaning particularly relevant in a specific context. A wonderful example is the way in which Charles Wesley experienced and thought about the death of Christ before composing the timeless hymn "And Can It Be?" Awareness of sin, the need for personal accountability, and the generous offer of salvation were characteristic themes (cultural representations) of the Wesleyan Revival in Britain. Charles Wesley wove these truths (individual concepts) together in the language of his time, inferring a fresh understanding of God's love (metarepresentation). Just pause to consider the profound lyrics of the first verse:

> And can it be that I should gain
> An int'rest in the Savior's blood?
> Died He for me, who caused His pain—
> For me, who Him to death pursued?
> Amazing love! How can it be,
> That Thou, my God, shouldst die for me?
>
> Amazing love! How can it be,
> That Thou, my God, shouldst die for me?[20]

The concept of metarepresentations has profound implications for understanding how we think and generate new ideas, not only creative ones but also analytical ones. To further explain the process, Sperber suggests that we generate new ideas when the metarepresentational module aggressively draws cultural representations "belonging to several cultural domains . . . [thereby] playing a major causal role in the generation of true cultural diversity."[21] We noted in chapter 2 that cognitive studies suggest there are modules in the brain dedicated to specific domains; cultural representations are one such domain.[22]

Earlier we noted that the transmission of culture is not simply replication but the transformation of concepts and representations. In the metarepresentational interaction of individuals, cultural representations are transformed in and by the process, leading to the formation and reformation of culture by the very nature of the process. For example, think of an informal conversation around a meal table when there is a breakthrough in understanding a problem that has vexed the group. The very atmosphere seemingly fosters the free flow of ideas among friends, creating the opportunity for metarepresentations to be

---

20. Charles Wesley, "And Can It Be?" (1738), http://library.timelesstruths.org/music/And_Can_It_Be.
21. Sperber, *Explaining Culture*, 150.
22. Bloch, *Anthropology and the Cognitive Challenge*, 60–67.

considered and collectively transformed. All this occurs without the pressure of a formal agenda, with its constraints of time and status.[23]

Individuals and Others: Theory of Mind

We begin to better understand the role of cognition in the formation of culture by considering the process of transforming mental representations of culture into cultural representations. Through studies in cultural anthropology, we learned to consider the importance of worldview, language, symbols, and artifacts. By viewing the process in cognitive terms, we introduce another dimension, known as "theory of mind." This refers to the ability to view others as "like me" in that they too are intentional in their behavior. Brown and Strawn describe theory of mind where "one infers the mental states of other persons based on their behavior, using memories of one's own experience."[24] Beyond simply reacting to the actions of others, a theory of mind focuses on the beliefs and desires that cause or motivate their behavior, thereby adding a reflective element to our recognition of others.

The ability to understand the mental states of others as well as one's own mind is also a "necessary condition for interpersonal dialogue."[25] Dialogue engages others in the process of reframing cultural understanding and in conceptualizing new cultural representations (artifacts, symbols, language, etc.). While producing cultural products may be an individual act (e.g., painting), it is the persons in a particular cultural context who will receive the production. The same is true of ideas as cultural representations. Through shared language, a particular group is open to countless possibilities, including complex and abstract ideas about the present, past, and future.[26] The degree to which persons thus relate to each other is yet another unique human capacity.

For example, consider a ministry team charged with leading a chapel service. They begin by securing the topic, whether assigned or of their choice; then they discuss the design of the service, identifying the important elements. Once the order of service and topics are decided on, they assign specific tasks,

23. These findings are relevant to Samuel Escobar's well-known critique of Western missiology for its overreliance on strategic planning, quantitative analysis, and efficiency, which he calls "managerial missiology." In support of Escobar, Valdir Steuernagel's response was a call for "kitchen table missiology," emphasizing the value of relational approaches to missiology. The articles may be found in William D. Taylor, ed., *Global Missiology for the 21st Century: The Iguassu Dialogue* (Grand Rapids: Baker Academic, 2001), 109, 124–25.

24. Brown and Strawn, *Physical Nature of Christian Life*, 57.

25. Warren S. Brown, "Cognitive Contributions to Soul," in *Whatever Happened to the Soul? Scientific and Theological Portraits of Human Nature*, ed. Warren S. Brown, Nancey Murphy, and H. Newton Malony (Minneapolis: Fortress, 1998), 109.

26. Brown, "Cognitive Contributions to Soul," 103.

such as leading songs, playing musical instruments, praying, and preaching, depending on the abilities and desires of the team members. During these discussions, each member is listening to the verbal and observing the nonverbal communication of other members. If this inference of the minds of others is appropriate, the discussion will be fruitful. In this case, doubtless previous experiences already indicate the range of acceptable ideas and actions, leading to an effective chapel service.

A theory of mind logically leads to a desire of the individual to influence the mental states of others in particular ways. Sperber describes it this way: "Human communication is both a way to satisfy such meta-representational desires and an exploitation of the meta-representational abilities of one's audience."[27] Metarepresentations and culture are linked in an important way. Communication in its various forms facilitates the transmission of cultural beliefs through the group (see fig. 3.3). In some cases, beliefs are transmitted "intuitively," such that the transmission goes without notice. For example, one enters a weekly meeting, sits, and organizes the agenda and other materials before the meeting starts. Others hardly notice this behavior because widely held cultural knowledge prescribes actions expressed in this type of regular event, aligning with the expectations of others and the individual's interpretation of the others' response.

In contrast, some "reflective beliefs" are metarepresentational, requiring greater understanding, usually brought out in the social discourse surrounding the belief. These beliefs are much more likely to draw attention because they appear counterintuitive, maybe even unintelligible or incongruous. Using the meeting illustration, when a new leader introduces a different structure—excluding persons normally present or changing the content, time, or frequency—greater attention must be given to communicating the rationale for the change. The structure and procedures are fixed in the organizational culture, so even if the leader has a right to make such a change, the degree to which members are given the opportunity to participate at the metarepresentational level will directly impact the reception of the idea. This may appear obvious, but experience shows that leaders often work through the metarepresentational process with limited input from those most impacted.

We focused on the individual or "self" in this section, drawing on current thinking in cognitive anthropology, building on our earlier consideration of culture and human nature. The next major consideration is the vital role family relationships play in the relational processes of human development. Drawing from studies in cognitive and social science, we will consider the role

27. Sperber, *Explaining Culture*, 147.

Figure 3.3
Social Selves and Theory of Mind in Transmitting Culture

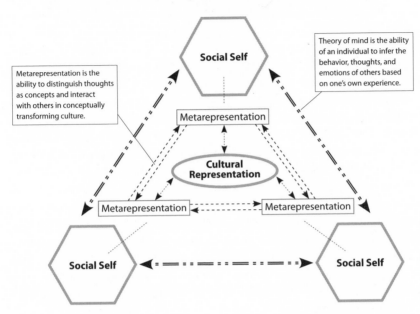

of family in the cognitive formation of individuals, particularly in relation to culture. Then we will consider the implications of this research for the way we respond missionally.

Relational Processes: The Effects of Family and Caregivers

The term "family" evokes a range of responses from each of us. When I think of my children and grandchildren, I experience a deep sense of fulfillment, that satisfying feeling of joy with the added element of longing to see them. For me, my children and grandchildren define family, evoking a sense of self-worth and solidarity. If I move to my parents' generation, the experience is altered by history as a product of my autobiographical memory. I choose not to include the wider extended family as core to my concept of self, due in large measure to the years of physical separation. My identity as an older person is selectively shaped by a lifetime of experiences. I retain little of my cultural roots, drawing instead on the diverse range of experiences with my wife and children during our years of service as missionaries and beyond. The element of choice operates not so much for inclusion as for exclusion. I selectively choose to construct my concept of family by affect rather than biology. In Strawson's terms, my narrative self fits the episodic profile: it is not the central focus of my story. Descola's explanation is more precise; my view is an "egocentric conception of a subject."[28] I have to pause to let that sink in, but as I do, it appears to accurately reflect my selectivity in defining the concept of family.

The opposite is true of my experience of Melanesians. We often observed that our friends did not exercise selectivity in including family members. The opposite was more the norm, observable in the use of kinship terms such as "small mother" for aunts, and "brother" or "sister" for cousins. The view of oneself was one of belonging, not one of individuality. Anthropologist Marilyn Strathern refers to this lack of individual identity in Melanesia as "dividuality," defining a person by their position and relations in the family or wider social network.[29] A humorous example was the problem of graffiti on the side of the church building. Young children would often be dismissed from Sunday school long before the worship service ended. Being playful kids, they found that the whiteboard markers made excellent drawing utensils on the smooth side of the building. The trouble for them came from their view of family. Once the artwork was complete, they would sign beside it using both their own name and that of their father, much to his dismay! Unlike mine, their concept of family strongly embraced a more extensive autobiographical memory.

This apparent dichotomy fits the profiling of world cultures that has characterized cultural anthropology, expressed in the phrase "the individualist west and the social relational rest." However, cognitive studies on the interdependence of human nature and culture provide a much more nuanced understanding of the diversity of cultures. Descola concludes that the theory of "dividuality" (group orientation) fits alongside or, in some cases, is even supplanted by the egocentric concept of "self."[30] The reality is much more complex than earlier assumed, leading not to the elimination of prior assumptions as much as to acknowledging the diversity of solutions to the problem of reflective individuation.

As I discussed this chapter with my friend and colleague Bambang Budijanto, he commented that after returning to his home in Indonesia he noticed that "digital technology and social media has significantly changed

28. Philippe Descola, *Beyond Nature and Culture*, trans. Janet Lloyd (Chicago: University of Chicago Press, 2013), 117. The subcultural theory builds on this selectivity in considering the role of personal networks in subcultures, as we will see in chapter 6.

29. Marilyn Strathern, *The Gender of the Gift: Problems with Women and Problems with Society in Melanesia* (Berkeley: University of California Press, 1988), 268–70.

30. Descola, *Beyond Nature and Culture*, 119.

the culture of parent/family and children, both in cities and villages."[31] The concept of family, while fundamental to the structure of culture, increasingly represents a diversity of understandings within societal cultures, even before adding the subcultures present.[32] This complexity makes it difficult to appropriate a cultural typology of family for our purposes. Instead, we will narrowly focus on the relational processes of adult-child interaction that influence the representation of cultural knowledge in the context of family and caregivers. If we are truly to understand our members as people, the relational processes begun in their family settings are an important point for learning more about their reactions and how their reactions influence the organizational culture.

Adult-Child Interaction in Family Life

A major contribution from the family to the cognitive formation of self is the genetic makeup of an individual as contributed by the biological parents. Life is formed in the womb of the mother through the most remarkable process, which normally results in the birth of a child whose physical and mental characteristics increasingly resemble one or both parents. That child, as a human, is endowed with mental capacities that are enhanced beyond those of any nonhuman species. The potential for the child's brain to mature into an adult brain is also present from the beginning. This amazing biological process has become an important part of the understanding of anthropology. I reconnected with the wonder of procreation through observing the life of my youngest grandson, born while I was writing this book. His rapid physical development and the early indications of a curious mind have reawakened my interest in the formation of persons.

Because physical and cultural processes are interdependent, a second major contribution to the child's cognitive formation is interaction with the family to develop personality, intelligence, and character.[33] This begins at birth when the infant engages the world, in most cases initially through relating to parents and family. Through this process, known in developmental psychology as "meaning making," the infant increasingly develops a complex mental

31. Bambang Budijanto, scholar, professor, and former Asia Regional Vice President of Compassion International, email communication, May 25, 2017.
32. For an extended anthropological discussion of the current views of kinship, marriage, and family, see Brian M. Howell and Jenell Williams Paris, *Introducing Cultural Anthropology: A Christian Perspective* (Grand Rapids: Baker Academic, 2011), 153–73; Robert L. Welsch and Luis A. Vivanco, *Cultural Anthropology: Asking Questions about Humanity* (Oxford: Oxford University Press, 2015), 317–39.
33. Brown and Strawn, *Physical Nature of Christian Life*, 53.

system.[34] The innate capacities engage with family members or caregivers as part of the daily routine, thereby socializing the child and making that child increasingly part of the family. As leaders, creating opportunities to discuss the familial and cultural practices in child raising among the members of your organization is an effective approach to facilitating the sharing of individual stories, particularly if there is an assurance of acceptance and appreciation of each individual's story.

Brown and Strawn provide an important foundation for understanding the interaction between children and adults in shaping intelligence, personality, and character.[35] I chose four relational processes that contribute significantly to healthy organizational culture. In this section we will introduce three relational processes and their implications: shared attention, interpersonal attachments, and empathy.[36] The fourth, imitation, will be discussed in the next chapter.

Shared Attention

A particularly significant process is that of learning to pay attention to the same thing (person, object, or event) with another person. From as early as six months, a child will respond to the interest shown by another person, and by their first birthday, the child will follow the gaze of another person. Whether looking in a given direction of the gaze or in the direction pointed to by a finger (or nose, depending on the culture), children learn to share attention as part of the interpersonal process. Brown and Strawn identify three important ways these skills facilitate the child's development.[37]

The first is that sharing introduces common sensory experiences as a basis for learning and communications. Another way of looking at this is to see how the act of sharing common experiences provides topics for conversation: for example, pointing out a cow in a field when walking with a toddler, assuming she sees it, and then talking about the milk you shared for breakfast. Another illustration is that talking about the Sunday school lesson with the children in the car on the way home from church fosters their spirituality. The connection to cultural knowledge is clearly set by this type of exchange. As the individual's ability develops, so does the depth at which the shared

34. Brown and Strawn, *Physical Nature of Christian Life*, 54.

35. Brown and Strawn, *Physical Nature of Christian Life*, 55. This section will draw on their insights from chapter 4, "How Bodies Become Persons," 53–70.

36. The missiological implications of interpersonal attachment are discussed in the context of Muslim-Christian attachment in the first book in this Mission in Global Community series. See Evelyne A. Reisacher, *Joyful Witness in the Muslim World: Sharing the Gospel in Everyday Encounters* (Grand Rapids: Baker Academic, 2016), 21–42.

37. Brown and Strawn, *Physical Nature of Christian Life*, 58–59.

attention can be discussed; as we have seen earlier, it opens the opportunity for both transforming and transmitting culture. The ability to share attention with multiple others through a common set of experiences or thoughts further transforms the cultural representations.

The second contribution of shared attention to a child's development is the child's ability to interact with others. Identifying a topic for interaction allows relational bonds to form. This may be anything from a shared facial expression, as is the case for babies, through to playing a game, to eventually sharing topics in conversation. To illustrate, my three-year-old grandson enjoys playing tag as often as possible, while my seventeen-year-old granddaughter called me recently to discuss political anthropology. The point is that shared attention to a common set of experiences not only grounds communication, it also allows for the acquisition and development of skills necessary for social relationships and skills necessary to the exchange of cultural knowledge.

The third contribution is the reciprocal relationship between the child and parent. Through sharing attention, they engage relationally so that each is required to respond. While a child is acquiring language, the reciprocity draws attention to the topic, naturally raising the interest of the child while also inviting the parent to respond with new vocabulary. As the child develops, this becomes a life skill, although experience indicates that it wanes, depending on the individual interest, ability, and experience of others. Assuming for the moment that this skill is retained at the level of shared attention, it fosters an important type of cultural exchange, whether culture is being learned or transformed. Even though this is normally in the context of children and parents, the process of shared attention applies to caregivers as well as to adults, colleagues, and coworkers.

Interpersonal Attachments

The second relational process is the forming of interpersonal attachments with parents. Studies in human development have consistently recognized the importance of the nature and degree of attachments formed with parents and caregivers during childhood. The study of attachments has become integral to the psychological study of human personality, asserting that interpersonal relationships are a primary motivation for human beings. It also supports one of the central themes of Christian scholars working in the intersection of human nature and culture, the importance of "personal relatedness" and "the partnering relationship with God."[38]

38. Brown, Murphy, and Malony, *Whatever Happened to the Soul?* Specifically, see Brown, "Cognitive Contributions to Soul," 101. See also Green, *Body, Soul, and Human Life*, 71.

Researchers have identified four attachment styles in the responses of family or other caregivers to a child.[39] The most relationally healthy is "secure attachment," developed by parents who for the most part are consistently available and reliable. The security experienced by children develops both an expectation of and comfort from parental responsiveness. In contrast, "insecure attachment" takes on three different styles, each with significant implications for the well-being of the child. "Preoccupied attachment" results from inconsistent parental responses, which induces anxiety or uncertainty in the child about the parent's reliability. A more severe form of insecure attachment is "avoidant attachment," when there is even less consistent parenting. The result is not just anxiety, but the expectation of disappointment, leading to reluctance to reconnect with the parent. The most disturbed form of insecure attachment is "disorganized attachment." Inherent in this style is chaotic and abusive parenting, leading to nonattachment, seriously impacting the child's mental health.

The direct link between attachments and culture is clearly significant. Strong attachments within the family (and with caregivers) provide a secure and loving environment for children to develop. Equally true, weak or inconsistent attachments put children at risk from a myriad of physical, emotional, and spiritual forces. We discovered in the early networking of ministries to children at risk that breakdown in family life was at the forefront of the crises. The importance of fostering secure attachments is critical in our organizations missionally, both internally and externally.

Empathy

Adult-child interaction in these relational processes is shown to foster empathy. The unique responses are modeled through the reactions of parents or caregivers when a child is hurt or frightened. The emotional connection is bidirectional; parents experience the child's emotion and the child experiences the emotions of the parents, positively or negatively. This process, referred to as "reciprocal attunement" and defined as recognizing that other individuals experience emotions and thoughts similar to those of the child, is an important element of a theory of mind. The best way to learn empathy is to be shown empathy. This is true of the child and continues into adulthood. It brings to mind Luke 6:31, "Do to others as you would have them do to you," and Matthew 22:39, "You shall love your neighbor as yourself."

A breakdown in any of the other relational processes will adversely affect empathy, leaving the child or adult struggling to separate their own feelings

---

39. Brown and Strawn, *Physical Nature of Christian Life*, 60.

from those of others. One result may be difficulty recognizing appropriate interpersonal boundaries. Another example is the widespread apathy and negative reactions to the plight of immigrants and refugees, illustrating the collective expression of a lack of empathy. Efforts to promote diversity in organizations are also impacted by the degree to which members are capable of and actually show empathy toward minorities or marginalized individuals.

As leaders of missional organizations, we need to cultivate all these relational processes among our members, not as a corporate requirement per se, but pastorally, with gentleness and respect for their families of origin. This cannot be overstated: for organizations to become truly intercultural, the practices relating to empathetic responses must be proactively and consistently cultivated. From observing those who excel in these relational processes, I have learned that the best way to invite learning is through hospitality—for example, exchanging insights over meals or in informal gatherings in smaller units, settings that allow for the sharing of ideas as individual stories, not lectures. Another important detail is to try to avoid making a single person the representative for a group or culture. The goal is to move from "us and them" to "us."

Responding to the affects of families and caregivers is exemplified in the efforts, begun in the mid-1990s, to improve the quality of work with children at risk. Viva Network, an international network of individuals and organizations working with children at risk, brought together a diverse community of scholars and practitioners for a series of global forums with the goal of understanding the issues better. Initially, participants struggled to make sense of the conditions in varied contexts in which exploited children lived, such as sexual exploitation, child labor, child soldiers, AIDS orphans, and so on.

The work of this organization, now referred to as Viva, provides an important case on two levels: (1) its mission is to provide resources that address the breakdown in the relational processes of the family by resourcing parents and caregivers, and (2) it exemplifies the type of organization that is shaping, catalyzing, and propelling itself missionally through an intentional approach to learning and responding to organizational (internal) and societal (external) culture. To illustrate these dynamics, I asked my friend and colleague Katharine Thompson to respond to the question, "What are you learning about culture that helps shape your organization missionally?" In her response, you will note not only areas of learning that are shaping the organization but also areas where further reflection is required. Viva's transparency of assessment is a key element in any healthy environment characterized by learning and integration.

Children and the Mission of God

Katharine Thompson, Oxford, England[a]

Viva grows locally led networks of churches and grassroots Christian organizations who are committed to work together so that children are safe, well, and able to fulfill their God-given potential. All of Viva's programs unlock local resources and inspire churches to serve children and families, in partnership with others.[b]

As I reflect upon the issues affecting children that Viva and our partner networks address—for example, trafficking and child sexual exploitation, violence against children, discrimination against girls, or family breakdown—it strikes me that we are working to address attitudes and behaviors that are deeply held within culture, attitudes and behaviors that contradict God's view of children as expressed throughout Scripture and that consequently put children at risk.

As I reflect, I can also see that these issues and trends in culture have morphed and shifted over the twenty-plus years that I have served with Viva, and our missional strategy has morphed and shifted as a result. However, in all our work we seek to advocate for a holistic biblical view of children and of good child-development practice, as well as to support local Christians as they seek solutions to issues children face. Throughout the process, we listen and learn from cultural practices and norms that value children and families, as illustrated in the following cases.

Family-Based Care in Africa

In Uganda, fifty thousand children are growing up in children's homes, but only a minority are orphans. Poverty or family breakdown leads many parents or family members to leave their children in institutional care, believing that there the children will receive the food, shelter, and education that the family struggles to provide. However, evidence shows that a child in an institution, even a well-run one, is significantly less likely to thrive. Tearfund UK asserts that "no orphanage can provide the care and nurture of a loving, supportive family."[c]

Research shows that long-term institutional care negatively impacts children's lives in many ways, including

- serious delays in psychological and social development
- attachment problems
- dependency mind-set

- trafficking and abuse
- separation from society

As a result of this growing understanding, the Christian view of mission is changing from one of rescue (e.g., taking children away from the family and local cultural context) to one of family reintegration and family strengthening, which values the local culture and the child's sense of belonging within it. This is a trend toward working within culture and listening to it—building on the biblical principles reflected in the local culture, for example, the value and importance of family.

Twenty years ago Viva started out networking children's homes and orphanages because they represented a good proportion of the childcare work of local Christians. However, along with our partner networks—for example, Children at Risk Action Network (CRANE) in Uganda—we are now advocating for a change in attitude, and indeed culture, in Christian mission and child development, promoting the widely held view that children are better cared for in families, be they birth families, kinship households, foster families, or families that adopt the children. Our collaboration—building with local government, NGOs, and churches—aims to equip and empower a move away from institutions toward family-based models of care.

This works to the strength of local cultures in Africa since they place a high value on the role of family and rely on the strength of the extended family.

Equity and Equality in India

The Bible tells us that all are of equal value (Gal. 3:28). The implication is that in God's sight, the value of girls is equal to that of boys. However, this does not play out in cultural reality. "It's a girl" is not a joyful birth announcement in parts of India, but rather a source of shame, despair, and anger. Viva partners estimate that up to 71 percent of girls are neglected by family members, and a daughter is considered a drain on the family, as the family must save for her dowry from the time of her birth. This tradition was outlawed in 1961 but still continues today and influences families' views of girls. A quarter of girls say they get less food than their brothers. Families are less likely to invest in a girl's education or health, as she will leave to join her husband's family in the end.[d]

This is why Viva is working with six city-based networks in India where five hundred churches and organizations are working together to change cultural attitudes and practices and ensure that girls are valued as much as boys. One of the activities is the Dare to Be Different program, which is mentoring twelve hundred girls in local schools to raise their self-esteem, help them understand their rights and responsibilities, and help them gain the confidence they need to make decisions about their future.

Volunteer mentors are trained to come alongside the girls and guide them through sessions concerning self-worth, purpose, protection, and wise choices. Girls who have been through the program are encouraged to share their learning with their peers and to develop advocacy groups to change attitudes toward girls. The networks are also hosting workshops with church leaders, parents, and community elders to focus on laws protecting girls and the value of educating girls.

Shift toward Home

In the last three years, Viva has begun to focus on issues affecting children and young people within Western culture, most notably in the United Kingdom. This in part reflects the significant issues arising in our culture, for example, family breakdown, struggling parents, and poor mental health and self-harm among youth. It also reflects the desire among our local church partners to reach out to vulnerable children and young people in their own communities. This is a shift in missional priorities—away from the needs in other countries toward needs at home.

Many cultural trends seem to be at play here, including rising secularization, rising nationalism, and rising inequality (or at the very least a perception of this). Experts point to the rise in types of self-harm as confirmation that more young people are experiencing serious psychological distress because they are under unprecedented social pressure: pressure to succeed at school, the damaging effects of social media, family breakup, growing inequality, children's body-image fears, a history of abuse (including sexual abuse), and increasing sexualization.[e]

Viva's decision to catalyze collaboration in Oxford is a shift in traditional mission focus to include building the UK church's ability to respond to vulnerable children in our own culture.[f] The decision recognizes, on the basis of our own primary research, that the issues facing children in our own context are serious.[g] So issues and trends in our culture are shaping Viva's mission. I believe it is positive, but not necessarily only so. For example, does it reflect the global trend toward nationalism? Is it a form of Christian nationalism?

[a] Katharine Thompson, MAICS (Fuller) is a cofounder of Viva Network from Oxford, England. Her area of expertise is in the field of developing networks for effective mission among children at risk.

[b] Viva's mission statement. For further information, see its website: www.viva.org/start-here.

[c] Markus Köker, Footsteps: Caring for Orphans, no. 101 (2017): 3, http://www.tearfund.org/en/Sites/TILZ/Resources/Publications/%7B567B7002-FF3D-4614-8D34-7F5197C8739F%7D.

[d] Jane Travis, "More Than a Dowry: India's Girls' Real Value," Life Magazine, December 2016, http://blog.viva.org/2016/12/06/more-than-a-dowry-indias-girls-real-value.

e Denis Campbell, "NHS Figures Show 'Shocking' Rise in 'Self-Harm among Young,'" *Guardian*, October 23, 2016, https://www.theguardian.com/society/2016/oct/23/nhs-figures-show-shocking -rise-self-harm-young-people.

f A more detailed rationale is available at http://www.viva.org/wp-content/Network-profiles /UK.pdf.

g The complete report on this shift, titled *Doorsteps: A Christian Response to Children and Vulnerable Families in Oxfordshire* (Oxford: Viva, 2015), is available on Viva's website at http://www .viva.org/wp-content/Doorsteps-report.pdf.

Reviewing and Reflecting on the Issues

Viva's commitment to be a learning organization is exemplified in its approach to action and reflection. As the cultures in the areas where Viva serves changed and morphed, its mission strategy also morphed and shifted to address the changing realities. One of the hallmarks of the Viva approach is interaction with the partner organizations in order to keep its mission grounded in the mission of God. The example of Uganda demonstrates how Viva's practice was informed by research and how, at the same time, the group held firm to a holistic biblical view of children. The partnership with CRANE in Uganda is responding to the change in understanding how best to care for orphans. The resulting shift to family-based models for orphans better facilitates the relational processes critical to child development.

The partnerships with churches and organizations advocating for the needs of girls (India) and vulnerable children (UK) demonstrate the holistic mission of God (unchanging) in the midst of serious culture shifts (changing) in both countries. It is encouraging to see the maturation of the movement over the past twenty years. The leadership of Thompson, along with others, has demonstrated the value of working with the members as people first, and adjusting to the needs based on their capacities to serve. Although not without challenges, Viva continues to be a major catalyst for people-centered partnerships, calling people to a vision of helping children reach their God-given potential.

Reviewing

The addition of "self" from the perspective of cultural knowledge provides a new synthesis to our understanding of the "total way of life of a group of people."[40] Expanding the concept of self to include the core, minimal, and narrative selves allows us to differentiate between those aspects that are universal (core), those that belong to other social species (minimal), and those that are uniquely human (narrative). This is most evident in the individual's

40. Howell and Paris, *Introducing Cultural Anthropology*, 36.

understanding of self, expressed in the ability to adjust to environmental changes. The narrative self reflects the understanding of our place in the group and our ability to adapt. This in turn is connected to how one remembers the individual pilgrimage to the current place and time, referred to as the autobiographical memory. Together the narrative self draws on the understanding of the individual life story and explicitly expresses that as a story of belonging.

An example of the impact of environmental changes on the individual self (narrative self) and the social self (culture) is the change in education toward online or distributed learning over the past decade. Traditionally, instruction took place in a face-to-face environment where instructors taught in a manner suited to their personality. The change in delivery systems from geophysical to online requires faculty to understand not only the learning-management system (software and technology) but also the educational philosophy underlying the new delivery system, and requires their own acceptance of the change as something worthy of adopting. Responding to the pragmatic issues of online education (new delivery systems and declining geophysical enrollments) is a driving force in culture change that is redefining the identities of teachers (social selves), and the testimonies of respected colleagues (narrative selves) who embrace the new system are critical to its success.

Understanding the important connection between the narrative self and the culture can help you implement change or strengthen practices more effectively by (1) providing time and space for dialogue surrounding the initiative, allowing for metarepresentations to be formulated or adopted, (2) finding ways to acknowledge those whose contributions, likely due to their ability to think creatively or analytically, are particularly helpful to the process, and (3) encouraging a new narrative by inviting individual narratives to be shared with others.

Exploring this interaction further, the faculty dialogue surrounding the new delivery system is an illustration of cognition at the metarepresentational level. Individual faculty members express opinions based on their individual understanding and biases (mental representations) in conversation with colleagues, moving toward metarepresentations that reframe or replace mental representations. The outcome, at least in my experience, is a move toward a new reality based on metarepresentations through learning, sharing, adapting, and integrating the new cultural reality.

These insights from cognitive studies that humans are both embodied physically and embedded in cultural communities also make us aware that "the self" has limitations that are determined by physical capacities and mental acuity. Both elements are impacted by the circumstances of our daily lives. This interdependence makes the refrain "I am so busy that it is hard to keep up" a serious wake-up call. We know well that this is not a mantra for good leadership, nor is it an indicator of a healthy organization. Our physical nature requires the same level of commitment to development as do our skills or abilities to lead. Further, our organizational culture should affirm a healthy lifestyle, including moderating the workload based on human capacity rather than only productivity. We can easily affirm this necessity, but it is not real until it becomes a common practice in the organizational culture.

The concept of the narrative self is another significant insight from cognitive anthropology. Rather than dividing between individualist and relational cultures, we find that a more valid comparison lies in the narrative self of individuals. Ranging from those who frequently, even elaborately, share their personal story (diachronic) to those whose need to tell their story less often (episodic), the link between the autobiographical memory and narrative self is a critical factor in being human. Building on this connection, we should consider where and when we give opportunity for appropriately sharing our personal narrative. As we share personal narratives with one another, they naturally become an integral part of creating and sustaining the story of our mission together. The organizational narrative cannot be told apart from the people who serve in the organizational mission. The very effort of telling and retelling the story should be linked to the mission in ways that affirm and inspire, thereby building a strong collective narrative.

An important part of the narrative self is the role of family in the lives of individuals. Families differ from one another within and across cultural contexts, as illustrated by my family compared to those of my Melanesian friends. By inviting discussion around family experiences, we can use relational processes developed from childhood to help us understand the similarities and differences of the various cultures represented by our colleagues. With the mission of the organization clearly in focus, we can facilitate a much more robust dialogue when we understand the importance of shared attention and interpersonal attachment. Providing a safe environment and physical space to interact opens the possibilities for greater interpersonal attachment and empathy for one another and those we serve.

Introducing this level of interaction may well be threatening to leaders as well as others in the organization. Controlling the size of the group (critical mass) will mitigate this problem, with the optimal range being five to eight people. A leadership retreat is an effective place to start modeling the type of reflection and outcomes desired; from experience I have found that this may mean reorganizing for a second round if the leadership struggles with unclear expectations. Depending on the size of the organization and the receptivity of the leaders, the time frame and communication of outcomes will vary, but the value of the process applies across the organizational landscape. The goal is not so much relational intimacy as deeper understanding of the cultural diversity that merges into the culture of your organization. This approach is helpful in reducing the threat level to those who are more likely not to share their story with others.

A theory of mind, as we have identified it, is an individual's recognition that other people, although unique individuals themselves, also have perspectives, feelings, and thoughts that are similar to those of other individuals. We understand that the development of empathy is tied to the development of a child's theory of mind. Therefore, the degree to which adults can feel empathy toward others depends on their history. Christian adults may feel a range of attitudes toward others, but our Christian commitment to loving others as well as our obedience to the mission of God compels us to show empathy. Facilitating opportunities to express and further develop empathy is vital to healthy cultural transformation.

Another important element of showing empathy is the degree to which it also helps others, particularly those on the margins, to positively experience the community. A majority of Christian organizations have a missional commitment to reflect the unity recorded in Romans 15:7: "So welcome each other, in the same way that Christ also welcomed you, for God's glory" (CEB). If this is integral to our mission, then it must be accompanied by the intentional creation of opportunities and space to express empathy for one another in word and deed. Our expression of empathy is not only for our community, but also to the world beyond the boundaries of our organization.

Reflecting

It follows that effective intercultural leadership requires deeper understanding and appreciation of the role of individuals in culture, including formation, transformation, and transmission of cultural representations. Consider the following questions from the perspective of leaders of your organization:

1. How does the concept of the "narrative self" relate to the development of leaders within your sphere of influence?
2. What are the primary venues for social interaction for members of your organization? To what extent does your organizational environment facilitate or impede metarepresentational exchange of knowledge about culture?
3. From the perspective of a theory of mind, which individuals in your organization have shown that they can provide stories that capture the

beliefs and attitudes of the community? How are those stories shared
among your group? Are they influential in shaping or catalyzing your
organization missionally?

4. Does your organization or leadership face major challenges that can
   be assessed through attention paid to the dialogue among your members or employees surrounding the issues? Are there ways that you as
   a leader can facilitate more robust conversations about your organizational mission in a less restrictive environment (e.g., kitchen table
   missiology)?

Beyond the context of the conversations, consider what we learn from the
anthropological insights about self, family, and caregivers. Even if the question doesn't relate to your situation, consider the implications for others in
groups that are related to you. Perhaps you can share your thoughts with your
contacts there. Here are questions for reflection:

5. How does the discussion of the interdependence between cognitive capacities and personal relatedness apply to the way you approach leadership development? Might some areas be neglected? If so, what steps
   might you take to broaden the impact of your efforts?

6. As you think of the families represented in your organization, are there
   ways you can facilitate both reflection and action for their well-being?
   How does the organizational environment facilitate or impede the commitment to family?

7. Considering the role of caregivers of children, are there ways that you
   could better provide for the individuals responsible for such significant
   missional impact? What approaches to ministry to families in the organization are currently in place, and who are the leaders?

8. Finally, are there practical ways you can foster both physical well-being
   and mental acuity among the leaders and members of your organization?
   Have you personally found a way to develop both aspects of your leadership? How can you ensure accountability for the steps you take (or have
   taken) to ensure a more effective organizational mission?

Chapter 4 will take up current work on the concepts of imitation and
rituals as they relate to both leadership and organizations. We will explore
perspectives and current work in cultural and cognitive anthropology as well
as anthropology of religion, drawing out implications for leading Christian
organizations.

4

Learning Culture Naturally

Imitation and Rituals

The Cape Town 2010 Lausanne Congress was deemed "the most representative gathering of Christian leaders in the 2000 year history of the Christian movement (*Christianity Today*)."[1] Having attended Manila 1989, I was keen to participate in the worship experience and dialogue with leaders from the global South and East in this setting where the knowledge of God's mission is met with rejoicing and obedience. In every session I encountered men and women from across the world, including personal friends from various countries I had visited during my twenty years as a missionary. It was a living witness of the church universal, just as I imagined it when studying ecclesiology in seminary. Certainly one could argue for greater representation in various elements of the program, but compared to other gatherings I attend, it was truly a "representative gathering"!

Stepping back from that great gathering, I should ask, How did we all learn to worship together so well, despite so many different church traditions and theological perspectives, not to mention the nationalities and ethnicities? To be sure, the presence of the Holy Spirit is the most accurate response. And I

---

1. Lausanne Movement, "Cape Town 2010: The Third Lausanne Congress on World Evangelization," accessed January 17, 2017, https://www.lausanne.org/gatherings/congress/cape -town-2010-3.

readily acknowledge that the Spirit's actual presence is a mystery that never ceases to inspire awe. We also share the Bible as our rule of faith and practice. But as with the Sunday school child who answers "Jesus" to every question, there is something more to be said. For instance, how do we learn these rituals of the Christian culture, in this case the evangelical culture? And what are the implications for our organizations and for us as leaders?

One could take many directions in responding, but for the purpose of exploring the concept of culture, this chapter focuses on imitation and rituals. In the first section we consider the natural relational and developmental processes of imitation from the perspective of cognitive psychology. The second section explores the mimetic basis for learning culture from the work of cognitive anthropology, providing important insights into the role of imitation in the transmission of culture. After reflecting on imitation and mimetics, in the third section we look at a case study of rituals and meaning from the Roma culture in Croatia. The fourth section considers the role of rituals in the transmission of cultural knowledge, from the difficulty of classifying them to performing formal and informal rituals as part of societal and organizational culture. We conclude the chapter with a review of the critical issues and reflection on the implications for our leaders and organizations.

Learning Naturally through Imitation

Cognitive studies in child development provide important insights into how personality, intelligence, and character are shaped by critical processes of the interaction between children and adults. Chapter 3 introduced the concepts of shared attention, interpersonal attachments, and empathy (emotional attunement). Here, following the work of psychologists Brown and Strawn on the physical nature of the Christian life, we will consider not only the influence of imitation in the relational process of children but also the unconscious imitation of others, and imitation as a means of Christian formation.[2]

The Relational Process of Imitation

The familiar experience of a child copying the behavior of a parent is one of the best examples of imitation. As a baby intently watches her mother, the baby copies actions such as sticking out her tongue or smiling, drawing

2. Warren S. Brown and Brad D. Strawn, *The Physical Nature of Christian Life: Neuroscience, Psychology, and the Church* (Cambridge: Cambridge University Press, 2012), 55–58, 78–82, 115–18.

positive attention to herself, which in turn ensures that this new behavior is part of her repertoire in the months ahead. It is as if the child is predisposed to imitate her parent, which is in fact true. Imitation is one of the most innate learning styles. This applies not only to behavior but also to attitudes, feelings, thoughts, and motivation. The fact that imitation includes perceiving what is happening as well as reproducing it underlines the importance of secure attachment in adult-child interaction, as we discussed in chapter 3.

A major breakthrough in the research reveals that acts that are seen and acts that are done are coded together by the brain.[3] Extensive research using brain scans indicates that the effect on the brain of observing others in action appears much like the effect of the action being actually done by the subject; this relationship is known as "perception-action reciprocity." This discovery led to the further discovery of "mirror neurons" located in the cerebral cortex of the brain. Although they were initially found in monkeys, evidence from recent research supports the presence of mirror neurons in humans. These mirror neurons account for the link between seeing and doing, known as "mirroring of neural activity."[4] The implications for learning culture at the individual level are significant.

To illustrate, think of the axiom often applied in medical education, "See one, do one, teach one," and relate it to a worship service. A person sees an unfamiliar action or a different practice in a familiar event (such as intinction of the bread into the wine in the Eucharist or kneeling at the rail for prayer) and constructs a mental image of how it is done, even a perception of the motivation and rationale for doing it, without any verbal communication. It is purely an observation of an action. This often results in imitation, doing it oneself. This may be the immediate response, such as joining the line of congregants to participate in the Communion service, or it may be to contemplate the reasons for particular actions while waiting one's turn to go forward. Normally, the person observes and practices until the task is mastered, after which they may well become the person others imitate—for better or for worse, since this process works with deviant behavior as well as appropriate behavior. The important point is that imitation is a natural ability including both observation for understanding and production for skill.

An important aspect of this perception-action reciprocity is that observing others also "primes the motor circuits" in our brain in preparation for "imitating the actions we are observing."[5] Marketers know this well, for example,

---

3. Brown and Strawn, *Physical Nature of Christian Life*, 56.
4. Brown and Strawn, *Physical Nature of Christian Life*, 56–57.
5. Brown and Strawn, *Physical Nature of Christian Life*, 57.

when the meal includes a particularly tempting dessert and the person in the ad is enjoying each bite. Or, more to our concerns, when a leader demonstrates the appropriate action rather than sending out a memo—in other words, leading by example. This is observable in children from the beginning, but it is increasingly significant in the preteen and teen years, as most adults know all too well.

One more important contribution of the research is support for a theory of mind, specifically one's capacity to draw inferences about the thoughts and actions of others through parallels from one's own experiences. It is the observation that others are "like me" or "not like me" that implies that their actions are or aren't in line with "mine." This is easily illustrated by experiences of driving a motor vehicle: for example, when a person allows you to turn into the lane ahead of them from a parking lot or slows to allow you to change lanes in heavy traffic, you immediately respond by joining the flow of traffic without any verbal communication. If you are like me, you notice many more instances where the driver does not yield, which I immediately attribute to the "not like me" category. This relational process of imitation continues through adolescence and beyond as one of the most significant factors in the formation of character and the learning of culture.

Unconscious Imitation of Others

Imitation is also a powerful force in shaping individual behavior, even that of adults. Although it is a continuous process, much of it goes unnoticed because we imitate others unconsciously. Simple examples include the contagious nature of a yawn, the effect of the first person to stand for a song, or the response to the first person to clap after a performance. The link to culture is obvious, but not always discernible without careful observation due to the unconscious nature of the response.

Psychologists researching the imitation of physical actions such as posture, mannerisms, or facial expressions describe it as the "chameleon effect."[6] The observation is that individuals "unconsciously and unintentionally" change their behavior to match that of people around them, thereby adapting to the context. This nonverbal exchange, while unconscious, acts to shape culture even more than spoken or written communication regarding the behavior. This is important to remember in training leaders, due to the variation of cultural perceptions about leadership. By participating with a leader, the trainee is

---

6. T. L. Chartrand and J. A. Bargh, "The Chameleon Effect: The Perception-Behavior Link and Social Interaction," *Journal of Personality and Social Psychology* 76, no. 6 (1999): 893–910, quoted in Brown and Strawn, *Physical Nature of Christian Life*, 79.

able to observe and hopefully imitate the action in context. This process of observing and performing the skill further reinforces perceptions of where it fits and even why it is necessary. There is no replacement for seeing it done.

The influence of unconscious imitation is so significant that researchers identify the imitation process as the "perception-behavior expressway," suggesting that simply perceiving the behavior of others automatically increases the chances of engaging in the behavior.[7] An implication of these studies is the significance of immersion for culture and language learning. It also follows that the choice of cultural informants is an extremely important part of the process, due to the chameleon effect. Unconscious imitation results in more rapid and complete mastery of the skill, in contrast to the more formal and theoretical classroom approach to training.

Beyond the influence of imitating behavior, research also shows that desires, motivations, attitudes, and even thoughts are "unconsciously primed" by imitation.[8] The current understanding is that despite the lack of awareness, people are influencing and being influenced by others continuously—an exchange referred to as "reciprocal imitation"—both in actions and thoughts. This capacity for unconscious imitation further reinforces our understanding that human nature and culture are interdependent.[9]

Imitation in Christian Formation

The use of imitation as a spiritual practice is common among Christians. Jesus commanded the disciples, "Follow me" (Mark 1:17). The apostle Paul instructed the Corinthian believers to imitate him even as he imitated Christ (1 Cor. 4:15–17). Thomas à Kempis finished the classic *The Imitation of Christ* in 1427 CE, relating Christian devotion to "the imitation of Christ." It is a simple yet profound appeal. As we have seen, the influence of both intentional and unconscious imitation reveals the strength of the "fundamental imitative character of human nature," further supporting the appeal.[10]

7. A. Dijksterhuis and J. A. Bargh, "The Perception-Behavior Expressway: Automatic Effects of Social Perception on Social Behavior," in *Advances in Experimental Social Psychology* 33 (San Diego: Academic Press, 2001), 1–40, quoted in Brown and Strawn, *Physical Nature of Christian Life*, 79.

8. For a brief review of the literature, see Brown and Strawn, *Physical Nature of Christian Life*, 80–81.

9. The power to influence the thoughts, desires, and behavior of others through imitation is at the center of the fields of communication and marketing. While I acknowledge this aspect of imitation studies, it is beyond the scope of this work; it raises issues that deserve significant reflection.

10. Brown and Strawn, *Physical Nature of Christian Life*, 115.

From the perspective of cognitive studies, the role of imitation in Christian formation is strongly supported by the contagious nature we noted for behavior, goals, attitudes, and even desires. For any organization committed to their calling as part of the mission of God, the formation of members individually and collectively is an important consideration. This goes beyond the specific competencies required in the job description to the nature of membership and spiritual maturity of the members in a Christian organization. Brown and Strawn make the important point that the church must "become a place where our imitation of one another results . . . [in] the desire to love and serve."[11] While affirming this primary role of local churches, we also must recognize that Christian organizations that are missionally committed to God depend on mature members in line with their mission.

The challenge of capturing the power of the imitation of Christ takes dedication and time to build what Lingenfelter refers to as a "community of trust."[12] To actualize the potential of imitation in Christian formation, it is important to consider the settings in which this may be achieved, ensuring sufficient time and opportunity for deeper relationships to form, as well as collective commitment to the organizational mission. Setting an expectation for Christian maturity as part of the organizational commitment is important, but facilitating the opportunity to regularly reflect on the actual practice as part of the routine of the group (team or department meetings) is critical to building these communities.

Drawing on the other relational processes, we can say that elements of the group must include shared attention, in the form of studies, shared narratives, and particularly opportunities to serve together in ministry and mission. Interpersonal attachments require a depth of intimacy that allows not only for conversations but also for critical feedback on mental representations and culture. We are painfully aware of the fact that imitation may be good or bad when it comes to behavior and attitudes. Without the ability to speak "the truth with love" (Eph. 4:15 CEB), it is difficult to move beyond superficialities. Finally, the cultivation of empathy not only requires good role models and appropriate understanding of a given situation, but it is also formed in the process of loving others. Evelyne Reisacher presents an important case for joyful witness, which includes the ability to show genuine empathy for the experiences and dignity of others.[13]

---

11. Brown and Strawn, *Physical Nature of Christian Life*, 117.

12. Sherwood G. Lingenfelter, *Leading Cross-Culturally: Covenant Relationships for Effective Christian Leadership* (Grand Rapids: Baker Academic, 2008), 81–90.

13. Evelyne A. Reisacher, *Joyful Witness in the Muslim World: Sharing the Gospel in Everyday Encounters* (Grand Rapids: Baker Academic, 2016).

With or Without Words: Mimetic Processes in Learning Culture

Mimetics is the broader field of study referring to learning actions that are sensory and body-based, requiring images, schemas, language, and movements for performance. It also refers to representing life or nature through imitation without the use of language. Anthropological studies of mimetic processes parallel those of cognitive psychology, demonstrating both the elementary skills present in nonhuman primates and, more importantly for our purposes, the substantially higher degree of mimetic skills in humans. Studies demonstrate the ability of even a small child to participate in sophisticated cultural processes through imitating the skills and practices of their social group.[14]

Children have been shown to have the ability to understand complex relationships between people and objects and events, even to the point of creating language to describe them and developing schemas for participating in the events.[15] This reinforces the significance of early childhood education as well as the importance of Christian formation for children, as demonstrated by the Viva partnerships in Uganda and India. These same mimetic processes continue to be crucial to learning throughout life.

Mimetics and Culture

An important function of mimetics in the transmission of culture lies in our ability to transform the "external material world," first into mental representations and then into public representations (and metarepresentations) that shape cultural realities through reciprocal imitation.[16] In addition to the material products of culture, social behavior and activities are generally learned mimetically as sensory, body-based processes, giving us the ability of competent action in institutions and organizations.[17] For example, knowing how to respond in a meeting or where to stand in proximity to the leader is learned mimetically. This was evident on many levels at Cape Town 2010, where, despite the enormous crowd, people found their seats on time and interacted with appropriate voice control, even when it required silence, all without direct instruction. Most of this skill comes from participation in our

14. Michael Tomasello, *The Cultural Origins of Human Cognition* (Cambridge, MA: Harvard University Press, 1999). His more recent work, *A Natural History of Human Thinking* (Cambridge, MA: Harvard University Press, 2014), thoroughly analyzes his work over the fifteen years between publications.

15. Tomasello, *Cultural Origins of Human Cognition*, 161.

16. Christoph Wulf, *Anthropology: A Continental Perspective* (Chicago: University of Chicago Press, 2013), 187.

17. Wulf, *Anthropology*, 187.

immediate small group or congregation. The resulting practical nonverbal schema, which requires no conscious precepts, takes control of our routine behavior as it is acted out in an unfamiliar scale of events such as Cape Town 2010.

A concept parallel to the sensory processes of mimetics is the public expression of culture, such as murals, music, and dance. Such works of art are imitations of nature through mimetic processes, not reproductions or copies of something. They portray the mental image of the artist.[18] As a consequence, the original object, used as a model for the work, is transformed into an expression (image) from the imagination of the artist as an interpreter. Interestingly, mimetic processes also impact the ability of others to appreciate this same work of art. Although knowledge of the context of an artist or the production process of a painting does not ensure that the artist's interpretation will be aesthetically pleasing to every observer, mimetics can affect the process of interpretation, both production and appreciation.

An example from the Cape Town 2010 experience demonstrates this concept. One of the significant new songs composed for the congress was "We believe in One God," based on the Nicene Creed. The song transformed the theological statement of the creed into a culturally significant form. The story of its origin was recounted to me in an email by Ed Willmington, the primary composer and conductor of the combined choirs and orchestra at Cape Town 2010.[19]

> The basic piece was written by Trevor Sampson, the main worship leader in Cape Town [2010]. Clay Schmit [Willmington's codirector] and I asked Trevor to write the ordinaries of the final worship service, wanting those parts of the service to have African origination. He is very gifted . . . [so] Clay and I spent time coaching and writing with Trevor in South Africa. . . . [When] he provided me with the basic song, he was singing and playing a keyboard in his studio in [Macassar], one of the townships around Cape Town.[20]

The debut evoked great joy as the congregation responded to Trevor's lead in the callback style of African singing, a culturally mimetic response. It was

18. For a very helpful summary of the relation of history and culture to the mimetic basis of cultural learning, see Wulf, *Anthropology*, 189–94.

19. Ed Willmington, personal email communication, January 31, 2017.

20. A compact disc of the official music from the opening and closing ceremonies was subsequently complied by Edwin M. Willmington, conductor of the combined choirs and orchestra at Cape Town 2010. It is available through the Brehm Center at Fuller Theological Seminary or online as a downloadable MP3 album entitled *Reconciled in Christ: Cape Town 2010* (Pasadena, CA: Brehm Center, Fuller Theological Seminary, 2013).

one of the most appreciated songs of the worship services. The song was subsequently included in chapel services at Fuller Theological Seminary and by special request during my service of installation as provost, in this case demonstrating the positive response of experiencing art as aesthetically pleasing.

Other actions that evoke aesthetic or intense emotional responses have also been identified as triggering mimetic processes—for example, the contagious nature of laughter or even the vicious cycle of violence.[21] The contagious nature of these processes, such as violence, is an all-too-present reality around the world. It is important to consider how Christian organizations, in harmony with their missional nature, can influence cultures through appropriating mimetic practices on a broader scale.

Practical Knowledge and Social Behavior

Wulf notes that "to a great extent" the learning of culture is mimetic and in that sense is part of the "processes of education and self-education."[22] Earlier I introduced the concept of a universal cultural schema, which is currently hypothetical at best; however, in the sense that culture is self-taught through mimetic processes, we do see at least a universal disposition toward culture in human nature. Further, given that mimetic learning is a "sensory, body-based form of learning in which images, schemas, and movements needed to perform actions are learned," we must consider its importance for leadership and organizations.[23]

Cognitive studies have linked the capacity for social behavior (action) to mimetic processes of cultural learning.[24] People develop skills that differ greatly from one culture to another, all through mimetic processes. This applies to a wide range of actions, such as games, the appropriate means of exchanging gifts, appropriate treatment of workers, and even ritual behavior. A specific example is the issue of respect shown by those in power to those who serve under their leadership. It is not uncommon for workers to comment on the way their boss treats the servers in a restaurant or the delivery person at the office. More to the point, inconsistencies in treating people from diverse cultural or ethnic backgrounds are a more powerful message than claiming to be committed to diversity. The reason is that practical knowledge, as determined by

21. Wulf, *Anthropology*, 193.
22. Wulf, *Anthropology*, 188.
23. Wulf, *Anthropology*, 188.
24. See Michael T. Taussig, *Mimesis and Alterity: A Particular History of the Senses* (New York: Routledge, 1993); Pierre Bourdieu, *The Logic of Practice*, trans. Richard Nice (Stanford, CA: Stanford University Press, 1990); Wulf, *Anthropology*, 194.

the wide diversity of cultural and social behavior, is in the end learned "using mimetic approximations."[25]

It is important to remember that unlike replication, mimetic processes generate skills that are both similar to and different from those of other people in other situations. Mimetic processes create the ability to adapt to the specific context through individual transformations of practical knowledge. The relationship between the practical knowledge and a given social behavior comes not primarily by the ability to conceptualize alternatives, but through the senses based on mental pictures, feelings, and imitating the social practice of others.

Another way of looking at the relationship of social behavior and practical knowledge is in the context of real-life situations, face-to-face, as contextually determined. Over time the repetition of social behavior becomes part of the mental schema of the individuals, appropriate to their daily experience and routines. It is based on the social forms and cultural norms of a given context. As individuals move across cultures, new experiences will create new ways of experiencing the world (due to cultural context), based not so much on a formal study of the new culture as on the lived experience of practices and relationships. In practice this is not quite as easy as it sounds. Yet for our understanding of culture and intercultural engagement, it has implications that are directly applicable to the changing global environment in which we live and work.[26]

Missiological Implications of Imitation and Mimetics

Thinking of the role of imitation in learning provokes us to consider how it might be used more effectively in leadership and organizational development. From childhood, we are imitating others, initially family members and caregivers, and eventually those who are part of our social group. We may remember how our imitation of others, often seen as "going along with the crowd," had both positive and negative effects on our formation. The influence of a strong youth group in high school or a campus ministry during college can make a significant difference to enduring faith.[27] For ex-

---

25. Wulf, *Anthropology*, 194.

26. By describing imitation, social action, and practical knowledge in this way, I have focused on the positive aspects of imitation and mimetics. There are many examples of both leaders and organizational practices that demonstrate the negative aspects of imitation and mimetics. I often use the phrase "indulging their idiosyncrasies" to describe individuals or groups that consciously refuse to learn from others.

27. The Fuller Youth Institute is actively involved in researching the influences of churches and youth work on Christian formation. The institute's goal is to turn the research into resources

ample, in many places, referring to one's participation in Scripture Union is a synonym for being a dedicated Christian. The same is true of belonging to a chapter of the International Fellowship of Evangelical Students. These dynamic Christian movements have appropriated the best elements of imitation as an approach to learning through regular meetings and by producing materials such as daily study guides and publications that contribute to the formation of mature faith.

Similarly, active participation in global networks broadens the opportunities to develop a more active theory of mind incorporating the thoughts and actions of believers from other cultures. As we noted concerning both relational and even unconscious imitation of others, the participant is influenced in behavior, attitudes, goals, and desires. Anthropology has long used the methodology of participant observation (finding understanding by observing the world from inside a given culture, rather than looking into that culture from the outside), which provides an important skill set for the study of culture, known as ethnography. The conscious and unconscious imitation of others is a powerful source of influence for an individual leader or organization. An important source for unpacking the cultural knowledge for others within the organization is found in the intentional dialogue that is facilitated by metarepresentations of cultural knowledge.

In chapter 3 we noted the importance of empathy when considering others, particularly from different cultural backgrounds. Introducing the stories and experiences of others (social and self narratives) facilitates the opportunity for individuals and groups to have a positive influence on each other that will most likely become a source of reciprocal imitation leading to cultural adaptation. In other words, by active participation in global networks of believers, we broaden the scope of the "fundamental imitative character"[28] of discipleship, which leads us to imitate not only Christ but others; thus we grow in our understanding of the glory of God as we see the kingdom of God work across cultural and physical boundaries. Reflecting on that understanding is foundational to the missiological concept of critical contextualization, the "ongoing process of embodying the gospel in an ever-changing world."[29]

Gatherings such as Cape Town 2010 provide important venues for sharing the physical products (public representations) of culture. Christians from all types of ministries, such as artists, musicians, pastors, missionaries, theologians, and missiologists, all have the opportunity to engage with others

---

to help the church become the best place for young people to grow. To access the resources, see http://fulleryouthinstitute.org.

28. Brown and Strawn, *Physical Nature of Christian Life*, 115.

29. Hiebert, *Gospel in Human Contexts*, 29.

with similar callings in what most often results in transformative reciprocal imitations through the various sessions of the event. New approaches to worship that include different artwork, styles of preaching, and other forms of liturgy create sources of learning that engage our understanding of the Bible and theology in fresh ways, while equally engaging human contexts, histories, and cultures. To be sure, we face challenges in broad areas such as finance, authority, representation of diversity, and the bracketing effect of congresses that fundamentally reduce the impact to those who participate; but that being said, these are not insurmountable, nor is a gathering on the scale of Cape Town 2010 the only way to create such global experiences. An important outcome of these opportunities is gaining practical knowledge of other cultures while also introducing new types of social behavior leading to mental schemas that engage the globalizing world.

The study of rituals follows logically from the study of imitation, again drawing on the work of cognitive anthropology but adding implications from the fields of anthropology, religion, and organizational studies. Before considering the current work in the study of rituals, we turn to a contemporary case study of learning from rituals both in everyday life and in the context of a local church. I asked a colleague who lives in a Roma community in Croatia, "What are you learning about the rituals in their cultural setting as the context of your witness to the gospel?" The case study highlights one of the most difficult aspects of understanding rituals: meaning.

Learning from Rituals

Melody J. Wachsmuth, Croatia[a]

I had arrived too early at the annual Roma[b] ball—it was 8 p.m. I thought people were exaggerating when they said it would go all night. I sat drinking coffee at a friend's home in the village, waiting to hear the fluid, improvisational melodies characteristic of Roma music in the Balkans. Finally the music started, and I walked over to the central field to find people standing in groups, waiting for the right song in order to dance.

The ball is a two-day annual event where Roma (and others who like the music) come from all around Croatia's eastern region to dance and socialize. At midnight on the final night, unmarried young women dress in their finest to compete for that year's distinction of being "Miss Roma." When the young women parade into the open-air tent, they are asked a few questions and then show off their dancing skills to the band's rollicking beat.

Identification—Rituals That Invite Shared Meaning

I wove my way through the crowd, accepting various invitations to enter a dance circle. My feet clumsily tried to keep up with the fast-stepping, roving beats. I saw people I had not seen in church for a long time, people who had walked to the ball from far-off villages—in fact, it seemed that everyone I had ever met in that region was there that night.

The next day in church, I felt like I had achieved a new status in the community—everyone smilingly referenced my dancing at the ball. By entering into their ritual of dance, it seemed, I had powerfully identified myself with them in a way that had formerly eluded me. Given their ongoing experiences of social exclusion, did this embodiment of shared meaning eradicate an unarticulated power structure?

Dancing is an essential performative ritual in Roma culture; however, in some Christian Roma contexts, it has been forbidden due to its association with drinking and social ills. Although the meaning of dance is different for me than for the Roma, joining in the ritual allowed me to momentarily share in their meaning. We are like two concentric circles, and the dancing occupies the shared space—a space I enter not with words or ideas but with bodily engagement.

Dissonance—Rituals That Create Clashes of Meaning

Social marginalization and poverty—a prominent reality of Europe's Roma populations—physically manifests in the way Roma communities are often separated from Croatian neighborhoods. I had been visiting Roma communities in this region for five years alongside a Roma Pentecostal couple who were evangelizing the people. Discipleship and relationship in this context is intensely personal—most of it happens through frequent visits to the home and over steaming cups of Turkish coffee and glasses of cola. In 2012, after two years of house visits, the Roma couple decided to open a church, and I continued serving alongside them during that process.

Herbert Anderson and Edward Foley, in *Mighty Stories, Dangerous Rituals*, argue that ritual, as embodied story, is a powerful medium that can merge the divine story with our story.[c] Although our small church consists primarily of new Roma Christians, we also have Croatians, Americans, and Dutch—a plurality of cultures, languages, perceptions, and experiences. As a cultural outsider but Christian insider, I wanted to explore how sacred ritual could join my story with that of my church community—to deepen the mystery of God's presence for all of us. However, not only do rituals invite identification and shared meaning, they can also unintentionally transgress cultural boundaries, revealing unarticulated beliefs and frames of reference.

I had introduced Advent readings and the Advent wreath as a way to connect our local church to the global church and enter into the hopeful waiting that marks the Christmas season. After I explained the meaning behind Advent, I invited a congregant up to do the first reading and light the wreath candle. Just as she was reaching forward to light the candle, the pastor came running up to stop it. Unbeknownst to me, there had been a stir at the back of the church because several people considered this ritual blasphemous, associating it with "Catholic" practice and "Tradition."

Croatia has a unique cultural context—although over 86 percent are Roman Catholic, a high percentage are nominal, and ethnic and religious identity are intertwined. Similarly, most Roma in Croatia identify as Catholic or Orthodox (if they have Serbian roots). Although we do not disparage the Roman Catholic Church in our Pentecostal church, some people who join the Protestant church associate any liturgy, ritual, or sacraments with an empty and corrupt Catholicism, particularly if family relationships have suffered as a result of their decision to leave the Catholic Church.

The aftermath of this misplaced ritual was difficult—someone threatened to leave the church if we lit candles again, others were confused as to why I had introduced the ritual in the first place. Although I had explained the meaning, ritual is much deeper than reflective knowledge—thus the visceral, urgent reaction against a perceived "dangerous" ritual. The dissonance of meaning unleashed by the ritual revealed the congregation's operating theologies. The obvious power of ritual, and of its guiding story, caused me to reflect on the potential of sacred ritual as an agent of change toward holistic transformation.

Ritual communicates and maintains social structures and stability—in the case of dancing, it is an invitation into an embodied joy, celebration, and identification with Roma culture. This bodily participation in ritual creates a momentary shared-meaning space and also reminds me that spiritual transformation should be holistic, that bodies are located in a particular social and cultural context. This power to connect and identify can also reveal the dissonance between cultural meanings—but perhaps this dissonance can help expose the limit of each person's contextual situatedness and therefore offer vision toward an expanded range of perception and understanding.

[a] Melody J. Wachsmuth (MAICS, MAT, Fuller Theological Seminary) has served as a mission researcher and writer in Croatia since 2011. Recently, her research has focused on the Roma in Southeastern Europe, highlighting both the growth of Christianity and the challenges facing these largely marginalized groups of people living throughout Europe. She also serves as a church leader in a Roma-majority church in eastern Croatia.

[b] The Roma, or Romani, referred to in some contexts (sometimes pejoratively) as Gypsies, are estimated to number ten to twelve million in Europe. However, they are not a monolithic group but instead consist of related groups of people who self-identify as Roma, Romani, or Gypsy, and

who may possess shared experiences or histories, shared language or related dialects, or shared cultural practices.
  c Herbert Anderson and Edward Foley, *Mighty Stories, Dangerous Rituals: Weaving Together the Human and the Divine* (San Francisco: Jossey-Bass, 1998).

What about Rituals? Knowing and Doing Culture

The account of ritual in the context of Roma culture highlights several aspects of rituals that merit careful consideration. In both situations, the rituals were widely known and repeated with sufficient frequency to be considered part of the culture. The annual Roma ball is both a celebratory event and a rite of passage for younger women. By participating in the festivities, Melody Wachsmuth moved closer to the people among whom she lives and works, through the "essential performative ritual." In the Advent ritual (including the readings and the wreath), she moved from participant to leading performer, introducing the well-known Christian ritual accompanying the Advent season. The outcomes of participating in these two rituals were surprising in their depth of response, the first positive and the second negative. The issue of meaning and the nature of the performance introduce the types of questions that are important to consider for both leaders and organizations.

Rituals Require Special Attention

The study of rituals is an enduring domain of anthropology, along with kinship and worldview studies; it is a consistent feature of ethnographies, or the study of cultures. Rituals are linked to the religious beliefs of the community, exemplified by Émile Durkheim's final volume, *The Elementary Forms of Religious Life*. He stresses the importance of practices (rituals) over beliefs as essential for sustaining religious community.[30] Beyond religious life, rituals are also inextricable from other areas of human existence, such as politics, education, business, family life, and mission. They assign meaning and even structure to human relations.[31] It is difficult to conceive any aspect of our existence that doesn't include some type of ritual.

Despite the ubiquitous presence of rituals, they are difficult to classify and understand since various participants and observers interpret the meaning differently, as seen in Melody Wachsmuth's experience. Defining rituals raises difficulties precisely because of these variables. The phenomena of rituals is equally complex, involving tradition, authority, performers, and activities.

30. Émile Durkheim, *The Elementary Forms of Religious Life* (New York: Free Press, 1912).
31. Wulf, *Anthropology*, 215–16.

Ritual studies have attempted to classify rituals according to the type of occasion to which they relate. Here are some examples:

- Rituals of transition (birth and childhood, initiation and adolescence, marriage, death)
- Rituals of institution or taking up office (taking on new tasks and positions)
- Seasonal rituals (Christmas, birthdays, days of remembrance, national holidays)
- Rituals of intensification (eating, celebrating, love, faith)
- Rituals of rebellion (peace and ecological movements, ethnic, gender, sexual identity, rituals of youth)
- Rituals of interaction (greetings, taking leave, conflicts)[32]

Another important category that stands with the rituals listed above is rituals of transformation, in which an experience that will transform the life of an individual or a group is anticipated.[33] While the overall classification helps with our discussion, it betrays a degree of vagueness when we try to apply it to a given ritual. For example, the annual Roma ball may be classified as a ritual of transition for young women, a seasonal ritual, and/or a ritual of intensification with regard to cultural identity. This raises an important point from the perspective of cognitive anthropology: while rituals tend to be "communicative acts" that convey "nontrivial information" to all those involved, both participants and observers alike, they resist precise identification of content and meaning.[34] At the same time, precision in performing the rituals is not only expected, it is critical to their nature. In the end, the vagueness surrounding rituals contributes to their power and even efficacy.

Repetition and Deference

One of the first things we notice about ritual is repetition.[35] Beginning with the frequency of performance, repetition relates to a variety of phenomena

---

32. Wulf, *Anthropology*, 216–17.

33. Hiebert introduced the concept of rituals of transformation in 1983 as "the combination of liminality, *communitas* (informal, temporary community), high expectations, and antistructural creativity [that] makes deep and lasting changes possible in short periods of time." Paul G. Hiebert, "Missions and the Renewal of the Church," in *Anthropological Reflections on Missiological Issues* (Grand Rapids: Baker, 1994), 170.

34. Maurice Bloch, "Ritual and Deference," in *Essays on Cultural Transmission* (Oxford: Berg, 2005), 123.

35. Bloch's extensive study of rituals in relation to cultural transmission occurs in several of his works, most notably in *From Blessing to Violence: History and Ideology in the Circumcision Ritual of the Merina of Madagascar* (Cambridge: Cambridge University Press, 1986). This section draws on his 2005 essay "Ritual and Deference," in *Essays on Cultural Transmission*, 123–37.

present in rituals. Common to ritual are repeated elements or phrases within the same performance, for example, hymns or songs within a worship service or the word "Amen" after prayers. Next is the repetition of whole rituals as repetitions of one another, as illustrated by multiple services on a Sunday. Finally, by their behavior, participants (actors and observers) guide others or even themselves based on previous occasions; in a sense they are merely "repeating either themselves or others."[36] The fact that many phenomena are understood as conscious repetitions and not original with the performers contributes to the significance. As such, all rituals involve "quotation," a term that refers not only to language but also to all repetitions of the originators.[37]

The concept of "quotation" may be illustrated in several ways, for example, in the use of printed bulletins containing the liturgy of the worship service. In organizations we use "Robert's Rules of Order" as the official parliamentary guide for conducting meetings, particularly those that involve corporate decisions that must be enforced or may be challenged. These are important considerations for pastors and organizational leaders; however, such regimented procedures should also be considered within the cultural context of operations. For example, parliamentary procedure is inappropriate in settings where consensus is achieved by prolonged discussions by the community, including restating (quotation of) key understandings repeatedly until it becomes the belief of all. In societies with a stronger sense of group identity, consensus is the norm, in contrast to more individualist groups in which majority rule or decisions by the individual is the norm. Before signing off on that observation, I should point out the relevance here of the African proverb, "If you want to go quickly, go alone. If you want to go far, go together," in further illustrating the importance of group process.

A second significant aspect of ritual is deference, that is, relying on the authority of another person or group to validate the truth of the ritual. This does not necessarily require the participants to understand the meaning or elements of the ritual, such as the use of Latin for celebrating Mass or singing a worship song in another language. In other words, truth is invested in the trust one has for the speaker or the speaker being quoted. As Bloch noted, deference "accounts for the rather odd possibility that one may hold something to be true without fully understanding it."[38] We could draw on many examples, but political campaigns and the reliance on sound bites and image as opposed to well-articulated factual arguments is a sobering

36. Bloch, "Ritual and Deference," 124.
37. Bloch, "Ritual and Deference," 125.
38. Bloch, "Ritual and Deference," 127.

illustration with implications for leaders of organizations, particularly when we're considering the integrity of the mission.

Generally, the cultural context organizes and regulates situations where deference to the quotation over understanding is acceptable. This may be observed in an appeal to the authority of "an expert" or to "tradition" or to history or the customs of the ancestors. A specific example is the common experience of people with no financial background listening to the finance report in a meeting, where the generally accepted accounting principles (GAAP) are meticulously followed and appealed to for validating the details of the balance sheet. If this experience of deference in daily rituals continues, the result not only means deferring our understanding, it means abandoning it. In practice, our social lives involve both searching for meaning and deferring our understanding based on trust in others. Another example is the trusted coworker with knowledge and competency who inevitably becomes the "go to" person when establishing a new ritual of practice. To summarize, ritual, from the perspective of cognitive anthropology, is the combination of "(1) quotation and deference, (2) consciousness of deference, (3) a lack of clarity as to who is being deferred to," with deference being the key.[39]

Ritual and Performance

Ritual and "performativity," as Wulf calls it, introduces yet another domain for consideration before we take up issues for organizational life. The focus of performance is on the "staging and the practical, bodily aspect of rituals."[40] Anthropological research in both culture and religion has identified a number of significant characteristics of rituals that help to clarify the nature of performance.[41] American anthropologist Roy Rappaport takes "ritual" to denote "the performance of more or less invariant sequences of formal acts and utterances not entirely encoded by the performers."[42] This terse definition points to the difficulties inherent in the vagueness identified earlier, specifically his use of "more or less" and "not entirely." Still, Rappaport's emphasis

39. Bloch, "Ritual and Deference," 129, 136.
40. Wulf, *Anthropology*, 222.
41. Wulf identifies twelve characteristics from his summary of the literature on rituals; see *Anthropology*, 222–30. In one of the most thorough works on ritual from the anthropology of religion, Roy Rappaport identifies five features of ritual from which I will draw my comments. See Roy A. Rappaport, *Ritual and Religion in the Making of Humanity* (Cambridge: Cambridge University Press, 1999), 29–50.
42. Rappaport, *Ritual and Religion*, 24. "Invariant" refers to the continuity and lack of significant change rather than to replication. "Encoded" refers to the establishment of acts and utterances when the rituals are constituted.

on ritual as performance introduces us to the important element of actually doing the ritual. We will focus our consideration of rituals on performance, primarily that which occurs in organizations.

Rituals, as we know them, normally include utterances that are predominantly verbal, and therefore symbolic, so that formal acts of ritual are invested with meaning.[43] Despite the emphasis on vagueness earlier, the meaning of the ritual is important to consider, but not as a template for understanding rituals in general. Instead, it is best to approach each ritual as a particular case, so that the search for meaning focuses on the performances and interpretations of the particular people, as illustrated in the Roma case. The importance of the form of rituals takes center stage in Rappaport's identification of the following five features.[44]

1. *Encoding by persons other than performers.* As in the concept of deference, the performers are principally acting and speaking via "quotation" from patterns encoded by others. This appears to only allow for established rituals and not new rituals emerging from current conditions or culture change. However, if we consider the metarepresentational level of interaction (dialogue) within a culture, we can understand that new rituals are most likely transformed from other rituals (cultural representations) through the dialogue surrounding the representations, for example, an organization's initiation of its first president or the first annual Christmas party. Further, the repetition noted earlier sets the pattern in place, allowing for new rituals to disseminate while also allowing for deference to be shown as the new rituals are passed on in repeated form. The emphasis here is that the ritual establishes "truth" through deference to the originators.

2. *Formality (as decorum).* The term "formality" means strict adherence to the form of the ritual. While the two terms "formality" and "decorum" are not synonymous, they do overlap. This is not a dichotomy between formal or stylized and informal or spontaneous performances. Rather, it recognizes a continuum of ritual behaviors that move from everyday (informal) rituals, such as greetings or farewells, to the formal and decorous, such as installations or worship services. Even informal or spontaneous rituals contain formalized expressions and actions, as in the curious example of offering best wishes to an actor (performer) with the phrase "Break a leg."

3. *Invariance (more or less).* The characteristic of invariance is a common feature in rituals, seen through repetition. To illustrate invariance, consider the worship service at Cape Town 2010. The liturgy was recognizable to most if not all of the participants, facilitating full participation from the

43. Rappaport, *Ritual and Religion*, 29.
44. Rappaport, *Ritual and Religion*, 32–50.

very first moments through the end of the congress. This was especially true during the Communion service. Although it doubtless differed in parts from those rituals of the home congregations of the delegates, the elements were handled in the same reverential manner, including reading from the Bible, denoted by the concept of invariance. Yet the principle of invariance also recognizes that invariance does not finally determine the ritual, so the concept is "more or less" invariant. For example, the physical response to songs of worship may include sitting, standing, raising hands, and dancing. The "more or less" must be added to "invariant" because of the very nature of what we identified as the transformation, in contrast to replication, of concepts and representations through the metarepresentations involved in the transmission of culture.

4. *Performance (ritual and other performance forms)*. There is no ritual without performance. It is a critical feature of ritual in the majority of situations; the notable exception is traditional liturgical rituals in which the order and content are recorded in books, which are carefully preserved for subsequent generations of performers. Yet even with the recorded text, the ritual is not a ritual until it is performed; rather, the text is a script for a ritual. Records or scripts function as a resource for the experiential learning required to perform the ritual. I discovered this the hard way in my first funeral service. While I had studied the liturgical elements of the event, I found that my first time as Pastor Doug was far more involved and significant than even my careful study of the liturgical text indicated.

5. *Formality (versus physical efficacy)*. Rappaport suggests that the term "formal" is made to carry the load for a number of other terms, including strict attention to the formal tradition—even the smallest details—and adhering to the form, repetition, frequency, and styles.[45] In this fifth characteristic, what is intended is in contrast to the assumption that the formal nature of the ritual will guarantee the desired result. Studies have generally not equated that which is done *in* the rituals with that which is done *by* the rituals. This is not to discount the possibility, for example, in rituals relating to spiritual warfare, that what is accomplished by the ritual may be closely related to what is done in the ritual. The significance of making the contrast is that the formality of rituals is integral to the transmission of culture, apart from the consequences or outcomes of the ritual.

Summarizing the role of ritual behavior beyond the realm of religion, German anthropologist Hans-Georg Soeffner observes that "ritual behavior is behavior that is fully formed, predictable, in a certain sense calculable, and it

45. Rappaport, *Ritual and Religion*, 46.

guarantees orientational security."[46] This element of "orientational security" is a critical outcome—as opposed to a guaranteed result—of both the repetition and the performance of ritual. I was reminded of this aspect of ritual during the substitution of players in a recent soccer match when a famous player ran in place, looked to the sky, and genuflected before stepping onto the field. The ritual itself calmed the nerves, focused the mind, and brought "orientational security" to the athlete, but she missed her next attempt to score a goal.

We will see that in organizational life, rituals, including the elements of repetition, quotation, deference, and performance, are also essential for transmitting organizational culture.

Rituals in Organizational Life

In her assignment to summarize studies in organizational culture, Stanford professor Joanne Martin identified rituals as a significant cultural form that "provides important clues" into the thoughts, beliefs, and practices of an organization's employees.[47] Her list of common types of rituals includes the following synthesis of the work of organizational culture studies:

1. Imitation rituals—focusing on indoctrination and orientation
2. Enhancement rituals—recognizing good performance
3. Degradation rituals—recognizing bad performance
4. Renewal rituals—strengthening group functioning
5. Integration rituals—providing opportunities to solidify interpersonal relationships
6. Conflict reduction rituals—repairing relationships
7. Ending rituals—transitioning a person from insider to outsider
8. Compound rituals—including two or more of the above rituals for a specific purpose[48]

A challenge to interpreting these rituals lies in the fact that early studies focused on the managerial perspective. For example, from the perspective of a manager, a degradation ritual may be important for establishing and retaining standards of performance (positive), while employees may interpret

46. Hans-Georg Soeffner, *The Order of Rituals: The Interpretation of Everyday Life* (New Brunswick, NJ: Transaction, 1997), 75.

47. Joanne Martin, *Organizational Culture: Mapping the Terrain* (Thousand Oaks, CA: Sage, 2002), 65.

48. Martin, *Organizational Culture*, 68–69.

it as evidence of an autocratic and punitive style of leadership (negative). More recently, critical studies have included the view of employees and other stakeholders, adding to the studies' value. Martin's list of rituals provides a helpful addition to those from religion and anthropology, bringing to mind similar rituals within our own organizational experience.

The importance of ritual in transmitting culture, internally and externally, in organizations is still in the early stages of consideration. The literature from organizational studies focuses on the symbolic elements of rituals, as illustrated by two influential publications. In the first, Bolman and Deal observe that "enacting a ritual connects an individual or group to something mystical, more than words or rational thinking can capture."[49] This makes sense when one considers that ritual is part of Bolman and Deal's "Symbolic Frame," which stresses the power and emotion carried by symbols in helping to make sense of the world. In the second work, Schein agrees: "rituals are symbolic," playing an important role in formalizing cultural assumptions and acting as a cultural artifact; yet Schein notes that rituals are not "easy to decipher."[50] Symbolism is an important element of ritual, as we have seen in the studies from anthropology, and rituals permeate the transmission of culture, leading us to reflect on the influence of rituals in our organizational mission.

Reviewing and Reflecting on the Issues

An important value of reading this book is its response to the question, "What are the implications of what we are learning about culture?" Using Cape Town 2010 as our main example provides a range of issues for reflection as we work through this chapter. Whether one attended the congress or any of the Lausanne gatherings is not critical, since the importance for our purpose lies in the broader context of global Christianity and involves issues that arise as a result of belonging to the global body of Christ. So our review and reflection draws on the global nature of our faith as Christians.

Reviewing

As we reflect on the question mentioned above, the practice of imitation is clearly a major means of learning as well as transmitting culture. The innate capacity of a human being to imitate others while not only recognizing the

---

49. Lee G. Bolman and Terrence E. Deal, *Reframing Organizations: Artistry, Choice, and Leadership*, 5th ed. (San Francisco: Jossey-Bass, 2013), 256.
50. Edgar Schein, *Organizational Culture and Leadership*, 5th ed. (Hoboken, NJ: John Wiley & Sons, 2017), 200.

actions but also approximating the motives, beliefs, and even desires of the actors opens a powerful avenue for Christian formation. By observing others, both intentionally and unconsciously, we are able to adapt to new approaches to spiritual formation through exposure to others. As we learn these practices, they go from simply mental representations (ideas) to actions based on a new understanding of the practice (metarepresentation).

This may be a positive experience of renewing one's devotion to Christ through new spiritual disciplines or through dialogue with other believers, which can shed light on difficult issues we face in a specific context. An example is the positive influence the revival in the Solomon Islands had on missions and churches throughout the Pacific beginning in the 1970s. The negative flipside, of course, is also possible, as seen in the flow of religious materials and media into those cultures with little or no reference to local issues or sensitivities of the recipients. The point is, through imitation, conscious and unconscious, we gain new insights and practices that help to form the cultural representations we need for addressing the big issues we face in this time of globalization.

The role of mimetic learning in the transmission of culture relates directly to the goal of reaching the whole world with the whole gospel. If we want to understand the thoughts and actions of others, there is no substitute for participating with representatives of other cultures in order to truly understand the incredible diversity of God's world. Further, in concert with thoughtful believers from other cultural contexts, we should expose ourselves to the specific cultural and social lives of a group of people so as to learn new ways of engaging the issues and building the relationships necessary for shaping, catalyzing, and propelling our organizations missionally.

In considering the nature of rituals, we added another dimension to the similarity and diversity we find among Christians around the world. Rituals born out of religious traditions, such as sacraments and liturgies, are most often transferred through both written records and experiential learning from seminaries or ministerial education. Further rituals of intensification and transformation, as noted in Hiebert's work, also account for the transference of styles of worship and rituals surrounding conversion experiences. However, when it comes to the role of organizations in transmitting culture, rituals are far more complex. For example, rituals are often tied to the value of specific roles, both socially and materially, as observed through rituals of installation, promotion, and disassociation (ending rituals), introducing complexities that are not as easily understood.

Leaders seldom focus on cultural and organizational rituals when considering the effectiveness of an organization in achieving its mission. Yet as we learn from the importance of repetition and deference, rituals play a powerful role in the transmission of culture. Through deference to others, to current leaders, or to traditions established by former leaders, organizational culture is transmitted to new members, as well as to the various constituencies we serve. When we fail to account for those rituals in assessing our mission, the integrity of our findings may be seriously undermined. For example, the loss of leaders trained within a particular church or missionary society to other organizations is usually attributed primarily to economic factors; however, we know from observation that the lack of rituals of integration that offer both appreciation and recognition plays a decisive role. Further, when members continue to feel deference toward leaders who are absent for whatever reason, the leaders who are present may enjoy significantly less allegiance.

One last consideration of organizational rituals comes from the performance of rituals. Remember that performance focuses on the staging and the practical physical aspects of rituals. Given the importance of performers, selecting or appointing those same performers becomes a significant element in the meaning and reception of the ritual. Again, those planning the ritual should consider who is being quoted and how that quotation will be perceived. Generally, it is wise to include a broad representation of the most significant constituencies within the organization while also representing those served by the organizational mission. If diversity is important to the organization, diversity is important in selecting the performers of the rituals. It is always interesting to observe the diversity in the audience compared to that of the performers of a given ritual. Considering the importance of the performers, planning and conducting formal and even less formal rituals should include a thoughtful assessment of both the performers and the decorum.

Reflecting

As we conclude, take time to reflect on the following questions as they relate to you, other leaders, and your organization.

1. How do you and your organization use imitation as a learning style? Are there ways that this could be strengthened or broadened, particularly with regard to developing skills vital to your organizational mission?

2. How do you account for spiritual formation as part of your organizational mission? Does your organization collaborate with other groups in sharing resources for spiritual formation?

3. Are there opportunities to partner with other groups or ministries to develop faith-based empathetic responses to others outside the organization or to those who may be marginalized within your organization?

4. In what ways are leaders in your organization learning from the mission of God globally? How are gatherings of international believers handled in your organization? Are there sufficient opportunities to facilitate the type of reciprocal imitation that leads to new practical knowledge and social behavior, reflecting the beliefs you share and furthering your organizational mission?

Rituals provide a significant type of imitation that has implications for us as Christian leaders. Consider the following questions to help apply the insights to your unique situation.

5. In what specific situations have you faced the same type of dilemma faced by Melody Wachsmuth when introducing the Advent ritual? As you think about the details, what were the primary issues, and how did you deal with them at the time?

6. Think of a particular ritual common to your organization, identifying both the elements and the performers. What type of occasion does it commemorate? What does that ritual mean to you and other leaders? To the members of the community? To those you seek to serve?

7. What opportunities do you have to participate in rituals that include a diverse representation of cultures? How could you draw more from those experiences in ways that would empower members of your organization?

In the following chapter I will introduce the issues of authority and trust from the perspective of exercising authority, institutional understandings, and the role of trust, drawing on cognitive and social anthropology as well as the anthropology of religion.

5

Authority and Culture

Whom Do You Trust?

The connection between authority and trust makes sense to leaders and followers alike. "If I trust you, I can work for you in good conscience." Walking across the campus reciting that thought was a comfort to me on several occasions, since my role at that time reported directly to the president of the seminary. I served two presidents as provost, and in both cases I trusted them. They empowered my position and were true to their word. It was a privilege to serve beside them.

Another experience too common for my liking is expressed as follows: "I have the responsibility, but not the authority!" I remember clearly hearing that or a variation of it from a number of people on leadership teams with me. It is natural to experience some lack of authority during the initial stages of one's appointment to a leadership role. It takes time to build trust, particularly among those who were marginalized during the selection process or at least perceive a lack of voice in the decision. The resulting deficit in authority requires both the one "in authority" and those "with authority" working together to fully legitimize the individual in the position.

A third response also occurs, perhaps not as frequently, but often enough to require further consideration. It is usually expressed as, "If you give me the authority, I will get it done." At first it appears to be a cultural problem, a differential in power distance.[1] On further reflection, there also appears to be a link to cognitive development in the individual as a complicating factor. Developing the ability to lead builds on an individual's theory of mind, that is, the ability to infer the thoughts and motivations of others. Interpreting the responses of others is subject to cultural understandings (e.g., power distance) but also the cognitive sense of acceptance and empathy for a given situation. It follows that intercultural leadership requires attention to the individual's interpretation of the thoughts and actions of others (theory of mind) in addition to the knowledge of culture and schemas (mental and cultural representations).

As I reflected on the topics to research and consider for this project, authority and trust emerged as an important choice, particularly since these experiences are not easily diagnosed and deserve to be addressed in intercultural organizations. The guiding questions for us are, How do you exercise authority as a Christian leader? How does trust factor into authority? And finally, who is in charge, and whom do you trust?

Authority and trust are the two primary considerations of this chapter. First, we will explore authority from the perspective of leadership studies and anthropology, as it is understood in relation to responsibility and accountability. Next, to provide a broader context to the conversation, we'll reflect on the theory and practice of authority in institutions in Southeast Asia. Third, we will explore the construction of authority as a natural part of social life, not a rigid construct of bureaucracy. After reflecting on the implications of these perspectives, we turn to trust as an inextricable element in authority due to the relational nature of authority. The case study later in this chapter is an important reflection by a scholar/practitioner based in Thailand, whose perspective as one who facilitates leadership development internationally is critical to our understanding. Finally, we review the concepts of authority and trust before concluding with an opportunity to reflect on the implications for our leadership and organizations.

Authority: Who Is in Charge?

The ambiguity and significance that surround the concept of authority are a major consideration for leaders, particularly those serving intercultural

---

1. The notion of *power distance*, as "the extent to which the less powerful members of institutions and organizations within a country expect and accept that power is distributed unequally," was introduced in Hofstede's work on a global approach to organizations and culture in 1980. See Geert Hofstede, Gert Jan Hofstede, and Michael Minkov, *Cultures and Organizations: Software of the Mind; Intercultural Cooperation and Its Importance for Survival*, 3rd ed. (New York: McGraw Hill, 2010), 521, see also 53–88.

organizations. Leadership studies indicate that "more and more people are finding that their jobs require them to influence others despite having no formal authority over them."[2] This sobering reality and the underlying issues relate not only to the organizational structure but also to how leadership is perceived both formally and informally. So we begin with what we mean by the term "authority."

Understanding Authority

The meaning of "authority" differs depending on the world in which it exists. According to Bernard and Ruth Bass's handbook, "Formally, authority is the legitimate right to exercise power."[3] Traditionally, the locus of authority is in the norms of the society and organizations in relation to their membership. One "in authority" has the right to command and expect compliance with their commands since the power to decide is also a right associated with authority. Authority is inherent in formal organizations; depending on the position and knowledge of the individual in authority, it is expected that leaders will exercise authority to control and direct others.[4] In contrast to *in* authority, some people are *an* authority, gaining their power not so much from a position as from their expertise, thereby creating a different path to leadership.[5] Their decisions are more likely perceived as a by-product of their expertise than solely as a right to exercise power.

Authority is also viewed from the perspective of behavior in relationship to followers, making their willingness to accept the commands a critical factor in the dynamics of authority.[6] Underlying these relationships are a variety of formal and informal contracts, some socially implicit and others legally explicit, that further impact the "willingness" of their acceptance. Still another element of authority as behavior is the perception of members in regard to their freedom to act and interact with others, accompanied by the right (informal or delegated) to take action and make decisions. This is governed by the "degree of freedom" that is allowed and the "initiatives" individuals feel it is safe to take, thereby responding to and exercising delegated authority.[7]

2. Richard L. Hughes, Robert C. Ginnett, and Gordon J. Curphy, *Leadership: Enhancing the Lessons of Experience*, 7th ed. (New York: McGraw-Hill Irwin, 2012), 104.

3. Bernard M. Bass with Ruth Bass, *The Handbook of Leadership: Theory, Research, and Managerial Applications*, 4th ed. (New York: Free Press, 2008), 353.

4. Bass and Bass, *Handbook of Leadership*, 354.

5. Bruce Lincoln, *Authority: Construction and Corrosion* (Chicago: University of Chicago Press, 1994), 4.

6. Bass and Bass, *Handbook of Leadership*, 354.

7. Bass and Bass, *Handbook of Leadership*, 354.

To illustrate, a team leader is placed in authority by the organization, either by the immediate supervisor or as part of a formal promotion or appointment by the executive leadership under an "explicit contract." The team leader will operate within the parameters of the organizational practices and mission; however, the exercise of authority also depends on that person's philosophy of leadership and the performance expectations of the supervising authority. A critical factor in the team leader's success is the willingness of the team members to recognize the authority as a "social contract." The degree to which the team members are free to do their jobs, including both the authority and the freedom to take initiative, is normally a determining factor in their support of the team leader.

Foundational to effective leadership is a shared commitment—by leaders and followers—to the values that undergird the authority, either formally or informally. In both traditional and behavioral views, the higher the status of the one "in authority," the more right they have to exercise power over those with lower status. The legitimacy of this understanding is based on the "norms and expectations held by a group . . . appropriate to a given role," based on the nature of the leader's appointment to the position.[8]

At the same time, "authority is not power," which is humorously illustrated by the Canadian National Research Council, which stated categorically, "No amount of legal authority over the grizzly bears of British Columbia would enable you to get yourself obeyed by them out in the woods!"[9] On a more technical level, J. M. Burns, in his landmark study on leadership, demonstrates that the relationship between authority and power is that authority is legitimated by the traditions of law, agreements, rights of succession, and religion, distinguishing it from power as sheer force and coercion.[10]

An earlier work on a social taxonomy of power associated with authority continues to provide an important perspective by identifying five bases: legitimate (legal), rewards, referent (potential influence), coercive (punitive action), and expertise (knowledge).[11] Although the topic of power is a significant area of study—for example, spiritual power or abuse of power—for our purposes the discussion of power will be limited to an element of authority.

8. Bass and Bass, *Handbook of Leadership*, 354.
9. Canadian National Research Council, 1943; cited in Bass and Bass, *Handbook of Leadership*, 355.
10. James MacGregor Burns, *Leadership* (New York: Harper & Row, 1978).
11. Hughes, Ginnett, and Curphy, *Leadership*, 125–34. The five bases of power were first identified in John R. P. French and Bertram H. Raven, "The Bases of Social Power," in *Studies of Social Power*, ed. Dorwin Cartwright (Ann Arbor, MI: Institute for Social Research, 1959).

Two contrasting structures help us illustrate authority in practice: bureaucratic and volunteer organizations. Formal, bureaucratic organizations (institutions, government agencies, hospitals, the military) have a hierarchy of superiors and subordinates, with higher positions having authority according to the official structure. It's still important that subordinates accept the authority of a leader, but the contractual basis of employment carries significant consequences for disregarding authority. In other words, "the power is in the position."[12]

In contrast, the exercise of authority in volunteer organizations (missionary societies, churches, and a variety of other Christian organizations) depends more on shared commitment to a particular cause or mission, since the appeal to contractual conditions is more a matter of interpretation than legally binding. Differences in the bases of authority, while significant, are in the end still a matter of the individual interpretations of the "rights, duties, obligations, privileges, and powers" of the people involved.[13] For Christian workers, it is often a matter of obedience to the call of God to serve in whatever capacity they serve within the organizational mission.

Responsibility and Accountability

Responsibility is given as part of any leadership assignment. The responsibility comes with the expectation that the leader will be accountable for carrying out the assignment. Few leaders lack awareness of their responsibilities, but as we noted earlier, an increasing number sense the lack of authority that should accompany the job. As demonstrated in an important study on the dynamics of leadership, authority is instrumental to a leader in fulfilling assigned responsibilities, validating the concern for "responsibility without authority."[14]

In practice, responsibilities are a combination of the actual job description, perceptions that workers or members have regarding the organization's expectations of performance, and the tendency of leaders to perceive their job as being broader and more far reaching.[15] These distinct understandings are negotiated as part of the leadership dynamics that characterize the organizational world, further highlighting the importance of the relationships between leaders and followers. A study of motivation and responsibility found

12. Hughes, Ginnett, and Curphy, *Leadership*, 575.

13. Bass and Bass, *Handbook of Leadership*, 356.

14. Edwin P. Hollander, *Leadership Dynamics: A Practical Guide to Effective Relationships* (New York: Free Press, 1978).

15. Bass and Bass, *Handbook of Leadership*, 360.

the most likely motivators to be a sense of doing what is right or legal, duty or obligation, and concern over consequence.[16] Or as Bass notes, "Alternatively, having a sense of responsibility may be a matter of how one evaluates one's own character."[17]

For the leader, accountability directly follows acceptance of responsibility, but in practice, the leader's accountability affects everyone in the organization. Reviewing critical studies in accountability, the key elements are acceptance of responsibility, answerability to authority, liability for performance, and willingness to serve the organization.[18] While these elements seem self-evident, it behooves those considering appointment to a position to reflect on their own ability and willingness to submit to accountability as a prerequisite for accepting a position. In my experience, submitting to authority is not an arduous task as long as we agree to be accountable in principle, which then establishes a shared ground for any personal confrontations.

Within organizations, accountability is normally built into the system through regular reporting to the supervisor either formally or informally, usually in a written report or a face-to-face meeting. This extends beyond the supervisor through the leadership to the regular organizational reporting to the trustees or directors. The flow of work is parallel to the expectations of accountability for performance. Although many challenges are associated with accountability, it is an intrinsic characteristic of human organizations.

Accountability is also a critical factor in authority and responsibility processes internationally, ideally based on the reciprocal actions of leaders in a context of trust and dependability in the partner organizations. From experience, I know there are two common concerns regarding accountability for organizations that operate internationally. First, donors have a stewardship concern, and they want formal accountability to ensure that their partnership or assistance will leverage the organizational mission. Second, the recipients have a relational concern: formal accountability processes suggest a lack of trust in their leadership.

One of the most explicit domains of accountability is that of finances, a perennial concern for nonprofit organizations and their supporters and central to the two common concerns of stewardship and trust. In his work on financial sustainability, scholar and leader Emmanuel Bellon identifies the tension between the polarizing effects of accountability and the universal

---

16. D. G. Winter, "A Motivational Model of Leadership: Predicting Long-Term Management Success from TAT Measures of Power Motivation and Responsibility," *Leadership Quarterly* 2 (1991): 67–80.

17. Bass and Bass, *Handbook of Leadership*, 360.

18. Bass and Bass, *Handbook of Leadership*, 360–61.

responsibility for owning one's actions.[19] In his analysis, he perceptively suggests, "It is very difficult to require accountability from others when one has failed to be accountable in matters regarding [one's] own processes and procedures."[20] It is in the best interest of all Christian organizations not only to expect accountability of others but also, and perhaps even more, to be accountable to others with greater transparency of organizational practice.

Moving from what we know about authority, responsibility, and accountability to how it works out in practice, we turn to the experience of positional and institutional authority. I asked my friend and colleague Siew Pik Lim to reflect on the challenge of exercising authority in institutions, an area she knows well as a woman in leadership within the plurality of the religious worlds of Malaysia.

Exercising Authority in Institutions

Siew Pik Lim, Malaysia[a]

James Bielo's analysis on how authority is made, reproduced, contested, performed, and negotiated drives this reflection on religious authority.[b] I reflect on the leadership model and practices of a selected number of Pentecostal charismatic churches in a Southeast Asian context. This reflection grew out of two observations. The first is the uneasy observation that congregation followers are increasingly subjected to a certain leadership paradigm in this faith tradition. Within this context, notable comments such as "I did not dare to talk to my pastor" or "I did not know that my pastor may be wrong" and confidential stories from friends, peers, and colleagues were laced with pain, distress, and guilt about leaving their churches due to differences and difficulty in following certain leadership practices. Second, I noticed that followers have legitimate concerns about leaders' behaviors, actions, and practices. Follower difficulties relating to leadership practices are primarily discussed in private and "off the record," as many of these followers have not had safe spaces to speak and be heard.

The organizational culture of these church institutions is consistent on these key elements: power centralization or high power distance, the leader's legitimate right to control resources, and followers' deference to leaders, who have greater power over decisions and actions than the followers do.

19. Emmanuel O. Bellon, *Leading Financial Sustainability in Theological Institutions: The African Perspective* (Eugene, OR: Pickwick, 2017), 125.

20. Bellon, *Leading Financial Sustainability*, 125.

The word "authority" does not feature prominently in the rhetoric of this tradition. Christian leaders are expected to apply biblical models and servant principles of leadership. If authority is referred to, it needs a qualifier of "spiritual" for legitimacy. The legitimizing factor often has to do with the leader's calling to a certain position, role, or ministry in the institution. In short, God's calling of the leader validates the authority of the leader.

Since the church is an established institution, authority is primarily bureaucratic and situated in the leader's role and in the existing organizational structure. An increasingly attractive type of authority is that held by influential, charismatic personalities who lead these institutions. From a particular theological standpoint, followers perceive and trust the "one-man vision" leader as God's anointed, first and foremost.

Illegitimate Authority

The first key issue in my reflection on authority is that there are correlations between authoritarian, high power distance contexts, hallowing of religious "larger than life" authority figures, and the propensity for leaders to exercise illegitimate authority. "Larger than life" leaders are often thought to possess "the ability to express themselves with great facility"; they also tend to focus on "the use of the Gifts of the Holy Spirit" and are looked upon as speaking on God's behalf, with their word "sometimes viewed on a par with that of Scripture itself."[c] There is a growing concern in the church and in seminaries about illegitimate authority, the tendency to overreach the authority and responsibilities of one's role.

I observed at least five patterns in the exercise of illegitimate authority that reflect these leaders' inclination to adeptly apply power autonomously, thereby transcending boundaries of institutional protocols and best practices and enabling themselves to carry out subtle, indirect tasks in the micro contexts of institutions:

1. A pastor or senior leader influences and conceals financial decisions and practices while extending his or her own authority over other areas of church governance.
2. A leader threatens followers when they diverge from the leader's expectations and wishes, and the leader maneuvers toward a desired outcome.
3. A leader's actions reflect a conflict of interest between the community's interests and those of the leader.
4. A leader rejects and overcomes queries perceived as challenging their authority.

5. A leader misrepresents scriptural teaching to justify their authority and to represent themselves as divinely appointed.

When authority is centralized on the leader and the leader has accessed as much power as they can, they can become "spiritual dictators" or institutional power brokers—posturing as if they are entitled to a personal power that is beyond their role, obligations, and responsibilities.

If indeed these "larger than life" leaders actually do possess divine authority and power as they believe, then they must make prudent choices and have good intentions and benevolent actions that bear well on the followers they lead. Still, other leaders in high-power contexts have chosen to do what is trustworthy, right, and good. These leaders understand their responsibility to set the right tone for the benefit of the community, choose a different approach to authority, and shift from acquiring power to giving away power.

Relational Authority

A second and related key issue in my reflection is the critical dynamic of *relational authority that is built on the intrinsic value of reciprocal trust.* The relationship dimension of authority and the equilibrium of harmonious relationships are integral issues for institutional health. The exercise of authority rests on reciprocal trust. In other words, relational authority, involving respect, deference, and compliance by followers, increases or declines in proportion to trust that the leader elicits from followers through actions, decisions, and behavior. Followers will accept power differential and defer to the leader if they trust the leader. The leader must reciprocate by leading with integrity, making reliable decisions, and managing resources in a way that accords due respect, concern, care, and consideration for followers and leadership situations. The leader is expected to act in the best interest of and maintain a harmonious relationship with the group.

There is growing concern regarding leaders who choose to appropriate power to control and manipulate, particularly in high power distance contexts. Viewed as betrayal of the social contract, such appropriation leads to the creation of factions by aggrieved followers in order to counteract the leader's authority. Disquieted followers are also caught in the double bind of either speaking up or exiting the leadership context quietly. Some followers choose to exit quietly, while others who choose to speak up can face painful consequences. Factions may arise and harmony be disrupted because the leader has diminished his or her authority and legitimacy by betraying the followers' trust.

Contextual Authority

The third key issue in my reflections is the unique dynamic in the Asian context, where *followers are amiable.* The rhetoric of biblical imagery relating shepherd to sheep and father to son strongly influences relationships between a leader and followers. A sheep trusts its shepherd to have its best interests in mind, and a son trusts his father similarly. Contextually, also relevant here is Choong's work on Confucian leadership, which asserts that Asian leadership models tend to acquiesce to the culture of patriarchy, paternalism, and autocracy.[d] I concur that practices of institutional leadership in the Asian context will continue to take cues from high power distance cultural values of patriarchy and paternalism, filtered through the lens of the father and shepherd leadership images. So, while I may critique tendencies to control and power posturing as overreaching leadership authority, the leaders in question may be convinced that they are leading in the best possible way for the institution and followers.

To the reader, I may seem overly critical about Christian institutions. I must therefore add the qualification that good leadership and institutions have clear lines of authority, obligations, and responsibilities. But when authority is misinterpreted to be more personal, it points to the challenges that I have highlighted above as growing concerns for a healthy church. The force of a "larger than life" personality that drives positional and bureaucratic authority can cause a well-intentioned person to lead with a misguided sense of authority and power, particularly when the leader is adept at producing results. I submit that prevalent issues of religious authority in my context need fresh theological and sociological resources to develop alternate paradigms for the promotion of trust and flourishing.

[a] Rev. Siew Pik Lim (PhD, Fuller Theological Seminary) is the president of Alpha Omega International College in Malaysia. An ordained minister in the Assemblies of God, Lim has expertise in institutional leadership and leadership development.

[b] James S. Bielo, *Anthropology of Religion: The Basics* (New York: Routledge, 2015).

[c] David G. Garrard, "Leadership versus the Congregation in the Pentecostal/Charismatic Movement," *Journal of the European Pentecostal Theological Association* 29, no. 2 (2009): 90–103.

[d] Gary K. G. Choong, *Counter-Cultural Paradigmatic Leadership: Ethical Use of Power in Societies* (Eugene, OR: Wipf & Stock, 2011).

Authority under Construction

The challenges of authority so well explained by Lim are attributable to the way we construct authority within our worlds. The exercise of authority is intrinsically asymmetrical and built into the organizational culture; the leader as an individual in authority is empowered by the organizational authorities in relation to the followers. The followers (congregation, members) in turn show deference, as illustrated by Lim, thereby drawing attention to the leader, while effectively generating an aura of confidence, respect, and trust.[21] Again, as Lim demonstrated, whether this attitude toward the leader is genuine or simply a "lived reality" due to the cultural context, it is interpreted "as if" it were genuine. Fundamentally, authority, as we have described it, is relational, a result of the social life of a group, community, or society. Acts of authority are based on the mutual understanding that an individual has the capacity to exercise authority, producing the intended effects. As Bruce Lincoln, a professor of religion and anthropology, asserts, "Authority depends on nothing so much as the trust of the audience, or the audience's strategic willingness to act as if it had such trust."[22]

Authority may be considered as being in the role of an intermediary between the extremes of coercion and persuasion.[23] Coercion implies that a punitive or violent act, or at least a distasteful outcome, will result if compliance isn't given, whereas persuasion uses verbal discourse, including the use of different types of communication and media. Authority is separated from the other two, but in fact plays a middle way, using some of the same techniques as the other two. Like persuasion, authority makes use of language to convey instruction or command action, while also dependent on a range of nonverbal "instruments and media" beyond simple rhetorical arguments.[24] The nonverbal may be part of the ritual use of dramatic presentation with costumes, props, and stages or platforms. Alternately, authority may draw from the domains of coercion when it builds on the fears or insecurities of others or uses threats of reprisals or redundancy to motivate. Importantly for our understanding, authority ceases to be effective and sustainable when it becomes either persuasion or coercion.

Previously, we explored the significance of deference, repetition, and performance in rituals. Each of these elements has a role in constructing authority, in addition to being a significant part of the cultural context in which the authority operates. Lincoln refers to "the whole theatrical array" of costumes, props, stages, and so on associated with authority.[25] These include symbolic regalia such as the robes and hoods of academia, the robes and stoles of clergy, special seating, designated parking, and an endless variety of other trappings that are symbols of authority. These artifacts and the rituals of installation or the rites of intensification (chapel, weekly services, regalia events) intersecting

21. Lincoln, *Authority*, 4. The concept of constructing authority is drawn from ibid., 4–13.
22. Lincoln, *Authority*, 8.
23. Lincoln, *Authority*, 4.
24. Lincoln, *Authority*, 5.
25. Lincoln, *Authority*, 5.

with each other are the elements used to construct the authority that is vital to making and sustaining the organization. The same is true of the places that signify the locus of the authority, be it a sanctuary, an office, a classroom, or some other location. These places, when inhabited by those in authority with the diplomas, insignias, or paraphernalia of office, determine the culture of authority as it is constructed by a given organization.

Lincoln identifies another significant aspect in the process of constructing authority: "authorized speech and significant silence."[26] For most of us, the role of authorized speech is critical to the culture of the organization. I can close my eyes and picture countless chapel services when the leader called us to prayer, silencing the auditorium, or when the pastor stood in the pulpit to commence a sermon, or when a group surrounded a kneeling individual at the commissioning of a new leader. All these highlight both the importance of speech as authorized by the organization and the response of silence. Both of these kinds of acts bear an intrinsic authority not only for the one who leads but also in the very act itself. The worship services of Cape Town 2010 also illustrate how pervasively these practices shape the cultures of our worlds.

The Other Side of the Coin: Trusting Others

The dynamics of authority are complex, defying any simple listing of attributes or skills. However, the more I reflect on authority and culture, the more primary is the consideration of trust. The relational foundation of authority and the trust factor account for a major source of influence in leadership and organizations. The key consideration for us is trust and the exercise of authority in the organizations we serve.

Understanding Trust

Trust is a centerpiece in the exercise of authority. It embraces a number of concerns as it intersects with the worlds of organizations, societies, and religion. In reviewing the anthropology of religion, Bielo even went so far as titling the chapter on authority, "Who Do You Trust?" The reason is based on a core anthropological commitment "that the problem of religious authority is fundamentally social."[27] We noted earlier that two primary types of authority are highlighted in the statements "She is *in* authority" and "She is *an* authority." The first is positional and the second is based on individual expertise. To

---

26. Lincoln, *Authority*, 9.
27. Bielo, *Anthropology of Religion*, 108.

illustrate this within a local church, the pastor is *in* authority, appointed by authority (e.g., by a presbytery or congregation) by virtue of ordination and/or giftedness, with the emphasis on skill and knowledge, whereas a member of the congregation who happens to be a professor of theology is *an* authority, irrespective of any position. So the question is not so much "Do I trust this religious authority?" as it is "Do I trust this person to care for me?"

To further illustrate trust as it relates to authority, consider the situation of a new church planted in a local community. The church-planting team is composed of a pastor and laypeople who choose to be part of the team, whether an international missionary team or a group of people dedicated to reaching their own community. In establishing the church, decisions as to the appropriate leadership structure may be either predetermined by the polity of the denominational affiliation or, in the case of congregational polity, left up to the leadership team. Once the structural question is settled, the more challenging questions relate to whom to appoint as leaders: Are they qualified both spiritually and socially? Do they have the necessary knowledge? Will they be respected as representing the authority of the church? To complicate matters, generation, gender, class, and ethnicity may also inform the appointments, further highlighting the contingent and relational nature of religious authority. In each case, the underlying question of trust is critical to the health of the young church.

In organizational studies, trust is associated with dependence and risk, in addition to undergirding the relational aspects of authority. One of the key concerns relates to the trustworthiness of the person or group being trusted in contrast to the potential naivety of those who are trusting. The emphasis here is on the relative confidence followers have in the actions of an individual, group, or organization. Of all the nuances in defining trust in the organizational world, the concept of "real trust" is helpful, since it means, "We trust someone . . . if we expect him not to be opportunistic even if he has both the opportunity and the incentive to do so."[28]

Thinking of "trust and trustworthiness" using the terms "reliance and reliability," respectively, helps us understand the instrumental nature of trust in an organization. This includes the obvious positive aspects such as ability, commitment, and vision as well as the negative aspects relating to deterring others from taking advantage of a situation.[29] In other words, how reliable are the trustees in a given situation? An important goal is to resist being

28. Bart Nooteboom and Frédérique Six, introduction to *The Trust Process in Organizations: Empirical Studies of the Determinants and the Process of Trust Development*, ed. Bart Nooteboom and Frédérique Six (Cheltenham, UK: Edward Elgar, 2003), 4.

29. Nooteboom and Six, introduction to *Trust Process in Organizations*, 4.

overly optimistic, particularly in ways that undermine the organizational mission—a very real problem when an organization faces the uncertainties of interorganizational or governmental negotiations and economic stability. Remember that trust in relation to people and organizations is grounded in the functions, positions, and roles people play within their organization.[30] In some social situations it may be appropriate to emphasize individual authority and individual relationships, but in the context of an organization, trust relates not just to an individual but also to the group; in that sense, in an organization, trust is corporate.

A consideration of the organizational use of trust is sobering and may even lead to pessimism. However, it need not do so if we focus on our organizational mission to ensure that we do not overstretch or encounter "mission drift." This is illustrated in the case of promises made by those offering investment opportunities or by political authorities. It is not hard to think of situations where an organization was enamored by the presentations of an investment group, even more so when they learned that other reputable organizations were also investing, taking inordinate amounts of risk that in turn ended in economic disaster. The same can be imagined of promises made by the political party in power, only to be overturned after an election or change of government. The point here is that in matters of organizational trust, it is prudent to be vigilant as to the degree of trust placed in a given person or group beyond what may be called for, underscoring the old adage, "If it appears to be too good to be true, it probably is!"

Leadership studies, compared to religious and organizational approaches to trust, indicate that trust comes as a result of the personal attributes of a leader. A helpful perspective is, "Whatever 'true leadership' means, most people would agree that at a minimum it is characterized by a high degree of trust between leader and followers."[31] Although always an important issue, trust is more prominent now, due in part to the erosion of trust in public leaders and greater levels of access to the thoughts and actions of people via social media. An interesting take is Fairholm's definition of trust in a leader as "reliance on the . . . authenticity of a person . . . in the absence of absolute knowledge or proof of . . . the truth. . . . Trust represents our best guess that [the person] is as he or she is purported to be."[32] As we think about authority and the importance of trust, we do well to remember Lincoln's observation that authority depends on "the trust of the audience, or the audience's strategic

30. Nooteboom and Six, introduction to *Trust Process in Organizations*, 5.
31. Hughes, Ginnett, and Curphy, *Leadership*, 151.
32. Gilbert W. Fairholm, "Leadership: A Function of Interactive Trust," *Journal of Leadership Studies* 2, no. 2 (1995): 11.

willingness to act as if it had such trust."[33] Followers are the critical variable in trust, since in giving the leader their trust, they are the most vulnerable party.

Lingenfelter's missiological approach to cross-cultural leadership establishes trust as a central dimension in his definition of a leader. The phrase he uses is "a community of trust," by which he means not only the "leadership team" but also the wider groups involved.[34] Trust in this sense is not a given, but rather is built through a process of leading, listening, and learning that expands as it is experienced. The significance of this approach is the weight it gives to the organic nature of the process; it is a "lived reality" that requires intentionality and commitment by those involved. This is in contrast to Lincoln's identification that even when trust isn't present, authority requires an audience (followers) to act "as if" they did trust the authority (leader). There is no room for acting "as if" in the scenarios described by Lingenfelter. When there are breakdowns or lack of trust, the community must take appropriate, definitive action, albeit in love.

Thinking Missiologically about Authority and Trust

Thinking missiologically about trust as a characteristic of authority presents us with the need to integrate all three perspectives: religious, organizational, and leadership. We begin with a missiological focus on the mission of God, recognizing that God's love for the world requires not only the broader goal of redemption and reconciliation but also that kingdom values characterize the mission in practice. Trust in the trustworthiness of God provides confidence to act in ways that conform to God's desire for truth and justice. Jesus's declaration in Matthew 28:18, "All authority in heaven and on earth has been given to me," precedes the missional response of our calling. In that light, a leader who seeks to live in a manner that builds trust in him or her as a leader, and who is also part of a community of trust, fits squarely with God's mission.

Looking at our organizational worlds moves us from trust in God to trust in each other. If we are to use our delegated authority from God to build trust, so that trust characterizes our authority, we must study and understand our contexts. Beginning with religious cultures, particularly our Christian cultures, how is our current use of authority perceived, and how is our history of using authority perceived? This raises a critical dimension of our practice of mission: When our practice of authority is received negatively—generating charges of colonialism, militarism, economic advantage, materialism, racism,

---

33. Lincoln, *Authority*, 8.
34. Sherwood G. Lingenfelter, *Leading Cross-Culturally: Covenant Relationships for Effective Christian Leadership* (Grand Rapids: Baker Academic, 2008), 19.

or the like—a radical redefinition of how we use authority may be required (irrespective of the merit of those charges). Typically, it is easier to find examples of these negative realities in the religious traditions of others than it is in our own, but the hope of building trust in our leadership and organization depends on the integrity of owning our history. Repentance and forgiveness have as crucial a place in our corporate life as they do in our private lives.

I remember participating in an event that illustrates well the absence of trust and the power of reconciliation. In 1989 it was my privilege to participate in a gathering of the Evangelical Alliance of the South Pacific in Suva, Fiji. The delegates represented various denominational and missionary organizations, along with local evangelical leaders from the Fijian community. After several plenary and breakout sessions, a well-known Pacific Island mission leader spoke in a plenary gathering. I was immediately struck by the powerful presence of this Tongan leader of a major mission movement. His speech began as a brief history of the relationship between expatriate missionaries and the Pacific Islander Christians in the missionary movement that spread across the Pacific. The leader rightly identified the first-generation believers' earliest involvement as a commitment to missionary "teams," even to the point of martyrdom. Then at one point in his presentation, his speech seemed to surge with energy as he told how expatriate missionaries and missions, using their broader resources, usurped the role of the Pacific Islanders in mission throughout the region and the world beyond. The uncharacteristic force of the accusations, merited as they were, penetrated the auditorium like an explosion, only drawing silence rather than uproar.

In the hours that followed, various groups of delegates met to discuss the significance of the presentation. Among these groups were those who, like me, represented the expatriate missions communities, while others represented those who were marginalized by the "overpowering" force of the Western missionary movement, as well as those who experienced marginalization within the various countries represented. It was a time of raw emotions and deep conviction. At a subsequent gathering, a recognized leader among the expatriate missionary group asked to speak to the gathering. As he walked up to the podium, he was joined by all of us who were associated with the mission organizations. By the time he spoke on our behalf, the stage was filled with a group in solidarity with our representative's words. His speech was simple and clear: we have sinned against you, and we ask your forgiveness. By the time the Tongan leader rose to join us on the stage, we were overwhelmed with the Lord's presence. Others joined him, and in the end "holy hugs" accompanied the shedding of tears. Then other groups rose to speak about their experience of marginalization and to seek the forgiveness of others. All of us in attendance were deeply moved, and also experienced the power of "speaking the truth in love" and repentance, not only for our current practices but also for our history.[35]

One of the significant insights arising out of the study of culture and human nature is that we are embodied through creation with natural abilities predetermined by virtue of our physicality, and we are embedded in a cultural context that gives us what we need to become what God intends us to be. It is truly a wonder of creation. As we develop from childhood through adulthood, our natural abilities engage with our cultural experiences, shaping us in response to the world God places us in. Our formation is an interconnected process physically, culturally, and spiritually. And the wonderful truth that we have affirmed often is that all of this is in the providence of God.

Such a strong affirmation should cause us to consider more deeply our role as leaders in discerning the gifts of those we lead and equipping them according to the mission God has given our organization. Each person with whom we serve is also loved, called, and being equipped by God in the same way we are as leaders. So when it comes to selecting and equipping leaders, we must start with discerning the gifting of the Holy Spirit in the individuals we are considering. While this seems straightforward, from experience I know that it is instead quite complex, especially when our goal is true diversity in our leadership teams. It isn't simply a matter of the organization (or you) identifying a potential leader and then teaching them how to lead. It requires the leader to be empowered to teach the organization how to be led. Remember, we noted that authority is principally social and relational.

To be culturally diverse in ways that are sustainable demands a significant social and organizational commitment to be "a learning environment," both in conscious, more formal ways and by allowing people to work in a context that does not hinder them from fully engaging in mimetic learning. As batting skills are developed through practice and as team athletic skills are honed through team workouts, the skills of leadership and followership are learned in the context of repetition. And in order to repeat the necessary instructive actions, people need abundant opportunities to lead and be recognized as one with authority to do so, and they need abundant opportunities to follow and to be affirmed for faithful following.

In practice, authority is based on long-established patterns in the organizational culture. Formal organizations typically have set patterns for appointing

---

35. The results of this significant gathering varied, but one of the more important outcomes was the embracing of the "Deep Sea Canoe" movement of Melanesian missionaries, which impacted most of the missionary societies in the region.

leaders, which include patterns for developing them, selecting them, and investing them with the authority of their particular position. Therefore, any plan to diversify the leadership, whether in terms of gender, ethnicity, or generations, requires a major commitment to assessing the entire system. As many of us have experienced firsthand, the challenge is not merely to appoint a single representative from a nonmajority group, but to establish new patterns within the organizational culture, patterns that address not only the opportunities and authority of the individual leader but, even more, require change to the culture of identifying, developing, selecting, and investing authority in diverse leaders in order to establish a broader base for succession planning.

Another aspect of the culture of authority is how the exercise of authority is built on trust in the individual in authority. Inevitably, the organization has a particular expectation concerning the exercise of authority, usually attached to expectations for decisiveness, efficiency, and results. Normally, a value is placed on relational skills as well, but that is overshadowed by expectations of performance, particularly when the related tasks have operational significance. This is further complicated by the number of leaders who easily conform to the organizational expectations due to their experience with the system and the trust that comes with it. And to be candid, in most cases their identification is with the majority culture, which is usually made up of older men from the dominant ethnicity.

Due to the God-ordained uniqueness of the individuals in authority, they have an intrinsic approach to the exercise of authority as part of their own story (narrative self) and based on cognitive relational processes (shared attentions, interpersonal attachments, and empathy), processes learned primarily mimetically. In general, mimetic processes unconsciously form the interaction between the brain and the contextual experience in which the behavior is acquired. We must not underestimate the context for the experiences, since the culture in which the leader is most experienced will establish the patterns and understandings that shape their leadership. The individual may know how to act in a given situation, but that knowledge is normally not easily articulated, and the behavior it generates may not even be conscious. When those mimetic processes take place in the context of the current organizational culture, particularly when there are limited examples of diverse leadership, the resulting social knowledge and concomitant skills will inevitably be socially acceptable as part of the status quo, restricting the impact and even the value of the diversity our organization is seeking.

Knowing the right clothes to wear and how to act in relation to the senior leader or donors are surface examples, but more important is knowing how to exercise authority with confidence in a given time and place. The lack of such knowledge is observable when those in authority delay decisions not only because they want to build consensus but because they lack the social knowledge or behavioral skills to move a group toward decision for fear of the consequences. Certainly, being raised in a different culture influences one's knowledge and skills, but how it does is not restricted to context; it is a matter of cognition. If we take seriously an organizational commitment to diversity, including in leadership, we must create opportunities to learn to lead and follow in a group whose members are more diverse than they used to be.

Depending on where your organization is in the process, it may be best to establish a diverse team to experiment with leading and following in ways that are truly sensitive to cultural differences, including granting authority to act and ample time for relationships of trust to be built. The lessons learned in this situation can then be disseminated across the organization and beyond. As we stated earlier, our development as individuals combines our natural engagement abilities with our cultural experiences in response to the world in which God places us. Keep that in front of the team so that when the team faces the inevitable annoyances in learning to work together, they can also see the uniqueness (and idiosyncrasies) as a gift from God. As we noted in chapter 2, we are as alike (embodied) as we are different (embedded) by virtue of being children of God serving the mission of God!

Every leader faces the challenge of exercising authority. If that leader belongs to a group that has traditionally been excluded from leadership, that circumstance adds new dimensions to the process of leading as one in authority. As I thought about examples of how this works out in practice, my thoughts went to Joanna Lima, a friend and scholar/practitioner with whom I served in mission leadership. I asked Lima to reflect on the challenge of exercising authority in missions. Based on her broader horizon developing leaders for international teams, she discusses her experience in both understanding and exercising authority. It is appropriate that the case study follows the concept of trust: as one who has built trust and works in a community of trust, she is well suited to illustrate the issues.

The Challenge of Exercising Authority

Joanna Lima, New Zealand/Thailand[a]

Leading is never simple. But in the mission context, where layer upon layer of complexity converge, it is unusually challenging. As a New Zealand woman, I came into mission leadership in a large, global, multinational mission with a set of largely unarticulated presumptions about leadership and how authority ought to be expressed. These culturally bound presumptions were deeply held and to some degree subconscious. Over time, I have become increasingly aware of how profoundly my cultural, theological, and even personal values shape every aspect of how I understand and express leadership.

As I reflect on the challenge of "exercising authority," three primary elements come to mind: first, the role of organizational culture and values; second, the specific challenges faced by women in leadership; and third, the impact of the culture outside the organization on exercising authority.

Organizational Culture and Values

Components of organizational culture, along with divergent interpretations of organizational values, can undermine authority without the leader or followers knowing it, particularly when organizational values are ambiguous or in tension with each other. For example, the term "servant leadership" is used liberally in many organizations, and while many of us would resonate with a desire to be a servant leader, in a given organization it may not be clear how to be one. Does that mean simply being responsive to the needs of those we lead, or is there room for visionary leadership? Can one engage in strategic leadership and be a servant leader concurrently? Can one exercise authority and be a servant leader? Of course many of us would answer yes to these questions—but we should be aware that there are highly divergent understandings of what constitutes authority and power, and particularly how they are to be expressed. Cultural and generational diversity can amplify this challenge.

Organizations that have a flat structure and emphasize a high degree of collaboration may be even more prone to misunderstanding authority, heightening the need for even clearer communication about appropriate exercise of power. This may be particularly true for mission organizations where members raise their own support and are considered volunteers.

Women as Mission Leaders

In addition to the challenges that all mission leaders face, women are often subject to another layer of complexity when exercising authority. Leadership literature in the business world effectively documents this complexity, describing women as encountering a "leadership labyrinth"—a helpful metaphor that highlights the fact that the journey into leadership for women can often be riddled with challenges and even outright animosity.[b] In the mission world, I suspect the journey is less likely to be marked by animosity and more likely to be slowed down through intentional or unintentional noninclusion. Diverse theological interpretations of the role of women can create a minefield for women in mission leadership—even in organizations that have taken a clear position allowing all members to lead. The socialization of this position can lag far behind the decision. Although I am privileged to serve as a senior leader in a mission that has embraced women in leadership, somewhat often I encounter others who are quietly mistrustful or openly apprehensive of this reality.

Once women are in a position of leadership, they encounter a new challenge. Undoubtedly some will question the appropriateness of a woman in that role—a challenge that men seldom encounter—and the questioning may come in a myriad of ways that impact their leadership. Men and women should both be aware that they may need extra energy and resilience to simply live in this tension.

The Societal Culture

The larger culture outside the organization can present another challenge to exercising leadership. Much research has shown quite diverse understandings and expressions of leadership across cultures. Of course culture is dynamic rather than static, and we struggle to talk about culture without stereotyping. I grew up in New Zealand, lived in Canada for a number of years after university, lived in East Asia for another decade, and married a Portuguese American (who lived in Japan for a number of years), and now we live in Thailand. It is impossible to say that my "culture" fits neatly into a box that is defined by one of my passport countries. Yet I recognize that the way I understand and express leadership is profoundly impacted by my culture, and the use of scales such as power distance, uncertainty avoidance (a society's tolerance for uncertainty and ambiguity), and long-term orientation (delaying short-term gain in order to prepare for the future) provides some helpful indicators for comparing the various influences cultures exert on any given situation.[c]

I pursued further research as I wrestled with the reality that even though our mission organization is very multicultural, the way that we expect people to exercise authority and receive it is profoundly shaped by a Western, individualistic, low power distance model of leadership, and is influenced by specific theological and missiological perspectives. We have to wrestle with the question of whether it is possible for multicultural, global mission organizations to be truly "culturally intelligent." This challenge is especially poignant in organizations where there is a "majority" culture—where one national culture is numerically dominant. Without extreme, practical intentionality, leadership appointments may be subject to the phenomenon of homophily—leaders are more likely to recognize leadership potential in others who most resemble themselves. If we're not self-aware of our own cultural influences and that of others, it is extremely easy to unintentionally offend and to exercise authority ineffectively. Leading effectively in multicultural organizations requires extra intentionality, sufficient feedback, and a lot of humility!

[a] Joanna Sears Lima (PhD, Regent University) serves as the international leadership-development facilitator for Pioneers and is based in Thailand. She has led multicultural teams in East Asia for many years.

[b] Alice Eagly and Linda L. Carli, "Women and the Labyrinth of Leadership," *Harvard Business Review*, September 2007, https://hbr.org/2007/09/women-and-the-labyrinth-of-leadership.

[c] Geert Hofstede, Gert Jan Hofstede, and Michael Minkov, *Cultures and Organizations: Software of the Mind; Intercultural Cooperation and Its Importance for Survival*, 3rd ed. (New York: McGraw Hill, 2010), 522, 529, 187–276.

Reviewing and Reflecting on the Issues

The case study, as Joanna Lima presents it, with such civility, invites us to respond intentionally with matching civility. The role of authorizing or conferring authority on a leader is no small matter. The individual who wears the symbols of authority or holds the office of leadership represents not only herself or himself but the entire organization and, by extension, the mission of God. There is no way to soften that responsibility; hence the wisdom of 1 Timothy 5:22: "Don't rush to commission anyone to leadership" (CEB). But we also face the challenge of providing increased opportunities to develop people and organizations for new forms of leadership, transcending the "majority culture" in creating new contextual realities. The path ahead seems to be in line with Lima's warning to avoid the phenomenon of homophily by extreme intentionality in giving opportunity to lead and creating opportunities for the organization to learn how to follow.

Reviewing

It behooves us to reflect on the implications of authority as leaders within Christian organizations. The threefold elements of authority, responsibility, and accountability, while well known to most leaders, play such an important role in our world that their relevance to the organizational mission should be continually reassessed. Similarly, where we find similarities between our context and Lim's in Southeast Asia, we need to consider appropriate ways to deal with practices that undermine the work of God's mission; changing such practices should be integral to the critical contextualization of our mission.

Authority, as we have established it, is important for leaders and organizations. Not only are the vestments and positions important to those "in authority" or who are "an authority"; they are equally important to the organizations and the "audience" (members) who respect the leaders who were appointed by those "with authority." This is more than a prepositional shift; it relates to the lived reality of the community. Authority is critical to organizations; as Bass notes, "Organizational effectiveness depends" on authority and responsibility.[36] The interrelationship of authority, responsibility, and accountability is a more complete view of the practice of authority. Conversely, as Lim suggests in her reflections, the illegitimate exercise of authority without accountability, sanctioned by the church, can weaken congregations (followers), particularly those whose members naturally defer to authority (high power distance contexts).

Authority as the middle ground between persuasion and coercion is a helpful understanding of its role in leadership. This is reinforced by the relational nature of authority, but it also draws attention to the behavior of the leader in authority. Learning to exercise authority in a manner that invites rather than sells or threatens is an important part of the task of leading. It is not so much a matter of finesse as of respect for the followers and the position of authority. To avoid the situation where the audience (followers) must act "as if" they respect a leader rather than genuinely respect them, leaders must earn and show respect.

The case for authority and trust being two sides of the same coin is convincing. Trust is the bond between organizations, leaders, and followers, without which there are serious consequences. Building trust is a primary task for any leader, particularly those working in intercultural contexts, as Lingenfelter so aptly demonstrates.[37] While trust is built, it must also be given if an organization is going to facilitate diversity in leadership. If leaders are to trust followers to respond appropriately and followers are to trust leaders to lead, leaders must provide opportunities for dynamic learning, since in the end trust is multidirectional (that is, intercultural) and not simply gained by virtue of appointment.

Reflecting

A common question of new members and outsiders is, "Who is in charge?" Reflect on the broader context of your organization, or one you are familiar with, in responding to the following questions.

1. What are the most common decisions that require permission or approval by someone in authority on behalf of your organization? What position does that person hold?

36. Bass and Bass, *Handbook of Leadership*, 365.
37. Lingenfelter, *Leading Cross-Culturally*, 21.

2. How do you and your colleagues view the use of power by those in authority? Is this congruent with the understandings of others in the organization? How does it compare to the more observable use of power in the culture(s) in which you serve?

3. If you were to call your team or closest colleagues together and ask them to define authority, what categories would you anticipate receiving from the exercise? What are the most important categories in your mind?

4. How does your organization go about constructing authority? What have you observed in the transferring of authority or the empowering of people to exercise authority? Do some areas need to be reviewed in order to bring them into line with your organizational mission?

The twin concepts of accountability and trust relate directly to the worlds in which you and I serve. Consider how this is the case, on the basis of the following questions.

5. Whom do you trust as a leader and person in authority? What makes you trust them? Do others share your trust in the leader? Why and why not?

6. How have you built trust in your role of leadership? Think of an example that helped you to learn more about the nature of trust. What were the most significant elements of the experience?

7. Are there opportunities for people from nonmajority cultures within your organization to grow in their capacity to lead? How could your organization strengthen its resolve to create opportunities for growth?

8. Asking the hard question, is your organization prepared to learn to follow the lead of someone whose cultural background will challenge some of the assumptions about authority and trust that are embedded in your organizational culture? How could you help to develop new approaches to be more intentional in leading and following interculturally?

In the next chapter we will explore the subject of "world making," drawing on extensive work and research from various sources, including anthropology of religion, social anthropology, and organizational studies. We will continue to reflect missiologically on intercultural leadership and organizations so as to shape, catalyze, and propel our organizations missionally.

6

Intercultural Realities

Four Worlds of Christian Organizations

In my various leadership roles through the years, I was tasked with writing reports for a board of directors (or trustees); these reports were then used as a base for other constituencies such as donors and friends. Every year it was a challenge to choose wisely between the more appealing achievements and the inevitable problems, usually related to budget or recruiting. "Integrity and transparency" were two words heading one side of my blank report sheet, while on the other side were the words "publicity and fundraising." They are not mutually exclusive, but neither are they always neatly compatible. The tough part was to tell the story in a way that invites people to listen, while informing them of the realities of our organizational mission. Finding the appropriate combination of strengths and weaknesses, opportunities and threats, was never easy.

The late Fred Craddock, distinguished preacher and scholar, describes a preacher's task as generating "the nod of recognition" in the listener and then the "shock of recognition."[1] I heard him say that in a sermon many years ago, and it stuck with me. His point, so eloquently phrased, is that people are inclined to identify with the cause or thesis if they are introduced to the familiar landscape of the picture at the beginning. It is a way for them to say,

1. Fred B. Craddock Jr., *The Craft of Preaching* (Atlanta: Chalice, 2013).

129

"Yes, I can see that," thereby committing their attention. But as we all know too well, every familiar scenario also contains shocking things, sometimes hidden and other times ignored or unseen for various reasons. Our job as leaders is to be honest in our communication, pointing out both the nod and the shock of recognition. Remember, honest communication is a marker of our uniqueness in creation. It also validates the experience of walking with God in the world God loves redemptively.

If we are to report accurately, missionally, then we must understand the various worlds in which we live. We must answer the broader question, How do we live in these worlds? Followed by, To what degree are we seeing the world as it is missionally? In this chapter we will apply Craddock's approach of generating the nod of recognition and the shock of recognition in responding to the intercultural realities of the worlds around us.

The chapter first introduces the concept of "worlds," focusing on the processes of constructing and maintaining worlds, especially religious worlds, as well as some of the influences on leadership and organization. Next, we consider the case of "the five faces of Islam," illustrating the complex concept of religious worlds. Building on the concept of worlds, as seen in the case study, the third section is an exploration of societal and organizational worlds and their impact on organizations missionally. The fourth section raises the concept of subcultures as an important general category of worlds occurring inside and outside our organizations. The chapter concludes by reviewing the critical issues of world making and then reflecting on the implications for leaders of organizations.

The Making of Religious Worlds

The concept of "world making," for our purposes, refers to the process of establishing, constructing, and maintaining a particular "world" as the lived reality of a group of people. It parallels the concept of worldview—beliefs, values, and feelings—adding the dimensions of time, place, and relationships, which make up the "world." To the individual living in that world, it is the convergence of the various aspects of life, which add up to the "way of inhabiting a world."[2] People who inhabit these worlds generally act in accordance with the premises of their world, even to the point of asking and answering their own questions. This is particularly true of religious worlds and the organizations that serve them.

2. William E. Paden, *Religious Worlds: The Comparative Study of Religion* (Boston: Beacon, 1988), 7.

Before launching into the concept of religious worlds, I offer a disclaimer for the perspective of why it is missiologically relevant to consider this approach. As we have asserted from the beginning, the *missio Dei* comes from the Triune God: Father, Son, and Holy Spirit. We who are called according to his purposes are servants of God as God fulfills the mission. In this book our missiological concern is with the context of God's mission. Hiebert's diagram of missiology in relation to other disciplines is a key to understanding the perspective of worlds.[3] Our study of religious worlds falls within the framework of human contexts, as we understand them, primarily as contemporary phenomena and secondarily as historical phenomena. In that sense we are following the call to the "exegesis of the culture" that is performed by critical contextualization.[4]

Many Different Religious Worlds

Anthropology has struggled to categorize religion within the framework of human endeavors. At times it has resisted religion as the enemy of scholarly anthropology, while at other times it has considered religion an integral part of the fabric of a culture.[5] An influential perspective among cultural anthropologists is that of Clifford Geertz, who claims that religion is a cultural system.[6] The significance of Geertz's claim from a missiological perspective is that we should consider religions as the lived reality of a group of people whose world is included in the gospel claim, "For God so loved the *world* that he gave his only Son, so that everyone who believes in him may not perish but may have eternal life" (John 3:16). Religious worlds, therefore, provide an important category for considering the religion of a particular group of people on the broader cultural landscape, with implications for Christian organizational cultures.[7]

3. Figure 1 in the introduction of the present volume is adapted from Paul G. Hiebert, *The Gospel in Human Contexts: Anthropological Explorations for Contemporary Missions* (Grand Rapids: Baker Academic, 2009), 32–35.

4. Paul G. Hiebert, *Anthropological Reflections on Missiological Issues* (Grand Rapids: Baker, 1994), 88–91.

5. See Brian M. Howell and Jenell Williams Paris, *Introducing Cultural Anthropology: A Christian Perspective* (Grand Rapids: Baker Academic, 2011), 176–78.

6. Clifford Geertz, *The Interpretation of Cultures* (New York: Basic Books, 1973). On the world scene, another perspective on religious worlds comes from the Harvard political scientist Samuel P. Huntington in his influential, if not also controversial, work *The Clash of Civilizations and the Remaking of World Order* (New York: Basic Books, 2011).

7. From the perspective of missiology and anthropology of religion, religious worlds is a "productive comparative category." James S. Bielo, *Anthropology of Religion: The Basics* (New York: Routledge, 2015), 82.

The concept of religious worlds begins by acknowledging that plural worlds coexist increasingly close to one another, yet each has its own distinct view of reality. To illustrate, in central Jakarta there stands a neo-Gothic cathedral, Saint Mary of the Assumption, directly across from the modern architecture of the Istiqlal Mosque, regarded as the largest mosque in Southeast Asia. On any given day, you can observe the faithful visiting each of these centers of their respective religious worlds while you are walking along the boulevard toward the National Monument to Indonesian Independence. In fact the *Pancasila*, the official philosophical theory of the Indonesian state, not only recognizes but guarantees the coexistence of these distinct worlds of Muslims and Christians. Using these large physical structures as symbolic of the different religious worlds highlights one of the major elements of a "world": place. In less public ways, every city and region hosts a diversity of religious worlds; it is one of the realities of globalization.

Place is a primary horizon for religious worlds, whether at the macro level, such as Mecca or Jerusalem, or on a more local level, such as a prayer closet or a Buddhist shrine. The sacred physical nature of the place is the essential requirement, not the scale or necessarily the location. This sacred nature relates to the concept of "dwelling," as not just a place to live or a place that represents religious beliefs, but a way that encompasses the embodied interaction with daily life. Bielo suggests that the term "dwelling" helps to differentiate between the inhabited place and the physical space itself.[8]

A second major horizon of religious worlds is the concept of time or "temporality," the lived notion of time: past, present, and future.[9] Temporality, to the religious world, explains the questions of origin of life, the afterlife, the spirit world, and the end times. Time as temporality is not simply a measurement, but is the ground for relating to the past and fostering identity. It also provides order to the religious life, including holy seasons and events of remembrance. From the perspective of cognition, the individual self interacts with others to maintain the religious world. This maintenance depends on the narrative that is created through cultural representations and metarepresentations in dialogue with others (contemporary or historical). Temporality also relates to the concept of deference in religious rituals by identifying not only respected leaders but also historical figures (e.g., church saints or venerated ancestors).

8. Bielo, *Anthropology of Religion*, 84. See also Steven Feld and Keith Basso, eds., *Senses of Place* (Albuquerque: School of American Research Press, 1996).

9. This is a major consideration in the mission theology, known as the "now" and the "not yet" of the kingdom of God. The perspective comes from the theology of the "already but not yet" developed by George Eldon Ladd, *Gospel of the Kingdom* (Grand Rapids: Eerdmans, 1990).

The horizons of place and time are inseparable in the making of religious worlds. Temporality frequently implies sacred space, as illustrated by the biannual General Conference of the Church of Jesus Christ of Latter-Day Saints, held at the LDS Conference Center in Salt Lake City. Through the use of technology, these gatherings draw a worldwide audience due to the significance of the place (Salt Lake City) and the ability to receive guidance from the church leaders. Events such as these are grounded in the practices across religious landscapes, acting as moorings in the making of worlds.[10]

I encountered a number of equivalent gatherings (missionary retreats) in a Jomtien Beach hotel complex in Pattaya, Thailand. Four major missionary societies were holding their annual East, South, and Southeast Asia area conferences at the same large hotel. It was fascinating, when walking past the various conference and breakout rooms, to overhear the presenters, many of whom could have been exchanged with little disturbance to content or theology! The point being, religious worlds as a comparative category has far-reaching implications for understanding our "normal" Christian organizational activities, including both place and time.

Understanding Religious Worlds

The approach to religious worlds that we are exploring is anthropocentric, rather than theocentric, focusing on behavior and world making, not theology or doctrine. Religions create their worlds by declaring their view of reality and specifying religious practices.[11] Rituals, such as those of transformation and intensification, play a particularly important role in maintaining and extending the religious world. Another common element is opposition to other forces within the world, seen and unseen. Using symbols to give meaning to these forces, religions are able to define reality through imagination as well as the defined narrative. Whether through art or rhetoric, the religious world offers answers to life's issues.

Missiologists experience the nod of recognition and the shock of recognition in regard to the forces of the unseen worlds when reading Hiebert's widely influential article "The Flaw of the Excluded Middle."[12] Originally published in 1982, the article opened new vistas for understanding the religious worlds of folk religion, magic, and astrology. These subjects were well

10. Bielo, *Anthropology of Religion*, 85.
11. This subsection draws on the discussion of understanding religious worlds in Paden, *Religious Worlds*, 53–65.
12. See Paul G. Hiebert, "The Flaw of the Excluded Middle," in *Anthropological Reflections*, 189–201.

known in anthropology and familiar to missiologists, leading to the nod of recognition. However, in the context of the world of religions, the middle is the area between religion and science that deals with the unseen influences of spirits and powers affecting daily life. They were excluded or not adequately understood by missiologists, leading to the shock of recognition. This growing understanding of the excluded middle led to a remarkable growth of interest in spiritual dynamics beginning in the early 1980s.

Understanding a different world means seeing that world as its adherents see it, resisting judgments that attribute motive and meanings that are foreign to their world. In reflecting missiologically on the Ten Commandments, we are reminded that the ninth, "Neither shall you bear false witness against your neighbor" (Deut. 5:20), applies not only to using fair measures and not lying about the neighbor but also to not attributing false beliefs and motives. When comparing our world to other worlds, we do well to compare our best thoughts and efforts to the best thoughts and efforts of others, rather than our best to their worst, which, my experience suggests, is more often the case.[13] As we will see in the case study, reporting on a given religious world using the realities of those who live it helps deepen our understanding of that world as it is, while avoiding bearing false witness by using stereotypes that tend to demonize rather than inform our various constituencies.

The concept of worlds is a very helpful tool in mediating ideas that are both different and common, given the interdependency of human nature and culture.[14] Behavior, as a primary concern in approaching religious worlds, is normally consistent with the history, particular people, and context in focus. By its very nature, observing diverse worlds is intercultural, requiring skills and language to interpret the contextual categories. When our reporting depends on sound bites or imposed beliefs, values, and feelings, we may unknowingly assume the role of world maker. Avoiding this error and rendering a fair interpretation requires great wisdom and discernment, since our annual reports reflect not only on our leadership and organization, but more importantly on the mission of God.

Like culture, humanly speaking, religious worlds are not principally the domain of an individual; they belong to groups of people, social institutions, and organizations. It is the group of people who give a world its plausibility over time. They are the ones who hold together the beliefs and actions,

13. Using sober judgment that upholds integrity while also holding firmly to righteousness and truth is a skill that is desperately needed in the world. For an excellent discussion of the subject, see Richard J. Mouw, *Uncommon Decency: Christian Civility in an Uncivil World*, rev. ed. (Downers Grove, IL: InterVarsity, 2010).

14. Paden, *Religious Worlds*, 54.

including reforming the world in times of crisis or when change is desirable or inevitable. The people themselves, as a collective, determine the religious roles and identities, using the stories and rituals that form their history. So it is in the gathered community that the sacred is preserved and defended. The missiological insight here is not only that the community maintains what is sacred but also that true understanding comes not from looking in from the outside as much as from observing the world from the inside. In anthropology this is known as participant observation.

The concept of world helps us understand religion as the place where people live, acting in ways that are consistent with their beliefs and in a real sense embodying their faith. It is little wonder why conversion to another religion creates such social and relational upheaval. While that gives us pause to reflect sensitively on the implications, from a missiological perspective it also reminds us why we are so committed to critical contextualization. One of the main reasons for introducing the concept of religious worlds is to consider what our own religious world entails as part of the process of thinking missiologically about our Christian organizations and institutions in the transmission of culture.

Using Howell and Paris's definition of culture as "the total way of life . . . that is learned, adaptive, shared, and integrated," we can make a case for each religion as a cultural world unto itself.[15] The total way of life includes the representation and transmission of culture, especially through the mimetic processes of imitation and ritual. Returning to Paden's most telling observation, "The guiding principle . . . must be that each religious community acts within the premises of its own universe, its own logic, its own answers to its own questions."[16] As leaders of Christian organizations, we do well to learn from these cultural insights, adapting where appropriate and sharing widely with our community in service to the mission of God in the diverse human contexts of God's world. To illustrate a contemporary challenge coming from the worlds of Islam, we turn our attention to John Azumah's observations.

The Five Faces of Islam

John Azumah, Ghana/USA[a]

It is very common to hear Christian apologists and critics of Islam say, "Islam is . . . ," "Islam teaches . . . ," or "Islam does not . . ." These are often, at the

15. Howell and Paris, *Introducing Cultural Anthropology*, 36.
16. Paden, *Religious Worlds*, 7.

very least, overly simplistic and misleading generalizations. As one leading Muslim scholar puts it:

> No one has seen "Islam" in its transparent glory to really judge it. But what we have seen are Muslims: good Muslims and bad Muslims; ugly Muslims and pretty Muslims; just Muslims and unjust Muslims; Muslims who are oppressors, racists, bigots, misogynists, and criminals as well as Muslims who are compassionate, liberators, seekers of an end to racism and sexism, and those who aspire for global justice and equity.

In other words, there are as many "Islams" as there are Muslims. The five "faces" of Islam outlined here represent various ways in which different Muslims understand and express their faith. These five faces (missionary, mystical, ideological, militant, and progressive) are more like overlapping circles than compartmentalized boxes.

The Missionary Face

Islam is the second largest missionary religion after Christianity. The Qur'an enjoins Muslims to "summon (all) to the Way of thy Lord with wisdom and beautiful preaching" (Q. 16:125). From the outset, conversion to Islam was almost always a by-product of conquests and commerce. However, in the nineteenth century, Christian missions inspired the formation of organized Islamic missions (da'wah), which have included state sponsorship in many Muslim countries since the 1950s. A good example of an Islamic missionary organization is the Tablighi Jamaat, which started in India in 1927 and can now be found all over the world. Muslims who view Islam mainly through the missionary lens seek to commend the best values of their religion while leveling polemical attacks against other traditions, especially Christianity. Well-known Muslim missionary polemicists include the late Ahmed Deedat of South Africa and Zakir Naik of India.

The Mystical Face

The mystical face represents the more esoteric or spiritual expression of Islam. Examples include Sufism, Islamic spirituality, and Folk Islam. Folk Islam predominates in the Middle East, Africa, and Asia, and is rooted in a strong belief in the supernatural: the spirit world, miracles, faith healings, dreams, visions, and visitations. Thus, mystical Islam bears similarities to charismatic or Pentecostal Christianity. Mystics practice spiritual exercises that include dhikr (remembrance of God), chants, music, poetry, dance, trance, and ritual meals. Whereas traditional Islam emphasizes the transcendence of God, mystical Islam teaches divine immanence and love. It teaches the need for a master or Shaykh, whose duty is to guide novices and meet the spiritual needs of the wider believing community. The spirit, rather than the letter, of the Qur'an is what matters to mystics. Followers engage in the magical use of the Qur'an for healing and other purposes. Organized Sufi orders include the Qadiriyya and Tijaniyya in the Middle East and Africa, Chishti in India, Mevlevi in Turkey, and Inayati in the USA.

The Ideological Face

Muslims who see Islam through an ideological or political prism emphasize the religion's legal and political content and believe that Islam is a complete way of life. The chief objective of ideological Muslims, also known as Islamists, is to Islamize the public sphere. The Qur'an is the only true constitution; an Islamic state is the objective, and enforcement of shari'a, or Islamic law, the means. All other systems are humanly created and false. The chief Qur'anic verse for Islamists is: "Ye are the best community that hath been raised up for mankind. Ye enjoin right conduct and forbid indecency; and ye believe in Allah" (Q. 3:110). Ideological Muslims take an extreme stance against other worldviews and teach a radical disassociation from and aversion toward any-thing non-Islamic. Examples include the Wahhabis and Salafis of Saudi Arabia, the Muslim Brotherhood of Egypt and Sudan, and the Ansar al-Sunna or Ahl al-Sunna in many African countries. Groups such as Hamas and Hezbollah are mainly ideological but have military wings.

The Militant Face

Almost always inspired by the teachings of ideological Islam, militants seek to achieve political ends through violence. They draw inspiration from parts of the Qur'an, a romanticized Islamic history, and selected texts and traditions. Examples include al-Qaeda, ISIS, Boko Haram, and al-Shabaab. Note that jihadi groups' citing of Islamic scripture and texts does not necessarily make them Islamic. For instance, although they regularly flout the elaborate and complicated laws governing the declaration and conduct of jihad, the rise of militant Islamic groups cannot simply be explained by violence in Islamic texts. Oppressive and corrupt regimes, dictatorships, weak state institutions, and misguided Western foreign policies have all contributed in important ways. The seeds of violence are clearly present in Islamic texts and history, but contemporary sociopolitical and economic factors constitute the fertile grounds for such seeds to sprout, take root, and spread.

The Progressive Face

The progressive face genuinely seeks reformation within Islam. Progressive Muslims read Islamic texts and sourcebooks critically. They call for independent critical thinking (*ijtihad*) in place of what they see as blind following (*taqlid*) by the vast majority of the faithful. Progressives are open to other worldviews and see themselves as engaged in a struggle for the soul of Islam. They defend the rights of minorities and promote gender equality in Muslim-majority countries. Progressives openly declare their stance against "those whose God is a vengeful monster in the sky issuing death decrees against the Muslim and the non-Muslim alike . . . those whose God is too small, too mean, too tribal, and too male."[b] Some are persecuted and exiled from their own countries. Progressive groups and think tanks include the Sisters in Islam of Malaysia, the Gülen Movement in Turkey, Muslims for Progressive Values in the USA, and Quilliam Foundation in the UK.

Conclusion

Each of Islam's five faces presents unique challenges to the church. Christians need to move past fear and prejudice in order to bring the gospel to Muslims (Acts 1:8). We need prayer warriors who will commit to praying for the Muslim World (Zech. 4:6). We need those who can participate in intellectual and theological discourse, helping the church to engage Islam in both the academic and public spheres. We should affirm courageous activists working for reform and justice. Certainly, the militant face of Islam poses a security threat that governments must confront (Rom. 13:4). Yet Christians must respond in love, seeking to understand and alleviate the sociopolitical factors that contribute to violence and extremism. The church can also reach out to and care for widows, orphans, and refugees left in the wake of warfare.

Finally, we must remember and behold the *human* face of Islam. Muslims are persons with names and loved ones. As an African proverb puts it, in times of crisis, the foolish build walls, but the wise build bridges. May we wise up and be Christian bridge-builders and peacemakers as our Lord and Savior implores us (Matt. 5:9).

This case study first appeared as John A. Azumah, "The Five Faces of Islam," in *InSights Essays*, October 2016, ScholarLeaders International, http://www .scholarleaders.org/insights-essay-archives/five-faces-islam. Used by permission.

[a] John A. Azumah is professor of world Christianity and Islam at Columbia Theological Seminary. Born and raised in Ghana, he earned his PhD at the University of Birmingham. He has taught at theological schools in Ghana, India, the UK, and the USA. Among John's books are *My Neighbour's Faith: Islam Explained for African Christians* and *The African Christian and Islam* (edited with Lamin Sanneh). John also serves on the board of ScholarLeaders International.
[b] Omid Safi, "Introduction: The Times They Are A-Changin'—A Muslim Quest for Justice, Gender Equality, and Pluralism," in *Progressive Muslims on Justice, Gender, and Pluralism*, ed. Omid Safi (Oxford: Oneworld Publications, 2003), 9-10.

The Making of Cultural Worlds

As Azumah so convincingly points out, the religious worlds of Islam are many and varied. His introduction to the five faces illustrates the unique role of religions in creating and maintaining their "worlds" by establishing the premises of their particular universe according to their own logic, and then, as was demonstrated in each of the five faces, answering their own questions, in each case acting according to their own premises. By approaching religious worlds in this manner, we can understand the worlds better and reduce animosity, moving from polemics, which often oversimplify or overgeneralize to the point of bearing false witness.

An equally important implication from the case study is that Christian organizations working in the Muslim worlds also suffer from Muslims' overgeneralizing, "bundling" together all actions done by "Christians" or "Christian nations," as if those actions were typical of all Christians. It is as common to hear generalizations such as "Christianity is . . ." or "Christianity teaches . . ." as it is to hear "Islam is . . ." or "Islam teaches . . ." The implication for leaders is that we must be aware of the biases and stereotypes that surround and even penetrate our work. Whether in matters of security or residence, the human tendency to demonize others knows no boundaries and is not limited to only one culture.

This book aims to take what we are learning about culture and apply it, so as to shape, catalyze, and propel our organizations missionally. Because cultures are dynamic, influenced by both internal and external factors, they constantly present new dimensions of what we consider as cultural, sometimes replacing the old ways, but more often simply expanding the culture. We acknowledge that culture, by definition, is learned, adaptive, shared, and more or less integrated. We learn from cognitive anthropologists that culture is "a non-genetic, very long-term flow of information, in continual transformation," with the key mechanism for continuity and change being communication.[17] Yet even with such broad parameters for inquiry, culture constantly challenges our understanding by redefining the boundaries of reality.

The concept of "world" gives us a helpful comparative category for further analyzing the influence of cultures on leadership and organizations. In addition to religious culture, we will identify three other major types of culture: societal, organizational, and subcultural, each presenting a "world" that helps define the boundaries of reality in our missional context. We will also consider

17. Maurice Bloch, *Anthropology and the Cognitive Challenge* (Cambridge: Cambridge University Press, 2012), 20–21.

some of the more significant elements of these three worlds as they represent the lived reality of various groups that intersect within the contexts of our organizations. We begin with the broadest category, societal culture.

Societal Culture

To move from the broad category of culture and its interdependence on human nature to a more applied approach, we must shift our focus, broadening our anthropological reflections to include the work of organizational and leadership studies. The broadest category of culture used in leadership studies is "societal culture."[18] We will adopt this purposely for the sake of imposing boundaries on what is included when studying the cultural context. This is in contrast to terms like "global culture" or "macro culture," either of which can assume more universal attributes and become unwieldy.

Societal culture is best described by the components Hiebert used in the earlier definition: "the more or less integrated systems . . . shared by a group of people who organize and regulate what they think, feel, and do."[19] Using the term "societal" requires identifying the broad group of people in focus while allowing for a level of selection according to the predominant patterns of behavior, products, and values of a society as they intersect in the context of our work at any given time. For instance, we may identify a national culture whose commonalities of citizenship, language, political system, commerce, media, and residence provide the integrated system that regulates and organizes social life, such as Turkish culture or French culture. Societal culture's far-reaching influence also shapes the components of the culture itself, such as beliefs and practices concerning self, family, others, social behavior, and rituals, thereby impacting the practices of all intersecting worlds. Practically, identifying the societal culture is useful for determining the cultural influences that permeate the "worlds" of organizations.

In most urban settings, the societal culture embraces a wide diversity of cultures, peoples, institutions, and activities, having both commonalities with other urban centers and unique particularities, which normally reflect historical and environmental factors. An organization that resides in that urban center must learn to accommodate the particularities while benefiting from the infrastructure and services available. Specific factors include things like

18. My choice of the term "societal culture" is based on the work of the Global Leadership and Organizational Behavior Effectiveness (GLOBE) Research Program project, which will be covered in chapter 7.

19. Paul G. Hiebert, *Anthropological Insights for Missionaries* (Grand Rapids: Baker, 1985), 30.

cost of living, travel time based on transportation patterns, affordability of facilities and housing, security, technology, and so on. While an organization will have some choice as to how to respond to the societal culture, it is seriously limited, forcing the organizational world, at least initially, to adapt accordingly. Societal cultures may not be national or regional; they may be the culture across a particularly large domain or social system such as education, medicine, politics, the arts, or certain professions.

Organizational Culture

The study of organizational culture has grown steadily in breadth and influence since the first publication of Schein's *Organizational Culture and Leadership* in 1985.[20] Definitions tend to identify general processes, the common elements being a focus on the boundaries that define the organization and the shared responsibilities of members (e.g., problem solving). Schein's review of cultural definitions includes what he refers to as the "basic taken-for-granted assumptions," including "beliefs, values, and desired behaviors that launched the group and made it successful," calling them the "cultural DNA."[21] These common assumptions become cultural representations for the organization, bringing meaning to significant events and practices as the culture is transmitted. The organizational culture that results from these dynamic processes is the lived experience of the collectives of members of the organization, which defines their reality.

An enduring question in the study of organizational cultures relates to cultural knowledge: Is cultural knowledge "generalizable," thereby opening the way for prediction, or is it always "context-specific," due primarily to the uniqueness of each culture? We explored these issues from the perspective of cognitive science in chapter 2, finding that the case for universal cultural knowledge as schemas has yet to be established. We also noted in chapter 4 that human beings learn much of their culture as "sensory, body-based" mimetic processes that form the practical knowledge displayed in social actions. In chapter 7 we will explore the work of a group of international scholars on the global dimensions of culture and leadership as an important area of further research.

20. Schein spent his career at MIT's Sloan School of Management. The fifth edition of his seminal work was published in 2017 in association with his son, Peter Schein. Edgar H. Schein, *Organizational Culture and Leadership*, 5th ed. (New York: John Wiley & Sons, 2017). Two other influential organizational culture scholars began to publish their research during that same period. Their efforts produced a major work on the subject, Harrison M. Trice and Janice M. Beyer, *The Cultures of Work Organizations* (Englewood Cliffs, NJ: Prentice Hall, 1993).
21. Schein, *Organizational Culture and Leadership*, 7.

Studies in organizational culture take various pragmatic approaches to identifying and exploring culture.[22] One pragmatic approach, "cultural knowledge as generalizable," is primarily a functional approach, leading to higher expectations for the organization. The outcomes that are hoped for, at least by managers, are profiles of a "strong culture," pointing to even greater levels of efficiency in meeting organizational goals. Another pragmatic approach is the "context-specific," treating cultures as metaphorical, leading to more descriptive outcomes. The hope for these studies is to learn more about the unique organization of cultures. The mediating voice in the midst of these differing approaches is an appeal to the work of Geertz for what he terms "thick descriptions," which seek to generalize within and not across the cultures.[23]

The elements of organizational culture that most reveal the understandings and realities of the members include the following:

1. *Organizational stories and scripts.* Stories generally contain two elements: the narrative that gives the details of the events, and the meanings or interpretations, usually setting out the moral. Scripts, which are often more succinctly stated, are the cognitive frameworks that support the stories.

2. *Jargon: the special language of initiates.* One of the first things to hit the outsider when they enter a new culture is all the jargon, especially the acronyms (often bearing little resemblance to the reality they abbreviate). These may include "technical jargon," such as the acronyms for departments, programs, or related groups (e.g., IT or HR). A second type of jargon is referred to as "emotionally laden jargon," such as phrases or descriptors that have ascribed meaning, such as "guinea pigs," "life-or-death situation," "back to the wall," "flat out," and "big dog."

3. *Humor: drawing the line with laughter.* In writing this I am reminded of examples of humor that were inappropriate, perpetuating stereotypes if not being outright racist, but I also remember humor that, while not funny to the uninitiated, had real value in helping to ease tensions or bridge awkward moments. This is particularly true in work teams that spend long hours together.

4. *Physical arrangements: architecture, decor, and dress.* Of all the elements covered, these tend to be the most accessible for gaining cultural

22. Joanne Martin, *Organizational Culture: Mapping the Terrain* (Thousand Oaks, CA: Sage, 2002), 40–44.

23. Geertz, *Interpretation of Cultures*, 25–26.

clues. However, in nonprofit organizations, decor is often chosen by the price, not value. One should always inquire about the importance of physical arrangements when trying to understand the culture of an organization.[24]

Along with these observable elements of organizational culture, two more elements should be considered: practices and themes. Under practices would fall the rituals we discussed earlier, drawing from the list offered by Martin. In addition to rituals, a multitude of written practices (regulations, handbooks, standards, etc.) help to define not only the practices but, by extension, the organizational culture. Also falling under practices are the everyday actions of members, which reflect the formal standards set by the organization, whether those standards are imposed as professional or legal or are intrinsic to the mission, such as theological or philosophical standards (Schein's "cultural DNA").

Practices can be divided into those that are formal and those that are informal. Formal practices most often identified as key to organizational culture are "structure, task and technology, rules and procedures, and financial controls."[25] In contrast, informal practices fall into the category of "That's just the way we do it around here." They tend to be more relational practices that include everything from social gatherings to fitness or sporting events. Informal practices tend to mitigate the rigidity of the formal practices, putting a "human face" on the work.

Themes, either espoused or implied, guide the interpretation of organizational culture and its processes. These range from the "core values" to key attributes of the organizational practice often repeated publicly for impact, such as, "Cape Town 2010 is the most representative gathering," or, "Our seminary is multicultural." Themes as espoused values provide an important source of information for explaining the behavior, reasons, and rationalizations of the organization.[26] Espoused values also tend to be used to create an impression for external audiences; leaders, therefore, need to know the societal culture to ensure that the espoused values fit the context to which they are addressed.

24. Stanford Graduate School of Business professor Joanne Martin identifies these categories along with rituals (covered in chapter 4 of this book) in her comprehensive overview of the work of organizational scholars on the topic of organizational culture. See Martin, *Organizational Culture*, 71–86.
25. Martin, *Organizational Culture*, 86.
26. Schein, *Organizational Culture and Leadership*, 4.

The importance of knowing the cultural context is easily illustrated in our personal experiences or the histories and names of our organization. Take, for example, Interserve: "Originally the Calcutta Normal School, Interserve has been known by many names in its one hundred and sixty plus year history: the Indian Female Normal School and Instruction Society, the Zenana Bible and Medical Mission, Women's Union Missionary Society and more recently the Bible and Medical Missionary Fellowship. Throughout these name changes, our dedication to those in Asia and the Arab world has always been at the forefront of what we do."[27] Equally, implied themes are important in that they reflect what people believe about their work or the people they serve. Implied themes are observable not only in behavior but also in material items, such as decor or purchases, and even in the equipment that is deemed necessary for the tasks. Identifying the themes of the organization is an important part of understanding its culture.

The two major levels of analysis of culture used in most conversations about leadership and organizations are societal and organizational. The choice of societal culture for comparative purposes provides us with a general category that conforms to the definition common to missiology, recognizing the complexities of macro or global analysis, such as linguistic regions (e.g., Francophone Africa), transnational identities, global economic concerns, and global environmental factors, which are beyond the scope of this analysis. In contrast, organizational culture is bounded by the specific articles of incorporation and the core documents adopted as part of establishing the organization or a branch in a new location. A practical way of identifying the boundaries is to ask about the requirements for membership or employment.

A third level of analysis of culture adds a dimension that exists in both societal and organizational culture. This sort of analysis focuses on subcultures, which collectively form the fourth world in which our organizations live; or, perhaps more precisely, subcultures live in our organizations.

Subcultures

In discussions of organizational culture, the concept of subcultures is commonly used to describe and distinguish from each other various groups in an organization. For example, Van Maanen conducted a study of organizational subcultures in 1991, identifying various subcultures among the employees of Disneyland. His study not only identified the subcultures but also ranked them in terms of social status, from "the upper-class prestigious Disneyland

27. Interserve, "Our Story," accessed December 29, 2017, https://www.interserve.org/connect/our-story.

Ambassadors and Tour Guides" to "the peasant status Food and Concessions workers."[28] While the study's results did not clearly indicate the degree to which the organization acknowledged or approved of the subcultures, they do highlight a differentiated structure. Other differentiation studies have examined broad ranges of subcultures all contained within the boundaries of the organizations, primarily along occupational lines.[29] This approach to subcultures, while helpful to specific organizations, lacks the descriptive or relational depth necessary for our purposes.

A more robust approach to subcultures, growing out of the work of both sociologists and social anthropologists, is based on personal networks of individuals as they relate within social contexts.[30] Social networks as an explanatory framework can address questions of social structure in diverse situations, where the presence of a group of people has identifiable cultural manifestations (resulting in a subculture). Additionally, relationships in subcultures are not limited by ethnicity, language, location, or kinship—the more common markers for cultural groups. As the concept of personal networks grew in influence, the breadth of studies produced significant new insights for the study of culture. Perhaps the most influential work for our purposes is that of Berkeley sociologist Claude Fischer on personal networks and the subcultural theory of urbanism.[31]

Approaching subcultures from the perspective of personal networks is an important corollary to the cognitive studies of "self" and "social selves" because it recognizes both human nature and culture. From the perspective of human nature, our initial relations are given to us by virtue of birth, including our relations with parents, siblings, and close kin, which are significant on multiple levels, as we considered in chapter 3. But over time, we move from those initial, given relations to others: some imposed, such as workmates, in-laws, and so on, others more a matter of choice. We move from prescribed

28. John Van Maanen, "The Smile Factory: Work at Disneyland," in *Reframing Organizational Culture*, ed. Peter J. Frost, Larry F. Moore, Meryl Reis Louis, Craig C. Lundberg, and Joanne Martin (Newbury Park, CA: Sage, 1991), 58–76.

29. Martin, *Organizational Culture*, 103.

30. British social anthropologist J. Clyde Mitchell edited one of the earliest works. Mitchell gathered some of the emerging scholars to address the dynamic changes in social structure that accompanied urbanization. See J. Clyde Mitchell, ed., *Social Networks in Urban Situations* (Manchester, UK: Manchester University Press, 1969).

31. The four most significant works by Claude S. Fischer for our purposes are *To Dwell among Friends: Personal Networks in Town and City* (Chicago: University of Chicago Press, 1982); *The Urban Experience*, 2nd ed. (New York: Harcourt, Brace, 1984); "The Subcultural Theory of Urbanism: A Twentieth-Year Assessment," *American Journal of Sociology* 101, no. 3 (November 1995): 543–77; *Still Connected: Family and Friends in America since 1970* (New York: Russell Sage Foundation, 2011).

relationships to choosing our relationships among those with whom we are compatible. As part of his findings related to research on social networks, Fischer concludes that "by adulthood, people have chosen their networks."[32]

Another important element for understanding subcultures is the powerful dynamic of cultural transmission within a given subculture. Cognitive studies have identified the formation/transformation of culture with the processes of mental and public representations as they are conceptualized individually (metarepresentationally) and exchanged with others, with sufficient frequency and breadth to become cultural representations. These processes are multilateral in the sense that culture is transformed as it is transmitted, not transforming unidirectionally or simply reproducing.

In his studies, Fischer observed that people build their personal networks within "their constraints and their preferences," which most often involves those who are similar to them in the critical areas of background, social status, personality, and general lifestyle preferences.[33] In the end, according to Fischer, "People tend to associate with people like themselves. In that sense, networks are 'inbred.' As a consequence of—and as a further cause of—this inwardly turned interaction, people come to share many experiences, attitudes, beliefs, and values; they tend to adopt similar styles of speech, dress, and appearance. . . . In short, they develop a common culture. . . . A set of people having overlapping personal networks and sharing a common culture is a *subculture*."[34]

The value of Fischer's approach to subcultures is significant when we consider the religious, societal, and organizational cultural frames (fig. 6.1). Subcultures exist in all sectors of society, even in highly collectivist and corporate societies—anywhere social networks are evident. Subcultures are forming and transforming in response to multiple factors; one of the most powerful is marginalization by societal and organizational cultures. Fischer's subculture theory of urbanism helps explain this phenomenon by observing that an increase in the size of a population, such as is found in cities, tends to "intensify the distinctiveness" of subcultures, because more subcultures will reach a "critical mass" such that they become a "world unto themselves."[35]

Another important dynamic for understanding the role of subcultures in organizations is the nature of intergroup contact in reducing or widening the differences between subcultures (fig. 6.2). The presence of subcultures within the broader culture (religious, societal, or organizational) makes it inevitable

32. Fischer, *To Dwell among Friends*, 4.
33. Fischer, *To Dwell among Friends*, 6.
34. Fischer, *To Dwell among Friends*, 6.
35. Fischer, *To Dwell among Friends*, 12.

Figure 6.1
Four Worlds of Christian Organizations

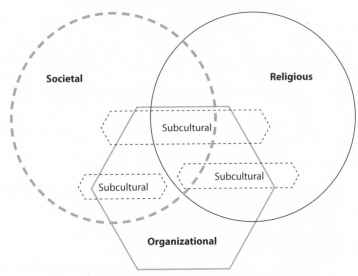

that they will encounter either the primary culture or other subcultures. The larger the primary culture, the more likely there will be social groups reaching critical mass and becoming subcultures. This results in more intergroup contact.

When intergroup contact is positive, it tends to reduce the homogeneity by allowing for the exchange of cultural practices, further transforming the cultures toward greater heterogeneity. As expected, the opposite is also true: when intergroup contact is negative, it widens the differences, further strengthening the distinctiveness and intensity of the subcultures. When that distinctiveness encounters aggression or discrimination, it leads to deviance and unconventionality, often resulting in intense encounters with the establishment.

Intercultural Realities and the Four Worlds

Moving from the description of the four cultures to the concept of "worlds" is an important part of relating the general concept of culture to the specific contexts of leadership and organizations. Culture exists not in a solid form that can be totally mastered but more in a fluid sense that, while being learned, is also adapting and shaping the worlds we know and integrating with our reality. In the description of "worlds" above, we noted that when the beliefs,

Figure 6.2
Subcultural–Organizational Intergroup Contact

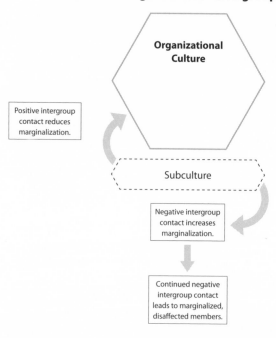

Organizational Culture

Positive intergroup contact reduces marginalization.

Subculture

Negative intergroup contact increases marginalization.

Continued negative intergroup contact leads to marginalized, disaffected members.

Adapted from Claude S. Fischer, *The Urban Experience*, 2nd ed. (Orlando: Harcourt, Brace, 1984), 40.

values, and feelings as the primary dimensions of worldview intersect with the issues of time, place, and relationships, we have a "world." From that perspective, we can begin to assess the impact of these dimensions as they engage with other worlds to better understand both the actions and reactions of the people who make up that world (fig. 6.1).

The intercultural realities for the individuals and groups who make up a particular world are accounted for in various ways. Fischer, in his presentation of the subcultural theory, included other factors as playing a part in each of the significant points of contact: positive, negative, and deviant. My first response to that approach was, "Brilliant. He is not claiming a universal cultural phenomenon, nor is he suggesting that all the dynamics are accounted for." Now I recognize even more the need to acknowledge other factors, due to the presence of extremely complex processes that engage people not only culturally but also physically, as human beings are guided by brain responses. This is yet another significant example of the interdependency of culture and human nature.

These processes are illustrated every day in the media, whether in a violent reaction by authorities leading to a senseless death or in a human interest story in which an individual without means to resolve their health problem is suddenly given a large sum of money or meets a doctor who is willing to help pro bono. The intercultural reality includes the psychological (e.g., empathy, flight or fight) and physical responses (e.g., social behaviors) of those involved. To further clarify, it is worthwhile to revisit the negative intergroup contact between a societal culture and a subculture. When subcultures experience discrimination or persecution, their subcultural responses intensify; frequently a stronger response takes the form of protests, political rallies, or boycotts, and in extreme cases it results in militancy against the societal culture. In the current technological environment, another level of response frequently comes from other subcultures that are philosophically or experientially in solidarity due to their own negative contact with the societal culture. This latter response is due not only to their own pain points, but also to the expression of empathy that is part of cognitive and relational processes. The responses are many and varied, but together they create the intercultural reality of life at the intersection of these "worlds," as demonstrated in the five faces of Islam.

While the intercultural realities will continue to engage us in the chapters that follow, we need to consider the concept of "four worlds." The concept of "world making" is explained by Paden's assertion that worlds act according to the premises of their "own universe," with their "own logic" and their "own answers" to their "own questions."[36] Each of the four worlds we considered in this chapter lives in its own universe. That may be a very tight universe in the case of a small organization or subculture, but even then, its history, mission, membership, and supporters are part of its universe. Obviously, the larger the organization or subculture becomes, the closer it comes to the critical mass necessary to acquire an influential position in relation to other worlds. At any given point in time the four worlds are interacting at many levels, all impacting the activities of the others while also being impacted by the others. And "at any given point in time" includes the history of the interaction of the worlds as well. Each world experiences its own questions and answers, though those questions and answers may collide with the interpretations of the other worlds.

The dynamics at work here are important considerations in the light of the *missio Dei*. We all fall into the trap of asking questions based on our own experiences and beliefs about reality, hoping to find what we are looking for. Because the worlds are collectives, present and past, they include all the

36. Paden, *Religious Worlds*, 7.

contemporary dynamics that make up the intercultural reality as well as the legacy of previous experiences. Just as Fischer notes that we each build a network, so also we make worlds together. The critical issue here is that we need to own our past and present with a view to the redemption and reconciliation that are central to sharing the gospel in human contexts, as illustrated in the 1989 conference of the Evangelical Alliance of the South Pacific in Suva, Fiji (see chapter 5 under the heading "Thinking Missiologically about Authority and Trust"). To do this effectively, we need to learn to ask and respond to the questions pertinent to the other worlds, a process that we know as contextualization. That includes struggling with the biases in the questions we are asking of our own organizations, religious worlds, and subcultures. To conclude this chapter, we will consider the "nod of recognition" and the "shock of recognition" by way of reviewing some of the dynamics of the intersection of the four worlds (fig. 6.1).

Reviewing and Reflecting on the Issues

By reflecting on the concept of world making as it pertains to religious worlds and the organizations that serve them, we are able to turn back toward our own religious world with fresh eyes. Remember that we are considering the human perspective; we must not confuse our perspective with God's mission or conflate our "religious world" with God's world. God's world is all-inclusive, containing all the cultural worlds as created by groups of people as their total way of life. Further, Christianity includes many worlds, far beyond the three easily identified major communions: Catholic, Orthodox, and Protestant. If we are to report accurately on our missional engagement with the world, then our reporting must openly acknowledge that the issues of our own religious world are integral to that engagement, recognizing that this is the quality of reporting most likely to generate the nod of recognition and the shock of recognition.

Reviewing

From the outset we acknowledged that our concept of world was intended to provide some comparison between the "cultural worlds" of our lived reality in human contexts. Choosing to identify worlds facilitates consideration of the distinct influences that culture has on aspects of our leadership and organizations. For example, if a church leader gains some notoriety in the press due to a scandal of child abuse, it reflects negatively on all church leaders and churches by extension. We know that from experience; it evokes the nod of recognition. But this negative reflection may also harm the reputation of *our* organizations, specifically, and thereby harm our ministries to children and youth in schools or social gatherings. When we find that to be true, reporting it to our constituencies is appropriate, leading to the shock of recognition. That seems obvious enough, but its significance is that it draws attention to the interrelatedness of contextual factors impacting our organizational work and that of other Christian organizations.

The category of religious worlds is very significant in a pluralistic society. Religious worlds are often associated with certain types of political or social platforms or with specific groups that influence our organizations, by aligning us with the extremes or even majority opinions that are counterproductive to our organizational mission. For example, in many Western nations the "enemy of society" is identified as Muslims. As Azumah so clearly set out, such generalizations harm the people being stigmatized (nod of recognition) and bear false witness against a neighbor (shock of recognition). This harm, in turn, tends to solidify subcultures, leading to an increase in deviant behavior, as seen in the increase of violent acts by a radicalized minority of the militant face of Islam and in extreme fundamentalist reactions against peaceful Muslims living in Western countries.

The comparative approach to religious worlds helps us see how important it is to understand the worlds as part of our redemptive witness among people of other faith traditions. To approach others without listening, while talking authoritatively about their faith, undermines the credibility of the gospel as we present it. I remind myself often that good news is intended to be good for the hearer, not a commodity for the speaker. A chaplain at the university where I served had a cartoon on the notice board outside his office. It was a series of strong statements by a zealous Christian, concluding with "Jesus is the answer!" Finally, after several scenes of this young fellow speaking out, another young person approached hesitantly and asked, "What is the question?" This is precisely the point. Our questions are best when open-ended and not rhetorical. We should be confident that the message of redemption in Christ is strong enough to withstand all types of questions. The process of finding the questions of a religious world is part of our missional task.

The use of a four-world approach (fig. 6.1) to analyzing the impact of culture provides for a more nuanced assessment of the influences that impact our organizational mission. For example, one of the besetting challenges to theological and missiological leadership development is the economics of formal education (in the societal world). The available financial resources to the established institutions in the West lag behind the costs of the educational infrastructure deemed necessary to provide the education. In other words, Western institutions have more educational capacity than financial capacity.

In the Majority World, in contrast, institutions typically face the challenge of both educational infrastructure and finances. Although the disparity is widespread, the global needs of theological and missiological education are beginning to be addressed.

Among evangelical Christian organizations that regard the education of Christian leaders as central to their mission, ScholarLeaders International (formerly Christian International Scholarship Foundation) is emerging as a significant contributor (organizational world). In the early years (1984–2000), the organization centered its mission on providing scholarships and support for students studying abroad, to help them "equip themselves and assume church leadership in their homelands."[37] By 2010 ScholarLeaders' organizational world significantly adapted to the changing societal worlds on the basis of what it learned in previous years, driven by deep and lasting relationships with alumni in influential positions worldwide.

The name change to ScholarLeaders International reflected a dynamic change in the group's organizational culture. It was no longer only a foundation for giving scholarships; it was a group of scholars (including the well-educated board and associated professors) whose vision grew to embrace the broader mission "to encourage and enable Christian theological leaders from the Majority World for the Global Church."[38] Reasons for the change are many, but one of the more important was the realization that the changing world of theological education, in response to the growth of the church (religious world) in the global South (societal world), was opening new opportunities for their maturing ministry (organizational world). Together, the ScholarLeaders "family" is an organizational world. Beyond the larger frame of reference, many alumni are in institutions where their participation in the ScholarLeaders initiatives forms a subculture within the broader organizational world of the institutions.

Each world has a culture that is unique, dynamic, and influential. As leaders of organizations, we have the privilege of sharing our stories of God's work on a global scale. This privilege comes with a responsibility for integrity, humility, and transparency in communicating the story to the wider world. I continue to be amazed at the breadth and depth of the mission of God across the world. We as leaders must remember that everything we report reflects on the entire body of Christ, as we know so well from Ephesians 4:4–6: "There is one body and one Spirit, just as you were called to the one hope of your

---

37. See the "Mission" page on the website of ScholarLeaders International, accessed June 3, 2017, http://www.scholarleaders.org/about/mission.
38. "Mission" page, ScholarLeaders International, http://www.scholarleaders.org/about/mission.

calling, one Lord, one faith, one baptism, one God and Father of all, who is above all and through all and in all."

Reflecting

The role of religious worlds transcends the traditional and geographical boundaries formerly assigned to them. Indeed most organizations are concerned about the extremes of religious fundamentalism across the world. As we think about the mission of our organization, we face the realities of lived religions that defy easy classification. Consider the following questions as they relate to religious worlds and your leadership and organization, or one you are close to.

1. How have you seen the "nod of recognition" and the "shock of recognition" in your experience with the missional work of organizations? Can you identify a specific example from your experience? If so, what impact did it have?

2. How would you describe the religious world that most influences your organization? What are two of the most significant premises that appear to be unique to that religious world?

3. How do place and time influence your religious world or, more specifically, your organizational world?

4. If you were asked to identify five faces of Christianity, what would you name as representative of the faith in your country of origin?

This discussion of ScholarLeaders International is intended to provide an opportunity to use the concepts of worlds and world making to assess our organizations. The analysis of the response by ScholarLeaders is far from complete, but it does illustrate the cultural worlds that will influence our assessments. Reflecting on the context of your organization from the perspectives of the four worlds and the intercultural realities that make up your world, consider your responses to the following questions.

5. What societal and subcultural worlds impact your organization? How are they organized to influence your immediate organizational world and the part of the *missio Dei* you are called to serve?

6. What are the subcultures within your organization? How is the organization addressing their needs, including offering opportunities for those subcultures to positively shape, catalyze, and propel your organization missionally?

7. Pushing it further, what cultural, subcultural, or religious world(s) do you most readily identify with, and how does that affect your service to the mission of the organization and the way you answer God's call to serve?

In the next chapter we will consider the issues of cultural influence and intercultural leadership. In thinking about leadership globally, we will also introduce research on global leadership and discuss the implications of that research before turning to intercultural leadership in practice.

7

Leading in Context

Cultural Influence and Intercultural Leadership

Once, waiting for a bus to take us to an evening meeting, I sat next to the internationally respected general director emeritus of Overseas Missionary Fellowship, J. Oswald Sanders. It was a real privilege for me as a younger leader. He had authored more than forty books in addition to his distinguished career in leadership, and his humility and wisdom were a living testament to the value of spiritual leadership—the subject of one of his best-known books.[1] Toward the end of our conversation, he shared a powerful insight with me. "As a newly appointed leader I once sat with Graham Scroggie at a Bible Conference, and as we discussed life and ministry he said to me, 'Sanders, never sacrifice depth for area!'"[2] After a lengthy pause, Sanders said to me, "McConnell, never sacrifice depth for area!" That charge, as much as any other in my life, challenges my thinking about mission, leadership, and the choice of where and how to serve. Although I have fallen short of depth on too many occasions, generally because of too many commitments (area),

1. J. Oswald Sanders, *Spiritual Leadership: Principles of Excellence for Every Believer* (Chicago: Moody Bible Institute of Chicago, 1967).
2. W. Graham Scroggie (1877–1958) was one of the great preachers and teachers of his time. Among his pastorates was the Metropolitan Tabernacle in London whose former preachers included George Whitefield and Charles Haddon Spurgeon.

as a leader I committed to carefully considering contextual variables (depth) and have found this practice invaluable.

To lead an organization on the basis of depth of understanding, you need to regularly ask questions about culture. Through practice, these questions will grow to include other issues such as the level of social discourse on the issues arising, the practices of other Christians (both contemporary and historical) in regard to the issues, and, through missiological reflection, the most appropriate actions to conform to the mission of God. In the last decade, in addition to what cognitive studies has taught us, research in global dimensions of culture and intercultural leadership has provided significant new depth to our understanding of the broad range of cultural influences so pervasive in organizational lives.

This chapter is concerned with the broader issues of culture as it relates to our organizations and leadership. We begin by taking a systems approach to culture and human nature that includes implications for our organizations missionally. In the second section we consider developments on a global scale, exploring the dimensions of culture and leadership. The third section introduces insights in intercultural leadership from a leading practitioner/scholar in Malaysia. In the fourth section we apply the concept of interculturality to our situations. We conclude by reflecting on how interculturality relates to our leadership and organization.

Cultural Influence: A Systems Approach

One of the central tasks of missiology is the process of exegeting humans, that is, studying humans and their contexts.[3] One can approach this task in many ways, but the most fruitful has been a systems approach (fig. 7.1). The basis is a comparison of systems within a given context, producing a "system of systems." As we observed in chapter 2, people are not born as blank slates ready to be imprinted by culture. Indeed, human nature plays a vital role in cognitive development, as does the environment. We must take this interdependence of systems into account when exegeting humans and their contexts. For example, a serious illness (physical system) may require oxygen and blood pressure monitoring (technological system), restrict regular contact with friends (social system), and in the end cause a theological crisis (cultural system). This illustrates the point that human contexts are composed

---

3. Paul G. Hiebert, *The Gospel in Human Contexts: Anthropological Explorations for Contemporary Missions* (Grand Rapids: Baker Academic, 2009), 127. For an excellent discussion of a systems approach, see chap. 6, 127–59.

of interrelated systems of which culture is the one that controls beliefs, values, and feelings. This interdependence of systems is also foundational to the "more or less integrated system" element in our definition of culture.

Figure 7.1
A Systems Approach to the Study of Humans

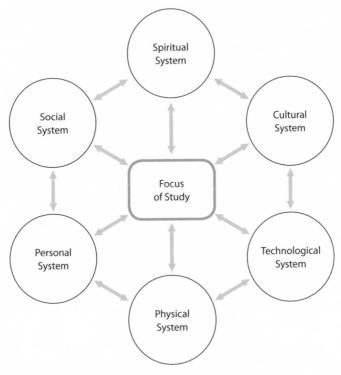

Adapted from Paul G. Hiebert, *The Gospel in Human Contexts: Anthropological Explorations for Contemporary Missions* (Grand Rapids: Baker Academic, 2009), 136.

Taking this a step further, a valid way to compare one culture to other cultures is a system-to-system approach. For example, if we consider close personal relationships in a Melanesian culture to those in the Australian culture, we have a reasonable basis for comparing the social systems of two different cultural contexts. The emphasis is on "reasonable," due to the fact that cultures are not transmitted as replications as much as transformations, so that every culture exhibits variations that reduce the accuracy of generalizations. Despite the lack of total uniformity in any given culture, the shared human systems between cultures allow for reasonable comparisons across cultures.

To illustrate, the traditional Australian concept of "mateship," based on a very individualistic context, refers to a close personal relationship of trust, shared commitments, loyalties, and generally a set of social relationships. In contrast, the Melanesian concept of *wantok* (loosely translated as shared "heart" language), based on a very collectivist context, also refers to a close personal relationship of trust, shared commitments, and loyalties, but involves a much broader set of social relationships including shared ethnicity or regional identity. By contrasting the unique approaches to the "social system," one can begin to understand the contextual relational significance, which is especially important when one is referred to as either a "mate" or a *wantok* while living in those cultures or when one is considering how best to convey the concept of discipleship.

The next step in understanding a systems approach is comparing a "system to systems" to more fully explore the implications of culture as a system within the systems that make up any given context.[4] For example, exercising authority in a position of leadership when a "mate" or a *wantok* works for the leader is a relational challenge to the organizational hierarchy, making it very difficult to supervise and even more difficult to enforce any policies that negatively impact the mate/*wantok*, especially in the collectivist Melanesian context. Another example is the common dilemma of how much to help children as they get older; do parents pay for physical needs, technological needs, social commitments, and so on, and when does this responsibility diminish, if at all? Depending on the social system, those responsibilities extend much further than biological children, as with *wantoks* in a Melanesian context. Leaders encounter a lot of ambiguity in this regard, especially in more collectivist societies. Do responsibilities to help one's social relationships (particularly extended family) entitle the helper to influence the one helped or to gain access to material resources? In businesses as well as nonprofit organizations, people regularly face the cultural dilemma of conflicting social and organizational expectations.

Considering the "system of systems" approach to the four worlds—societal, organizational, religious, and subcultural—we recognize, as we exegete the human context, that each is a "cultural system" connected to the other systems. For example, a local Anglican congregation in the Eastleigh suburb of Nairobi known as "Little Mogadishu" is influenced by the social system (family, friends, social networks), physical system (air, water, land, etc.), and technological system (communications, transportation, sanitation, etc.), while also being influenced by the cultural systems of the four worlds: Kenyan

4. Hiebert, *Gospel in Human Contexts*, 137.

(societal); Anglican Church of Kenya (organizational); Muslim (religious); and the critical mass of Somalis (subcultural). As we begin to consider the intersection of the four cultural worlds that most demarcate our "context," particularly as they relate to leadership and organizations, we must also include the influence of the other systems.

In this broader frame, systems are integrated so that causality is multidirectional; as a result, an action in the social system will likely affect all the other systems (cultural, physical, technological, etc.).[5] It is, therefore, difficult to isolate a single system from all the others. As much as we may wish to restrict our focus to a single system or culture, the ripple effect of the transmission of culture within the integrated system-of-systems consistently impacts our organizational worlds. As Hiebert noted, "Ultimately in exegeting humans it is important that we take a system-of-systems approach."[6]

Cultural Influence

A particularly significant concern for organizational leaders is the depth of influence one culture can have on other cultures or systems, illustrated by a leader whose *wantok* (societal culture) is an employee (organizational culture). We know that a culture is a more or less integrated system of beliefs, feelings, and values created and shared by a group of people. As such, the cultural system includes the subsystems of patterns of behavior, signs and languages, rituals, belief systems, and worldviews. This is important since identifying the cultural influence within a systems approach must include the complexity of subsystems. The same is true of the subsystems in the social system: relational, economic, political, and legal.

To illustrate the relationship between systems and subsystems, consider the interactions between the human systems based on the cultural beliefs and values regarding the rights and freedoms of the individual in the United States. These cultural beliefs and values are actualized by political and legal action in the respective American social subsystems. Changing values with regard to persons with disabilities as seen in the Americans with Disabilities Act of 1990 impacted human systems, most obviously the four systems and the four organizational subsystems noted in figure 7.2. The rules governing discrimination immediately required proactive responses by human resource departments; adjustments to the practices of members toward others, normally included in the member code of conduct (antidiscrimination clauses);

---

5. Hiebert, *Gospel in Human Contexts*, 133. Often recognized by the negative effect as illustrated by global urbanization.
6. Hiebert, *Gospel in Human Contexts*, 136.

appropriate technological assistance (e.g., special equipment for the hearing impaired); and changes to the facilities (e.g., wheelchair ramps and handicapped parking). All of these responses, which not only comply with the laws of the nation but also recognize the need to care for the well-being of others (love in action), clearly indicate the tremendous power of a cultural sphere of influence.

Figure 7.2
**Cultural and Systems Influence:
Christian Organizations in the United States**

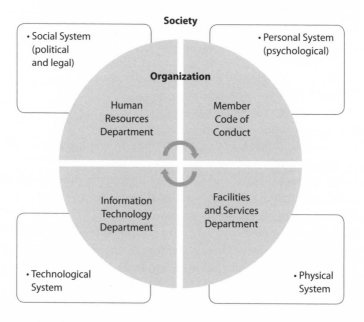

An area that has attracted less attention is the collective cultural influence of Christian organizations based on their differing cultures of practice. While we tend to see our organizational culture in isolation, other cultures and human systems tend to encounter the variety of Christian organizations as a unified religious world, thereby aggregating the beliefs and practices of that world, which multiplies its influence. In some cases that is advantageous to the individual organizations. For example, in the United States during the George W. Bush administration, faith-based and community initiatives were recognized for their contribution to "America's supply of compassion" and ability to provide important social services. As a result the federal government launched the Faith-Based and Community Initiative, which provided a "comprehensive effort to enlist, equip, enable, empower, and expand the work of faith-based and community organizations."[7] However, a more sobering reality confronts us when the media labels the actions or beliefs of a segment of the Christian community as indicative of "evangelicals" or when a highly visible member of the Christian community falls into disrepute or broadcasts support for a dubious cause or public figure. The resulting shame is often ascribed to the wider Christian community. John Azumah's case study on the five faces of Islam in chapter 6 is another example of the variety of cultures within any one religion and how the various cultures cannot be conflated.

Missiological Considerations

The reality of cultural spheres of influence raises a number of important missiological implications for Christian leadership and organizations as illustrated by macro-level examples. First, as leaders evaluate their roles within and outside their organizations, they should develop and carefully monitor their personal sphere of influence. When a leader has a good reputation, it reflects well on the individual, the organization, and Christians more broadly (Prov. 22:1). While we each could name leaders whose personal failures drew negative attention, we should be all the more vigilant and thankful for those who remain strong and finish well. At a time when global interconnectivity is ever expanding, the boundaries of our membership in the Christian community are disappearing, so the question we must answer is, "How do my actions affect my Christian brothers and sisters around the world?"

A second missiological consideration moves beyond personal influence to cultural influence: not only the way our organization reacts to the influences of the cultures around us but also how we influence other cultures by our collective actions. What is true of the individual is also true of the organization, perhaps even more so. Others observe our behaviors and our ethical and moral beliefs, and then they interpret them within their own worldview. We should monitor many practices and beliefs in the light of our organizational mission, but we should pay special attention to the publicly recognizable implications of our work, such as operational integrity, fiduciary propriety, legal compliance, and so on. Undergirding our corporate responsibilities to society is our witness to the redeeming love of God for all the world (Mark

7. George W. Bush, "The Quiet Revolution: The President's Faith-Based and Community Initiative: A Seven-Year Progress Report Letter from President Bush," George W. Bush White House Archives, February 2008, https://georgewbush-whitehouse.archives.gov/government/fbci/qr3.html.

16:15; John 3:16). Inherent in the mission of God is reconciliation, including vigilance and intentionality in our care for the poor and marginalized (James 1:27), consideration of the impact of our decisions on various sectors of the community locally and globally (Matt. 22:37–40), a commitment to civility and a civil society (Rom. 12:9–13:10), and a commitment to be an influence for righteousness and advocacy that witnesses in humility by doing justice and loving mercy (Mic. 6:8).[8]

The third missiological consideration is the contextual relevance of our mission in practice. I have observed that Christian organizations with which I am associated follow carefully the changes in the worlds in which they work. Characteristically, these healthy organizations adjust their business practices as appropriate, carefully adhere to national laws, change member care as appropriate, and implement new strategies for leadership. In most areas, information is available on how to improve organizational service. We should also be concerned about the ever-widening gaps between various sectors of the church and about Christian organizations that negatively impact the health and growth of the mission of God. Each of us could make a list of the most significant issues from our vantage point, such as those often raised in mission circles. Here are some examples:

1. Groups of people who have no access to the gospel (unreached peoples)
2. Serious limitations to the distribution of biblical and Christian discipleship materials where the church is growing rapidly
3. Concern for the persecuted church
4. Care for children and the vulnerable
5. Material resources, including adequate food supplies
6. Access to clean water
7. Adequate housing
8. Fair access to education
9. Fair access to health care

I often wonder if it is time to give greater attention to coordinating our individual organizational mission while encouraging the multiplication of missional responses in light of the staggering population growth and concomitant needs. We live in a time of unprecedented need and, by God's goodness, unprecedented opportunity to serve.

8. The issues of civility are examined in depth in Richard J. Mouw, *Uncommon Decency: Christian Civility in an Uncivil World*, rev. ed. (Downers Grove, IL: InterVarsity, 2010).

Thankfully, our churches, missions, and other Christian organizations have a long history of working internationally across a multitude of cultural barriers. However, despite our noble history, many vexing issues remain that challenge our ability to respond. Particularly relevant to our concern is the worldwide need for godly leaders who are discerning and wise. This sits at the intersection of organizational leadership and cultural contexts, raising the question again about what we are learning that will help in shaping, catalyzing, and propelling our organizations in missional response.

Leadership and Culture

In the study of leadership, particularly as it relates to organizations and cultures, an important question is, Are there cultural representations that apply globally—universal dimensions if not schemas—and if so, does that inform our understanding of leadership? The question gained notoriety through a landmark study published in 1980 by Dutch scholar Geert Hofstede, titled *Culture's Consequences*.[9] Among many significant findings, perhaps the most influential were five dimensions of culture identified by Hofstede as generalizable. While cultures differ in their response to each dimension, the dimensions identify basic commonalities that each society confronts.[10] The five dimensions are power distance, uncertainty avoidance, individualism, masculinity, and long-term versus short-term orientation.[11]

9. Geert Hofstede, *Culture's Consequences: International Differences in Work-Related Values* (Thousand Oaks, CA: Sage, 1980). Another significant study introduced the cultural differences between "low context" and "high context" cultures: Edward T. Hall, *Beyond Culture* (Garden City, NY: Anchor, 1976). The usefulness of these macro-level studies for missiological reflection on leadership and organizations is clearly shown in James E. Plueddemann, *Leading across Cultures: Effective Ministry and Mission in the Global Church* (Downers Grove, IL: IVP Academic, 2009).

10. By the early 1990s many missiologists added the concept of generalizable cultural concepts to their steady diet of ethnographies and texts on anthropology. The most influential book was Geert Hofstede, Gert Jan Hofstede, and Michael Minkov, *Cultures and Organizations: Software of the Mind*, 3rd ed. (New York: McGraw-Hill, 2010). This study unpacked the complexities of Geert Hofstede's previous work, making it accessible to those working in intercultural settings. It remains one of the most significant works and is now in its third edition. Like Hofstede's work, the publication of the GLOBE study (discussed in the next section) found rapid acceptance in our intercultural studies of organizations.

11. Hofstede, Hofstede, and Minkov, *Cultures and Organizations*, xix–xx. Geert Hofstede explored "differences in thinking and social action that exist among members of more than 50 modern nations." He argued that a person receives "mental programs," or schemas, from their family of origin and develops them through the course of their life, and that these schemas carry "a component of national culture." The definitions of all the dimensions are included under the section "Dimensions of Culture" below.

The GLOBE Project

Other scholars picked up on the nature of cultural universals and their relationship to management. The studies were particularly motivated by questions of diversity in approaches and the impact on global business interests.[12] Significant interest in macro-level studies surfaced among scholars around the world, leading to a large-scale study known as the Global Leadership and Organizational Behavior Effectiveness Research Program (GLOBE), launched in 1992. This study involved sixty-two different societies from all the major regions of the world, drawing together 170 social scientists. I include it here because it involves an ongoing collaboration resulting in publications that are expanding the field of intercultural leadership.[13]

The project scholars gathered at the outset to generate some of the essential understandings, including a working definition of leadership. They arrived at a consensus on a universal definition focusing on organizational leadership: "the ability of an individual to influence, motivate, and enable others to contribute toward the effectiveness and success of the organization of which they are members."[14] Based on this definition, the research proceeded on the assumption that cultural forces influence leadership behavior and that the GLOBE study would fill the substantial knowledge gap regarding the cross-cultural forces relevant to leadership effectiveness and organizational practices.[15]

Dimensions of Culture

The GLOBE study is based on the five dimensions of Hofstede's work. It expands the concepts of culturally generalizable and independent variables

12. See, e.g., Harry C. Triandis, *Individualism and Collectivism* (Boulder, CO: Westview, 1995); Fons Trompenaars and Charles Hampden-Turner, *Riding the Waves of Culture: Understanding Diversity in Global Business* (New York: McGraw-Hill, 1993).

13. Among the publications are the following three volumes. The first is Robert J. House, Paul J. Hanges, Mansour Javidian, Peter W. Dorfman, and Vipin Gupta, eds., *Culture, Leadership, and Organizations: The GLOBE Study of 62 Societies* (Thousand Oaks, CA: Sage, 2004). This first volume contains the macro-level project, which used both qualitative and quantitative measures as an etic study. The second volume is Jagdeep S. Chhokar, Felix C. Brodbeck, and Robert J. House, eds., *Culture and Leadership across the World: The GLOBE Book of In-Depth Studies of 25 Societies* (Mahwah, NJ: Lawrence Erlbaum, 2007). This volume is an in-depth study of twenty-five of the sixty-two societies using measures in a more emic approach. These two volumes represent phases 1 and 2 of the project. Phase 3 is represented in Robert J. House, Peter W. Dorfman, Mansour Javidian, Paul J. Hanges, and Mary F. Sully de Luque, *Strategic Leadership across Cultures: The GLOBE Study of CEO Leadership Behavior and Effectiveness in 24 Countries* (Thousand Oaks, CA: Sage, 2014).

14. House et al., *Culture, Leadership, and Organizations*, 56.

15. House et al., *Culture, Leadership, and Organizations*, 67.

and further facilitates reflection on leadership effectiveness across cultures. The group of international scholars reviewed the literature relevant to leadership and culture from other large-sample studies and identified nine dimensions. These quantitative (measurable) dimensions of culture have replaced those identified by Hofstede as the benchmark for assessing the intersection of culture and organizations. The nine dimensions range from a high to low level of importance in a societal or organizational culture. Briefly defined, they are as follows:

1. Assertiveness—ranging from showing deference to being strongly assertive and confrontational
2. Future orientation—the extent of involvement in future-oriented behaviors, such as planning or delaying gratification (e.g., retirement plans)
3. Gender egalitarianism—a group's view of differentiating gender roles
4. Humane orientation—the emphasis put on fairness, generosity, kindness, and altruism
5. Institutional collectivism—the commitment to encourage and reward sharing resources and collective action
6. In-group collectivism—the expression of pride, loyalty, and cohesiveness in the group or family
7. Performance orientation—encouragement and reward for improving performance and excellence
8. Power distance—the expectation of members regarding the distribution of power
9. Uncertainty avoidance—the desire to avoid uncertainty by clear rules and norms[16]

The identification of these nine cultural dimensions in societal and organizational cultures provides leaders with the opportunity to reflect on how each team, work group, department, or division within their organization responds to these dimensions of culture. For example, in-group collectivism (esprit de corps) may exist within a regional office or between regional offices, fostering an "us and them" attitude toward leaders and directives from the headquarters of the organization. Those in the headquarters, on

16. Of the three major works published through the GLOBE study, the one most accessible and helpful for leaders is House et al., *Strategic Leadership across Cultures*. The definitions and more in-depth discussion of the nine dimensions are found in chap. 1, esp. pp. 12–17.

the other hand, tend to see everyone within the organization as "us," creating a challenging situation, particularly during times of budget cuts. A logical implication is that it behooves leaders to assess their areas of responsibility in each of the cultural dimensions and make adjustments that lead to greater cohesiveness.

Understanding cultural dimensions also provides a broader base for evaluating leadership as part of a regular assessment of an organization's mission. Consider, for example, a newly appointed department leader who tries to exercise control over a situation by making a necessary but unpopular decision that assumes unequal power distance (authority), while members of the department had a relationship with the predecessor (trust) that allowed for greater equality or shared power. Part of the development of that new leader is to recognize and work with the unique culture within their sphere of responsibility.

One other implication to consider is the value of including proficiency in each of the dimensions as an "effective and valuable" set of skills in our organizational leadership development programs.[17] As part of the curriculum for the development programs, the nine dimensions could be addressed through the use of case studies, combining a number of dimensions or selectively working with an individual dimension that is currently challenging the leadership of the organization. In time, the training should support organizational goals for greater diversity and intercultural competency. To illustrate, I regularly use case studies to expose students to insights from the nine dimensions and other significant perspectives as part of my approach to teaching leadership and missiology, a method I learned from Paul Hiebert.[18]

Schemas and Cultural Dimensions

From the beginning of Hofstede's work, the presence of cultural dimensions was attributed to the "mental programs," which we know as schemas, embedded in the thought processes of individuals and the collective culture. The cognitive processes of cultural transmission of these dimensions are not simply replications brought about by formal training processes, such as an orientation program. Instead, the dimensions are learned primarily through

---

17. House et al., *Culture, Leadership, and Organizations*, 67.

18. From 1984 to 1986, Fran and Paul Hiebert gathered case studies and prepared a book on the use of case studies in missions, published as Frances F. Hiebert and Paul G. Hiebert, *Case Studies in Missions* (Grand Rapids: Baker, 1987). Alan Neely subsequently published a more inclusive approach, Alan Neely, *Christian Mission: A Case Study Approach* (Maryknoll, NY: Orbis Books, 1995).

observation or imitation as experiences and are transformed by the individual through the process as personal cultural beliefs and values. The schemas, therefore, operate as a map that guides responses to leadership and organizational practices, judging them as effective or ineffective. Because these dimensions are retained as schemas, they are embedded at an unconscious level, thereby subtly influencing reactions in a given situation.

Schemas are also very complex in that even though cultural dimensions are retained as schemas at an unconscious level, they also relate to assumptions of appropriate behaviors by the group collectively. On a practical level, this means that changing the practices related to a dimension such as gender egalitarianism in a particular cultural context is often a difficult and time-consuming task. Observing the process of change within societal culture supports the notion that the younger generation tends to be early adopters of changes in social norms, values, and practices (e.g., technology). Although there are many other variables, such as demographics and education, generational societal changes have a powerful effect on organizational culture.

To illustrate generational changes in cultural dimensions, consider gender egalitarianism. In my first years in mission leadership after returning to my home culture, a noticeable change in gender roles was influencing younger recruits for missionary service. On college and seminary campuses, discussions were characterized by gender equity both in roles and support systems. Use of colloquialisms and slang terms, particularly of women (e.g., "girls" or "gals"), was no longer acceptable. Social institutions were beginning to recognize women in leadership, and students were strongly supporting the change. Men were taking more active roles in raising children, partly due to the introduction of paternity leave. On a practical level, women (married or single) and men (married or single) expected to be recruited, equipped, and assigned. This meant that provision for accommodation, access to educational choices for children, frequent home assignments, retirement plans, and so on were viewed as nonnegotiable.

In contrast, during visits to various mission projects and gatherings of veteran missionaries, the assumption was normally that married women would have a prescribed role typically associated with the family and supporting the team or group, whereas married men and single missionaries (women and men) would be assigned roles that were directly related to the core mission by the predominantly male leadership. As the generation transitioned, this distinction was less pronounced, so that by the time I completed my second term in a mission director role, women were entering leadership roles within the missionary society and several new appointments were functionally "joint appointments" of a wife/husband team. This changing understanding of leadership is also reflected in the findings of the GLOBE project through the study of strategic leadership across cultures.

Assessing Global Leadership Dimensions

Among the many other GLOBE findings, six global leadership dimensions were recognized as intercultural leadership attributes, skills, and behaviors. Like the quantitative dimensions of culture, the leadership dimensions were identified by scholars reviewing other research and literature and then were tested through their research. I include the dimensions to highlight the relevance of the ongoing study of leadership and culture associated with the global project. Based on the key findings in the CEO research, criteria used by members to assess leaders provide important insights for organizations. The assessment findings for each of the six global leadership dimensions are:

1. *Charismatic/value-based leadership.* Charismatic leaders inspire their followers with a desirable and realistic vision that is developed based on appropriate analysis and high performance expectations. They are viewed as sincere, decisive, and credible because of their integrity and willingness to sacrifice their own self-interest.
2. *Team-oriented leadership.* Team-oriented leaders are loyal to their teams and care for the welfare of their team members. They use their administrative and interpersonal skills to manage the team's internal dynamics and to create a cohesive working group.
3. *Participative leadership.* Participative leaders believe that employees can contribute to decision-making and should be engaged in the process of decision-making and implementation. They also believe that debate, discussion, and disagreement are a natural part of good decision-making and should not be suppressed.
4. *Humane-oriented leadership.* Humane-oriented leaders are unpretentious, show humility, and are reticent to boast. They are empathetic and likely to help and support team members in a humane manner by offering resources and other forms of assistance.
5. *Autonomous leadership.* Autonomous leaders have extreme confidence in their own abilities and lack respect for others' abilities and ideas. They view themselves as unique and superior to others and as a result prefer to work independently and without much collaboration with colleagues or direct reports.
6. *Self-protective leadership.* Self-protective leaders have a deep desire to succeed [or to be perceived as effective] among a group of colleagues and direct reports who may act as competitors for the leaders' position and

success. To protect themselves, they defer to positions of power, hide information that might advantage potential competitors, follow rules and policies to avoid risk, and interact carefully with others to ensure they leave a positive impression.[19]

The global dimensions represent leadership attributes that combine a broad range of behaviors, skills, leadership styles, and even personality traits. Their presence in the cross-section of leaders from the twenty-four countries studied provides an important comparative basis for understanding organizational leadership across cultures. Remember that within a given societal culture, some leadership types and schemas will predominate, reflecting the particularities of the culture, which in turn influences the organizational leadership. For example, the research demonstrated that in Russia, a high power distance society, the societal expectation of "strong powerful leaders" is one important variable in the continuing role of Vladimir Putin as a leader.[20] In every society, the prevailing societal view of leadership is an important point of comparison for leaders of Christian organizations to consider as part of their assessment of the mission and culture of their organization.

In contrast to the Russian case, an organization study conducted by Jim Collins and associates wanted to avoid the role of the top executive as the key factor in great organizations, in part due to the prevailing opinion that leadership was everything; so he asked the research team to focus on other variables in the study of successful organizations.[21] As the study progressed, it found enormous evidence that supported the importance of leadership in the success of the companies. The discovery, by now well known to most students of leadership, is that top leaders (referred to as level 5) were one of the most important predictors in the success of "great companies."[22] The prevailing organizational view of leadership at the time was that a leader should be a strong charismatic visionary whose big personality was able to determine the

19. House et al., *Strategic Leadership across Cultures*, 322–23. The global leadership dimensions are a synthesis of 112 attributes identified in the analysis of relevant literature supported by the research done by House et al. for this volume; these attributes, in turn, provided twenty-one primary leadership dimensions that, by a process of quantitative analysis, were collapsed into six global dimensions. For a complete explanation, see House et al., *Strategic Leadership across Cultures*, 322–24.

20. House et al., *Strategic Leadership across Cultures*, 18.

21. Jim Collins, *Good to Great: Why Some Companies Make the Leap and Others Don't* (New York: Harper Business, 2001). Deviance from cultural behavior must be factored into our studies, as was supported in the GLOBE CEO findings (322).

22. Collins, *Good to Great*, 22. For a full description of the leadership levels 1–5, see Collins, *Good to Great*, 17–40.

course of organizational culture.[23] Instead, the research showed that level 5 leaders built "enduring greatness through a paradoxical blend of personal humility and professional will," thereby demonstrating that dominant views of leadership are not necessarily determinative for effectiveness.[24]

The identification of the six dimensions of global organizational leadership provides us with an important, widely recognized perspective for assessing leadership within our organizations. With so many different types of leadership in every organization, depending on size and mission, identifying them using the global dimensions helps with comparing and evaluating the organizational culture in relation to the societal culture. By way of a reminder, the cultural understanding of leadership exists in the schema of the individuals that make up that culture even more than on the pages of the official organizational documents. An effective means of accessing this knowledge is through informal discussions using open-ended questions on leadership followed by a broader survey drawn from the insights gained in the discussions. When thinking about organizational leadership, we must also consider the power of schemas in controlling behavior and expectations, as well as the difficult, time-consuming process of changing schemas of practice.

Another significant consideration for our purposes is that the global leadership dimensions align well with the concept of four worlds for understanding cultures, as noted in the previous discussion of cultural influences. The GLOBE consensus of these dimensions was based on the understanding that organizations have clear boundaries and structures that are comparable across cultures. Their focus was on the interaction between societal cultures and the organizational cultures. By expanding the two cultures to include the subcultural and religious worlds of our study, the findings of the GLOBE project can be used as a basis for considering the four worlds: societal, organizational, subcultural, and religious.[25]

Since the GLOBE project has continued for twenty-five years, it has become a major research domain in the fields of leadership and organizational studies. The more than two hundred scholars who have worked on the project represent an intercultural movement in scholarship similar to those in medicine, education, and other global interests. It is significant for missiology in that the GLOBE study takes seriously the contextual variables that

---

23. E.g., Jack Welch's approach to leadership is considered to be winning as opposed to losing, demonstrated in his tenure at General Electric. See Jack Welch with Suzy Welch, *Winning* (New York: HarperCollins, 2005).

24. Collins, *Good to Great*, 20.

25. The inclusion of subcultures as part of the findings was significant to the GLOBE study as discussed in Chhokar, Brodbeck, and House, *Culture and Leadership across the World*, 9–10.

characterize good missiological research. It is also important for the sake of helping us as leaders of Christian organizations to understand and evaluate the plethora of books, articles, training programs, and media productions on leadership. Too often these works are based on much smaller cultural samples or, worse, have no reference to the context of the leadership or are limited to an individual's perspective from their individual experience of leadership. I include this level of detail to provide some important additional categories for comparative purposes in the study of culture relating to leadership and organizations. Adopting this recognized use of terminology and categories will help us describe our intercultural leadership practices in a more transparent and understandable way.

Moving from the macro-level influences of culture to the implications for leaders, we will consider the insights from my friend and colleague Nam Chen Chan. His work on culture and leadership demonstrates the increasing depth of understanding in intercultural studies globally. Chan's reflection on the concept of intercultural leadership from his studies and experience as a church planter, pastor, teacher, and leader in Malaysia reveals his insights into the relational nature of Christian mission.

Intercultural Leaders in Christian Organizations

Nam Chen Chan, Malaysia[a]

As a fledgling cross-cultural church planter and pastor, I was concerned simply with how I could traverse cultural barriers as an individual to effectively lead my congregation. I saw everything in the single dimension of bridging two cultures: between the congregants, all from one ethno-cultural group, and myself, from another culture. It was a rather naive perspective of intercultural leadership, even for the situation then. For today's Christian nonprofit organizations in far more diverse contexts, it is grossly inadequate. Cultures in contemporary societies are highly dynamic and multidimensional. Intercultural leaders therefore have a deeper and more critical role of blending efficiency with increasing measures of "interculturality" into the missionality and "soul" of their organizations in order to facilitate an interpenetration of cultures as a core value and practice.

Unique Organizational Cultures

German scholar Stefanie Rathje proposes that contemporary societies are best understood as multicollectivities of smaller collectivities of different types and sizes. Individuals can be members of multiple collectives and are often adept with the cultures of more than one collective.[b] Nonprofit Christian organizations such as local churches and mission agencies may therefore be viewed as collectives where individuals, usually of their own volition, choose to be members. Each has its own unique organizational culture, which is initially shaped by the founding members but is modified and reshaped by later leaders and influential members.

This understanding raises a number of related critical questions for the Christian organization seeking to realign itself in contemporary contexts of immense ethno-cultural diversity that are also constantly reconfiguring. Does the organizational culture facilitate or repel diversity? Who or which group determines the ongoing reshaping of the organizational culture? How are the decision-making processes that direct the organization's future forged?

The fact is, an organization may espouse diversity, but assumed norms, values, and practices shaped by the dominant ethnic group can turn away other groups, with the former none the wiser. This dominant group may not even be a majority, but they determine the cultural ethos through a combination of factors that also include historical precedence, education, and socioeconomic status. Instead of enrichment through hybridization with new cultures, the organization pressures assimilation into unessential norms assumed by the dominant group.

Interculturality—Blending and Embracing Cultural Differences

Therefore, the role of intercultural leaders is to integrate organizational efficiency with what may be termed "interculturality." A relatively new term coined to advocate mutuality and reciprocity when variant cultures encounter each other, interculturality fosters an interpenetration of cultures in ways that lead to creative change and re-integration.[c] It is a paradigm that goes beyond sensitivity and cultural respect geared merely toward creating a cultural space for the "other." Rather, it is an openness that empowers the individual and the organization to critically blend and embrace variant cultures.

Since the crossing of cultural boundaries is a core missiological concern, intercultural leaders thus play the role of shaping a missionality and an organizational "soul" in nonprofit Christian organizations, both of which are characterized by interculturality as expressed in the organization's values, norms, and processes. Cultures-by-default, or in this case, reshaped cultures, tend to perpetuate the dominance of groups already in control.[d] Thus, intercultural leaders are acutely sensitive to the power dynamics at play. Different cultures also have different strengths, but none are perfect, and all are tainted by sin. Intercultural leaders therefore creatively draw out the best from an organization's *mélange* of cultures, in the same way that an orchestra conductor would from his ensemble, to create and integrate for the best intercultural synergy and effect.

More comprehensive definitions of leadership rightly include cross-cultural interaction as an activity that can emanate from any person or group within the organization to influence and effect change.[e] However, the nature of interculturality impinges upon the personhood of the leader, regardless of position. Requiring more than generalized intercultural competence, the deeper dimensions of interculturality imply that true intercultural leadership is embodied in leaders engaged in authentic intercultural friendships. In this regard, the development of friendships of this type within and through the nonprofit Christian organization aligns with primary concerns in Christianity and missiology—meaningful relationships and the crossing of ethno-cultural boundaries.

[a] Nam Chen Chan (PhD, Fuller Theological Seminary) is the executive director of AsiaCMS. He is a scholar and practitioner who served as a denominational leader and seminary lecturer in his home country of Malaysia. His expertise is in church and culture, intercultural leadership, and missiology.
[b] Stefanie Rathje, "The Definition of Culture: An Application-Oriented Overhaul," *Interculture Journal* 8 (2009): 35–58.
[c] Franz Xaver Scheuerer, *Interculturality: A Challenge for the Mission of the Church* (Bangalore, India: Asian Trading, 2001); Birgit Breninger and Thomas Kaltenbacher, eds., *Creating Cultural Synergies: Multidisciplinary Perspectives on Interculturality and Interreligiosity* (Newcastle upon Tyne, UK: Cambridge Scholars, 2012); Agnes M. Brazal and Emmanuel S. de Guzman, *Intercultural Church: Bridge of Solidarity in the Migration Context* (Alameda, CA: Borderless, 2015).
[d] Sherwood G. Lingenfelter, *Leading Cross-Culturally: Covenant Relationships for Effective Christian Leadership* (Grand Rapids: Baker Academic, 2008).
[e] Ronald A. Heifetz, *Leadership without Easy Answers* (Cambridge, MA: Belknap Press of Harvard University Press, 1998).

Interculturality in Practice

As Chan insightfully notes, applying the concepts of interculturality to Christian organizations that value diversity opens a number of significant opportunities for growth. To move from acceptance, observable in behaviors recognizing differences, to including more explicit ideas and perspectives from other cultures to eventually reaching more implicit cognitive and affective processes and schemas requires that leaders consider a number of practical changes. The extent of the change, from adaptation to complete restructuring, depends on the organizational needs and level of commitment to interculturality. Many areas could be included, but for the sake of understanding the approach in specific domains we will consider four: committees, subcultures, adapting practices, and intercultural friendships. It is important that implementing change be viewed as a process over time, in harmony with new insights about culture as it applies to the organizational context.

Committees as Communities of Trust

The organizational committee structure is usually either established to accomplish regular work as it arises within a given domain, for example, a finance committee, or tied to specific tasks relating to organizational processes such as recruitment and member care. Another common committee is the one that manages the organization, that is, the president's cabinet or executive team or committee. In each case, the primary task is to oversee particular departments or divisions, according to each member's individual expertise. In larger and older organizations, the number of committees tends to be higher, in many cases increasing as part of the developing bureaucracy. The culture of committees normally develops around workflow management, with specific tasks being delegated to subcommittees or individuals who report back to the committee for approval.

Although we tend to think of committees as work related, they are also hubs for social interaction and support. I suggest that we consider appointing committees as communities of trust where cultural differences are discussed as part of the organizational learning process, and, in turn, these insights are applied to the work at hand. To achieve this, the approach to appointing committee members must be adjusted to ensure that greater diversity is included. This requires reconsidering appointments based primarily on position. Unless or until there is broader diversity in leadership positions, appointments should include people who are able to contribute alternate views on issues and practices. An alternative is to move from workflow committees to intentional learning communities that are assigned work, traditionally belonging to committees, as part of their learning as a community. Ensuring that the communities have representative skills and knowledge from various groups within the organization will help with the change.

To illustrate, a large Christian institution had a clearly defined committee structure including standing committees, management committees, and executive committees. The primary consideration for membership on the committees was a supervisory position in a department or division related to the work of the committee. As a newly appointed leader considered the membership in the leadership council, the breadth of diversity in the employees exceeded the representation on the council. The leader, in consultation with others, initially decided to appoint several members based not on their role but on their contribution to the diverse learning community. After a number of initial challenges, the group began to work together in a pattern that included considering the cultural implications of each item on the agenda. Not the least of these items was proactively implementing the organizational commitment to diversity in searches and appointments. The overall result was a greater awareness of cultural differences that in turn fostered a greater degree of interculturality in the leadership of the organization as well as genuine intercultural friendships.

Subcultures as Cultural Assets

Every organization should actively engage subcultures as resources. Subcultures, as we defined them in chapter 6, are based on social networks that are chosen rather than assigned, bringing together a set of people with overlapping personal networks who share a common culture. These subcultures may have traditional commonalities, such as ethnicity, language, or location, or the commonalities may be based on beliefs and values, experiences, attitudes, recreational or artistic interests, or occupations. The two major considerations of subcultures are critical mass and the experience of intergroup contact—either positive, leading to inclusion in organizational life and structure, or negative, further marginalizing the group and strengthening its members' feelings of exclusion. Although in larger societal or organizational contexts subcultures have a greater presence and influence, individuals or smaller groups within a context may also identify with a larger, external subcultural group from another context; for example, a few individuals who identify with an ethnic group within an organization may primarily identify with a larger, external subculture of that same ethnic group in the societal culture.

In considering this domain, I made a list of subcultures that exist at Fuller Theological Seminary and was forced to move from primary subcultures to secondary subcultures to adequately account for the uniqueness of each group. I identified fifteen primary subcultures, and many more when considering secondary. For example, one expects that the faculty are a primary subculture (as are staff and administration); however, a closer look identifies a secondary subculture for each of the three schools (intercultural studies, psychology, and theology), a subculture for each of the major academic disciplines (theology, biblical studies, ministry, missiology, marriage and family therapy, and clinical psychology), and subcultures within those disciplines (Old Testament, New Testament, systematic theology, leadership, anthropology, etc.). By the time I considered our only professor of ethnomusicology, I decided that I had taken it too far. I return to the point that critical mass and intergroup contact help us assess the particular experience and contribution of each subculture.

From the perspective of interculturality, these domains of cross-cultural interaction provide a rich source of cultural knowledge and experiences for the community. However, these domains may fail to be such a rich source, depending on how the various domains interact within the organization. Even with the risks, a proactive approach to positive intergroup interaction that includes and engages the various committees and subcultures, at parallel levels and across the levels of the organization (depending on size and complexity), allows for influence and relationships to build. From experience, I've learned that in larger organizations the result of a proactive approach is more often mixed, with many group interactions being exemplars and others being disasters. Perseverance is one of the most important attributes in any organization committed to being truly intercultural. While there is no all-inclusive means of ensuring positive outcomes, an intentional and systematic commitment to building friendships has been shown to be fruitful. Equally, if the organization lacks inclusion and appears to be satisfied with the status quo, it will lead to disgruntled members and a lack of trust in the organization and its leaders.

Finally, it's essential that the members of each group (subculture) see *themselves* reflected in the leaders of our organizations. There is no shortcut to actually being intercultural. The influence of other cultures on the organization must be reflected in the diversity of leadership as well as in the organization's interculturality. Diverse leaders should be proactively recruited, and the organization must also fundamentally commit itself to diversity of leadership by equipping culturally diverse members to be leaders at all levels within the organization. Subcultures are a gift to the organization not only for cultural insights but also in that they provide potential diversity in leadership.

Adapting Practices for Interculturality

Once an organization commits to interculturality, it will need to adjust many practices, not the least of which are those related to communication. Organizations continually face challenges in the process of communicating actions, decisions, and developments. Small organizations or teams can handle these challenges somewhat informally, even as part of a regular time of fellowship. In my first appointment as a missionary, the mission community met weekly for prayer. At our prayer meetings, over tea and biscuits, we regularly shared announcements. We were a small group, so the announcements covered the appropriate topics, reducing the need for more formal approaches. This practice, while acceptable for a small organization, does not meet the needs for accountability in larger, more complex settings.

More formal communication must address issues of accountability to the governing structures of the organization and beyond to external accountability (accreditation, government departments, audits, etc.). Organizations normally adapt to the various levels of communication necessary to meet needs and requirements, so that over time their communication practices become routine and even part of the schemas controlling appropriate behavior. To change these routines will inevitably create tensions and may even contravene regulations. To manage the tensions, it is best to consider adjusting current practices to make space for increasing interculturality within the organization. Since the most common means of formal communication includes agendas, minutes, reports, and periodic formal gatherings to disseminate relevant information, those kinds of communication are a good place to start.

To illustrate, if committees are viewed as communities of trust, then the agenda for the formal meetings should be reviewed to include either a regular "agenda item" or a recognized time in the meeting to review the most recent examples of behavior that either exemplifies good interculturality or prompts discussion of ways to develop better practices. This requires a culture change in managing meetings, since it takes time in the meeting. Again, this is predicated on a commitment to develop interculturality in the organization. An example of this change in a large organization was introduced by a CEO who dedicated one of the three monthly meetings of the leadership team to the presentation and discussion of issues of cultural diversity. The presenter was given thirty minutes for the formal input, and then small groups discussed key questions, after which the leader debriefed the responses.

Once this is part of the set agenda, leaders need to ensure that the formal record (minutes) of the meeting includes a brief summary of the details; this can also be a copy of handouts or the presentation. Since the formal record of the meeting is the legal document required by external authorities, the organization must keep such records as part of its regular activities in reporting to accreditors, auditors, or trustees. The group can save work by omitting from the minutes anything except the motions passed, declined, or tabled—thereby also omitting anything extraneous that is better left out of the official record. This information should be disseminated to members of the organization who were not present. Usually the information is sent through an intranet posting, written text, email, or other form of information sharing that includes the presentation (or summary) and encourages comments and feedback. Thus the group can impact the wider organization with insights gained through these regular presentations or discussions devoted to interculturality, ensuring that these insights become part of the individual practices as well as the organizational culture.

An alternative to the formal approach, particularly applicable in smaller organizations or groups, is to intentionally apply creative approaches to regularly scheduled events. Often, for example, an organization will include songs in other languages or testimonies by individuals from different cultural groups in fellowship gatherings, chapel, or worship services. Similarly, inviting diverse members to share films, music, or other artistic presentations, can be a powerful means of "seeing through the eyes of others" as part of the commitment to building a relational basis for interculturality. Proactive approaches such as these are consistently reported to be the turning point in the commitment of individuals to intercultural relationships and lifestyles. Relating this to affective worldview change, these turning points are mental representations of culture that interpret experience and transform one's thinking. An experience of mine illustrates how a small change can yield a new best practice. A team I served on decided to start including a meal in its weekly meeting. Each member in turn was given the responsibility to provide a favorite food for a meal, which was then the subject of discussion as to its significance either to the individual's family or to the culture in general. The meal's importance might derive from their "home culture" or from its significance to the individual. As a participant in that team, I have very fond memories of each culture represented and the individuals who participated, resulting in deeper intercultural friendships.

Intercultural Friendship

Chan's observation that "true intercultural leadership is embodied in leaders engaged in authentic intercultural friendships" is a foundational missiological consideration for the practice of engaging interculturally. The example of Jesus and the disciples points to the significance of genuine friendships, even across different positions socially or spiritually. Jesus, speaking to his disciples, said, "You are my friends if you do what I command you" (John 15:14). Jesus's use of "friends," instead of "servants," reflects the level of trust and harmony in their relationship. While obedience characterizes a follower or servant, in this case Jesus makes it clear that he and his disciples share a common mind and a common commitment to understanding God's will. When Jesus spoke to his disciples as friends, he was reflecting "the highest ideals of love in human friendship. In turn, these ideals reflect God's own love for the world."[26]

Friendship is also reflected in the missionary work of the apostle Paul. One of the most extensive examples is found in Romans 16, in what is a listing of his personal relationships and, in that sense, friendships. To illustrate, in Romans 16:5 (NLT), the apostle asks, "Greet my dear friend Epenetus," an early follower of Christ from Asia. The first sixteen verses of this final chapter

26. Marianne Meye Thompson, *John: A Commentary*, New Testament Library (Louisville: Westminster John Knox, 2015), 329.

of Romans are a "who's who" list of coworkers in Rome. Again in the Letter to the Philippians, the apostle includes Timothy and Epaphroditus as friends and coworkers, asking that the believers welcome Epaphroditus "in the Lord's love" (Phil. 2:29 NLT). The work of missionary teams, such as those who accompanied Paul, has long been a model in support of Chan's observation that a primary concern for such teams is "meaningful relationships and the crossing of ethno-cultural boundaries."

While the concept of friendship is understood differently in various cultures, the concept of close personal relationships is common. The study of social anthropology illustrates the need for recognizing the difference between "friends" and personal networks. The earliest studies focus on friends of friends as a relational category, whereas subsequent studies of cultural differences move in the direction of personal or social networks characterized by social support and frequency of contact.[27] From a missiological perspective, engaging the concept of personal networks as a common cultural phenomenon is a good place to start in moving toward a biblical understanding of friends as part of discipleship, further illustrating the concept of interculturality.

Reviewing and Reflecting on the Issues

One of the important insights from reflecting on human systems was confirmed by Hiebert's observation that "taking a system-of-systems approach reminds us of our interconnectedness with the whole of God's creation."[28] It is so easy to make our own worlds the center of the universe, thereby reducing the grandeur of creation. By opening new vistas of integration, we can instead learn about our worlds in ways that will significantly impact our individual and collective mission, in the *missio Dei*.

Reviewing

In intercultural work, we need to be able to compare one culture with another, not in order to judge the relative merits of cultures, but to understand the beliefs, values, and feelings that express the culture so that our message and actions accurately reflect the gospel of Jesus Christ. Beyond individuals are the local churches, missionary societies, and Christian organizations that embody the message, sharing it through their actions and communication,

27. E.g., Jeremy Boissevain, *Friends of Friends: Networks, Manipulators, and Coalitions* (Oxford: Basil Blackwell, 1974); and Claude S. Fischer, *To Dwell among Friends: Personal Networks in Town and City* (Chicago: University of Chicago Press, 1982).
28. Hiebert, *Gospel in Human Contexts*, 137.

thereby raising the stakes on how we are perceived by the world around us. By carefully assessing the various cultural influences, internally and externally, we can better contextualize our mission. The opposite is also true: to assume that our practices are appropriate based on the past alone is to inadequately understand our context in this rapidly changing era of globalization.

The global studies of organizational leadership are developing more informed approaches to the societal, organizational, religious, and subcultural worlds in which we exist. By drawing on global dimensions of culture and leadership that are recognized broadly as relevant for evaluating organizational leadership, we can better assess our effectiveness in particular contexts. One of the important outcomes of these insights is the ability to review our leadership development programs to ensure that we are equipping leaders prepared for the complexities of the worlds in which they serve.

Chan reflected on the role of intercultural leaders as facilitating "an interpenetration of cultures as a core value and practice." We are not crossing from one culture to the other, influencing another culture unidirectionally; instead, we are part of the constant "interpenetration of cultures." This fact alone should move us toward an organizational commitment to interculturality. It is not simply a matter of adding another set of tasks, but rather a perspective we live out in the daily routines and evaluations we make in fulfilling our organizational mission.

Reflecting

Cultures shape our beliefs, values, and feelings in ways that deserve deep reflection, especially when we think of the implications for our organizational mission. To reflect on the influence of culture on organizations and leadership, both individually and with your coworkers, is a worthwhile exercise. These questions are intended to facilitate that reflection.

1. Think of a current issue you face as a leader, for example, a health problem afflicting one of the leaders in your organization. What human systems are impacting the situation, and how are you managing the implications?

2. How does your organization influence the worlds in which you are situated? In what ways can you as a leader increase the influence and witness of your organization at the points of intersection with broader cultural, social, or other human systems?

3. Which of the global leadership dimensions are most prevalent in the leaders with whom you associate? What are the strengths and weaknesses of each approach (e.g., participative or humane-oriented leadership)?

Considering the call to authentic intercultural friendships as leaders is a good way to conclude our reflections. Here are a few questions to guide you.

4. Who are your closest friends from other cultures? What do you know about their cultural understanding of friendship? Are you aware of the expectations they place on your relationship? Answering these questions together, both of you sharing openly, is an important exercise for both strengthening and deepening your friendship.

5. How does your work in a Christian organization affect your ability to meet and befriend non-Christians interculturally? Are there changes that would better facilitate your opportunities, and if so, how would you engage differently?

6. Do your intercultural friendships influence the way you understand and communicate the gospel? If so, are there areas that remain unexplored as part of your growth as a disciple of Christ? If not, how can you learn more from your friends?

In the final chapter, we will review what we are learning about culture, leadership, and organizations.

8

Responding Missionally

Learning into Practice

David Livermore, in his work on cultural intelligence (CQ), rightly identifies a significant problem in the literature of leadership and management that has bothered me for years. As he puts it, "Many leadership and management books give us the idea that leadership is a universal skill set that works the same everywhere . . . but it just doesn't jive with the realities of leadership in today's multifaceted, globalized world."[1] This idea of a universal model is borne out of the same desire for predictability seen in the nature-versus-nurture controversy resulting from cognitive studies, discussed in chapter 2. While it would be very helpful to find one approach or one universal set of skills that would solve all our problems as leaders, the worlds in which we live are just too complex. Our goal should be not a single approach, but rather to accept the challenge and privilege of learning as a lifelong quest to better understand the worlds God places us in and calls us to serve missionally. In the words of theologian Veli-Matti Kärkkäinen, "Christian faith proposes

1. David A. Livermore, *Leading with Cultural Intelligence: The Real Secret to Success*, 2nd ed. (New York: AMACOM Books, 2015), ix. Both this book and his volume *Cultural Intelligence: Improving Your CQ to Engage Our Multicultural World* (Grand Rapids: Baker Academic, 2009) are important resources for leaders and members of organizations working interculturally.

a solid, historically based but also history-transcending hope based on the faithfulness of God, who raised from the dead the crucified Son in the power of the Spirit."[2]

The purpose of this book is to help us explore what we are learning about culture and how it applies to Christian leaders of organizations serving God's mission. Each of the preceding chapters explores areas relevant for leaders and organizations. In choosing topics, I considered the significance of the scholarship surrounding each topic and the influence that the topic had on the missional work of organizations. I was particularly concerned to address issues as they relate to the intersection of culture, human nature, individuals, and collectives. The hard work of selecting and writing will be complemented by the hard work you do in reflecting on the implications for your organizational mission as it is enfolded into the mission of God. If we are to continue to grow in our understanding as Christian leaders, we need to build on these cultural insights.

This final chapter reviews what we are learning about culture, leadership, and organizations, and draws out the implications for each major topic. The underlying assumption of my work here is that fundamentally our calling as Christian leaders is to respond missionally. To guide us, I will discuss the topics as they arose in the preceding seven chapters, drawing from the questions in the reflecting section at the end of each chapter and applying the insights to our task as leaders. The goal here is to apply what we are learning about culture to help shape, catalyze, and propel our organizations missionally.

Thinking Missiologically

Thinking missiologically requires us to consider not only our individual calling in light of God's mission, but also the mission of our particular organization. As followers of Christ, we acknowledge our call to God's mission of bringing redemption and reconciliation to the world through the presence and power of the Holy Spirit. It is God's mission from beginning to end. We submit to the authority of Scripture as the norm for understanding and critiquing all realities. In turn, we must be aware of the historical and theological implications of the work we do and why we do it. Through the process we must remind ourselves that culture is a missiological constant, requiring careful attention to the contexts in which we serve. Acknowledging that God works with particular people in particular places as part of God's creation and the object of God's redemptive purpose, Christians from across the globe move forward to take "the whole gospel to the whole world."

As leaders, we are aware that some decisions are momentous for the mission of our organizations. Generally, these decisions are very seriously considered and, depending on the scale, they may involve careful research and consideration at the highest level of organizational governance. From experience, I know that the process will also involve considering issues such as the missional nature of the potential actions, as well as being concerned about whether our mission is drifting because we're overextending our resources and personnel. Whether the enthusiasm for a new initiative carries it through or the concerns dissuade us from the project in favor of concentrating on the core mission, the processes are normally in place to guard the organizational mission. A good rule for leaders is to approach missional decisions from the perspective of exchange, determining which of the possibilities will best align with the organizational mission and, in the majority of cases, what current commitments will be replaced by this new or renewed initiative.

A concern that is highlighted by what we are learning about culture involves the decisions that are more common and seemingly less momentous. The routine decisions that are smaller in scale but more frequent effectively shape the organizational culture. That culture is shaped, for example, by the regular personnel decisions assigning individuals to locations with specific duties and preparation to assume an organizational role. When asked about personnel decisions, most leaders will acknowledge that they are among our most significant missional responsibilities. Yet in practice, factors such as the immediacy of the need or limited resources prohibiting either a more thorough search or more extensive training lead to decisions on the basis of availability and expediency. The role of providence should not be discounted in our actions, but neither should it be used to justify precipitous actions. As a dear friend used to say, "Hope is not a strategy!"

As leaders, we must continually reassess our approach to decision-making in light of our organization's principles and practices and, more importantly, in light of our mission. We must ask how our decisions, principles, and practices support our organizational mission, and in doing so we must remain committed to strengthen or change those decisions, principles, and practices that are no longer missionally appropriate. Our understanding of God's mission of redemption and reconciliation provides a realistic frame of reference for considering each of the elements of our organization in light of its contribution to the mission. Often the presenting need for revising our practice comes from significant cultural and systemic changes in the worlds in which we work. Wycliffe Bible Translators shifted its mission significantly in response to changes in vernacular language use and technology-assisted translation practices. Seminaries, in adjusting to online education due to changing demands for theological and missiological education, are also shifting practice and refocusing their organizational mission. A careful review of the cultural context should be an integral part of every decision. To make more accurate decisions, decision makers should consider input from diverse sources and, wherever possible, acknowledge that the participants themselves are representative of that diversity. We do this because culture is a missiological constant.

For example, an organization with a history of working with the poor may choose a simple lifestyle that fits well with the local people. One of the biggest challenges for intercultural workers who cross socioeconomic barriers from more affluent contexts is finding a sustainable lifestyle that identifies as closely as possible with the local population. The missional significance of this issue is supported by studies of the incarnational model of ministry that positively correlate with the receptivity of people in evangelism and church planting.[3] In my experience, as leaders we should prayerfully select the lifestyle of workers based on the location of service, approaching with both discernment and input from local leaders wherever possible.[4] As Andrew Walls observes, "Christianity is . . . an ongoing dialogue with culture."[5]

As we reassess our principles and practices, we should also reassess how we approach our mission biblically and theologically. Organizations serving God's mission should regularly read the Bible missiologically and reflect theologically on how others have responded to similar situations. Ask yourself, What have I learned from the response of Christians to a significant issue facing my organization? How is our mission reflective of "the mission of God to bring about the redemption of the world"?[6] Establishing a regular opportunity to think missiologically with specific expectations for the outcome of the study is more than a good discipline; it is vital to leading an organization missionally.

---

3. Paul G. Hiebert and Eloise Hiebert Meneses, *Incarnational Ministry: Planting Churches in Band, Tribal, Peasant, and Urban Societies* (Grand Rapids: Baker Academic, 1996).

4. E.g., given the expenses of an urban lifestyle—accommodation, modes of transportation, recreation, clothing, childhood education—a local high school teacher could afford a median lifestyle as a city dweller. In other cases, living in a shanty town or squatter settlement provides an incarnational presence that reduces the lifestyle barriers. Organizational practice is a critical element and one that requires careful consideration, as evidenced in the case of the Numa family in chapter 2.

5. Andrew F. Walls, *The Missionary Movement in Christian History: Studies in the Transmission of Faith* (Maryknoll, NY: Orbis Books, 1996), xvii.

6. Scott W. Sunquist, *Understanding Christian Mission: Participation in Suffering and Glory* (Grand Rapids: Baker Academic, 2013), 7.

Finally, it is wise to periodically seek the records or reports of past actions that have significantly impacted your organization, either in shaping the culture, catalyzing significant new responses, or propelling you forward missionally. You can do this by assigning the task to a team, preferably rotating the members to widen the base of understanding. The team can interview those who were involved in the situation or ask them to respond to questions in writing. Any written histories are also helpful, such as those that consider various periods in history, as they will direct you to more contextual histories to supplement what you find through oral history.[7] Once you are confident that you have an accurate picture, gather the leaders to consider the implications and celebrate the history. If such an event is already part of the calendar, so much the better. The goal is to turn your eyes collectively toward God with thanksgiving in recognition of God's faithfulness and to set a precedent for your leadership.

Human Contexts

Every culture, by its very nature, has a distinct worldview with unique characteristics that regulate the way people think, act, and feel. The result is a shared way of life that explains reality according to the particular group. As we observed in chapter 2, important new insights from cognitive studies are adding to our understanding by considering the physical nature of human beings as well as their cultural contexts. The interdependency of human nature and culture, sometimes referred to as nature and nurture, most accurately identifies humans as embodied beings who are also embedded in their specific context. With that in mind, what does it mean for us?

We're learning, for example, how individuals experience and store cultural representations as mental representations. The mind of an individual may contain a vast number of these, each resembling an object or symbol. These are not exact replicas of the actual object or symbol; instead, they are encountered as public representations through the senses (sight, smell, sound, taste, touch) as transformed by the process into mental representations. Consequently, there are likely as many opinions about what something is or does as there are people. Thus, to understand the culture, you need to seek many sources of information and look for similarities and patterns in the information.

A leader needs to provide the organization's members with opportunities to participate actively in dialogue. Human knowledge comes from a combination of innate capacity, individual interaction with the environment,

---

7. E.g., Scott W. Sunquist, *The Unexpected Christian Century: The Reversal and Transformation of Global Christianity* (Grand Rapids: Baker Academic, 2015).

and interpersonal communication. If we fail to provide sufficient time and resources for this interaction, we not only undermine the learning process but also underestimate the value of human ingenuity as a gift from God. Culture-making is an active process of observing, transforming, and transmitting cultural representations. Each member of the organization depends on mental schemas for understanding and participating in the mission. This also means that all members are active participants in developing the acquired schemas representing the knowledge base of the organization. We do well as leaders to carefully review our approach to our human resources and make the appropriate changes in order to truly empower members.

It follows that using symbols and frequently referring to them is integral to establishing and maintaining an organizational identity. It is also important to make sure the historical use of the statement or symbol does not conjure up images or events that are actually counterproductive. For example, in a conversation I had with a group of pastors from the Balkans, they reflected on the historical use of the cross by various groups, including the armies of the Crusades and, more recently, those who invaded Kosovo displaying the Serbian Orthodox cross. The process of considering the contextual issues demonstrates the significance of historical and contemporary elements of culture as it is embodied and embedded in and through us as human beings. The insights from cognitive studies give us a new appreciation for the interdependence of culture and human nature.

Members and Others as People

The notion of "self" aids our understanding of culture as a total way of life of a group of people, made up of individuals. Anyone working interculturally must devote significant time to understanding the individual and collective narratives of the people. This principle applies equally to the people your organization serves and the members you lead. You can hear these narratives in many settings, especially in conversations relating to hospitality, such as a lunch gathering, an evening in a family home, or an informal gathering in a park or community center. If you cultivate the practice of listening to others, you will hone important communication skills, including your ability to ask questions and to discern when to be silent and when to share your own story. Try to communicate a caring attitude in ways that are contextually appropriate, likely respecting gender and generational factors. People don't always need to tell a story, but effectively communicating that you are willing to listen strengthens your member care.

The same is true for those who are the focus of your mission. For example, experience with humanitarian crises demonstrates that people react to physical deprivation at the level of their core selves and at the minimal level of self, reacting in time and space. They do not necessarily respond in culturally consistent ways. So organizations initially must deal with the physical needs, plus the fear, hostility, and uncertainty generated by the crisis. However, leaders must also be aware from the beginning of the role of the narrative self, that is, the ability to perceive oneself in relation to the world with memory of the individual story. We noted that the story of life is important to every individual, even if they do not readily share it with others. To see individuals and groups as important is to take the time to listen to and get to know their stories. Thus we must always recognize the dignity and history of the people.

Generally, an important part of a person's story is their faith tradition or that of their community. Exercising sensitivity to the context is important for knowing how to share your faith with others. In my own experience, caring for the immediate concerns of a person or group builds trust and will open the door to conversations at deeper levels, such as sharing your faith. Again, the work of Evelyne Reisacher is helpful to our understanding of witness and evangelism.[8]

We should also consider contextually appropriate ways to express empathy. The process of "reciprocal attunement," or sharing emotions, is bidirectional and extremely important, particularly when one moves from an individualist society to a more collectivist society. I remember once falling off my motorcycle in the highlands of Papua New Guinea. I was scraped up and feeling both embarrassed and in pain. A group of local men waited to see if I would get up and then burst into laughter. It caught me off guard, but I soon found myself laughing heartily along with them. I later confirmed that the response was the most empathetic, since it took away the shame of the incident and allowed each of them to express "empathy" Melanesian style. I am not suggesting that this response is normative, only that what constitutes an empathetic response may well be unique to your area. As a leader, work on your ability to empathize with others, and make it a regular topic for discussion within your organization. Empathy is also a key to building bridges to other cultures and people, showing genuine interest in, and learning from, the differences. In the end, it is a very effective expression of love, critical to the role and responsibility that individuals have in creating culture.

8. See Evelyne A. Reisacher, *Joyful Witness in the Muslim World: Sharing the Gospel in Everyday Encounters* (Grand Rapids: Baker Academic, 2016). Another helpful resource on the topic of evangelism is Paul Wesley Chilcote and Laceye C. Warner, *The Study of Evangelism: Exploring a Missional Practice of the Church* (Grand Rapids: Eerdmans, 2008).

Learning Culture Naturally

Learning naturally is not a goal; it is a reality. As we noted in chapter 4, the vast majority of cultural learning takes place at the level of imitation. Formal language studies build on the principle of imitation through listening and repetition, but the principle also applies to nearly every area of learning culture. With as little delay as possible, intercultural workers should cultivate the ability to observe and practice—to practice participant observation, studying culture by learning from people through the cycle of participating, observing, and reflecting. It sounds simple, and it is. The value is in its effectiveness as a discipline that enables the learner to achieve naturalness in relating to others. The discipline can work with any type of repetitive behavior, such as learning to drive in the city, but it isn't limited to that. Watch the way respected leaders speak to people, conduct meetings, dress, sit, or stand, since many leadership behaviors can be learned through imitation. Remembering the details is critical, so practicing frequently and writing down those observations for further reflection, if applicable, is essential.

People also imitate unconsciously; we readily observe this in children at play. They pick up language, gestures, games, and a range of behaviors at a pace that makes adults envious. We also make adjustments as we grow in understanding, as one discovers when initial relationships become trusted friendships. The result is new insights into a deeper level of culture learning. One of the most helpful skills is the ability to laugh at yourself when you make a mistake. A leadership axiom I often quote is, "Be a leader who makes new mistakes." Try to learn from each mistake, but don't let it stop you. As you work with other leaders, extend to them the same privilege of learning. And remember to choose wisely whom to imitate, since imitation can lead to bad habits too.

Learning the whole range of rituals is an interesting process for leaders and members of the organization. This includes the various types of rituals within an organization, as we saw in chapter 4, as well as those in the wider societal, religious, or subcultural worlds. There is no better way to learn the culture of rituals than to participate in them. Don't limit your experience to church-related events; determine what are good events or rituals that are part of the societal culture, and practice participant observation. Also remember the advice from 1 Corinthians 10:23–33 regarding not giving offense. It is best to talk to the elders in the local fellowship or other leaders in a given context to determine the shared understanding of what is appropriate. That will change as your organization learns more about the culture, but initially it is best not to move beyond the consciences of the local believers and those you serve.

Authority and Trust

Newly appointed leaders often struggle to know the limits of their authority, which is a very natural experience, as we saw in chapter 5. It becomes more complicated if there is no period of transition for learning from the previous leaders what is expected and the nature of authority. In the context of a group that is closer in age to the leader, it is best to work toward a team-oriented or participative approach, identified in the global research project described in chapter 7. That will likely work for those in your own organization, at least initially. When the circumstances surrounding the exercise of authority are extreme, you will have to judge how best to act in the situation. Some situations may require more formal authority, such as governmental relations or interorganizational negotiations. In that case, it is wise to ask those with more experience, if time and circumstances allow.

In the long term, exercising authority is a critical part of leadership development. A leader's style will directly impact the way she or he handles authority. It is important to keep the elements of responsibility and accountability in mind, as they are necessary in any style the leader develops. Remember that the style of the leader should adapt wherever possible to the needs or maturity of the followers. As we noted from Bass's work, followers expect those in authority to act responsibly in ways that link their actions and words.[9]

Surprisingly, research on leadership has taught us that silence is important in exercising authority. Don't be a leader who has to fill the silence, especially in intercultural contexts. You can practice silence in your role in a ritual or in a meeting while listening and considering the options. However, although respect is often equated with the willingness to listen, leadership also requires the ability to act decisively, exercising the authority of the position. Learn to keep these two in tension. There really is no such thing as balance in the pressures of leading Christian organizations. We must be able to pull hard in whatever direction without letting go of other important things.

As we noted in chapter 5, trust is the other side of the coin. From experience, I know that trust is usually given as a gift of grace at the beginning; you may suffer occasional and painful exceptions, but in general you start with a small but important reservoir of trust. Then you earn or lose it as you grow in your leadership. Even after many years in leadership positions, I find that trust is not uniformly distributed across the organization. It depends on both macro- and micro-level issues in intercultural settings. I wish it were different

9. Bernard M. Bass with Ruth Bass, *The Handbook of Leadership: Theory, Research, and Managerial Applications*, 4th ed. (New York: Free Press, 2008), 360–61.

and that a specific approach would protect your trust, but apart from daily vigilance you can't do much to change the dynamics. Don't be discouraged: as leaders who are primarily followers of Christ, we can ask God for wisdom and discernment confidently. It is wise to become a student of trust interculturally. Experiences of gaining and losing trust will teach you more about faith than most other experiences. In every situation, a leader should strive to be reliable (trustworthy) for those who follow.

Recognizing Worlds

Using the concept of religious worlds can be problematic with some of our constituents, especially those whose faith was harmed by studying comparative religion in college. Be discerning in how you describe or use the term "religious worlds." That's why there is a disclaimer in the first part of chapter 6. Selecting this particular category facilitates the conversation of leaders and members with outsiders—for example people of other faith traditions—in a way that builds understanding with them on the basis of our shared humanity. Finding particular categories to discuss helps us build trust and understanding. For example, asking about issues of righteousness or purity in the religious tradition of the other allows for important understandings of culture. Another example would be exploring how other religious worlds handle bereavement, a common human experience. It may be awkward at first, but no matter what the situation you find yourself in now, become a student of the major religious traditions among your neighbors. As an aside, asking if the other person can help you learn about their world is an honest place to start building the relationship. You will have to judge the receptivity to such conversations in your specific context, but maintaining a learner posture is the most acceptable approach in my experience. The case study on the five faces of Islam will be useful for you as a starting place with the diverse populations whose religious traditions influence our worlds. Whatever approach you take, ensure that you are accounting for the influence of religious worlds on the mission of your organization.

The use of "societal world," "organizational world," and "subcultural world" as a way to explore our worlds is a good approach for leaders to understand and describe culture. Try to identify the various experiences and influences according to the world in which they originate. It is often like detective work, but it does cultivate a skill we need as intercultural leaders. For now, it is best to begin with the societal culture or a subculture that is easily accessible. Once you gain more fluency, you can focus on other subcultures and societal cultures. Learning about or reviewing the history of your own organization will help you understand its organizational culture.

In my experience, organizational leaders tend to underestimate the importance of the cultural identity of their members, assuming to the detriment of the organization that everyone shares the common identity of the organization. As a result, leaders may not be sensitive to the differences, thus allowing practices that unwittingly or flagrantly discriminate against others. These types of infractions, known as microaggressions, refer to common—verbal or behavioral—indignities that insult others, particularly with regard to physical differences. Allowing these actions undermines Christian unity and stands in direct opposition to the love of God at the heart of the *missio Dei*. Again, we must own the reality that culture is a missiological constant.

Cultural Influence

Approaching humans as intersecting systems is a very good way to appreciate the contribution of cognitive science to our understanding of culture. From my colleagues in psychology I have learned the importance of embodiment and the role of cognitive development, which contributes to my knowledge of culture. This knowledge was greatly helped by studies on the notion of self. For years, my focus was group oriented, even though I lived in a highly individualistic culture, both societally in the United States and organizationally in an institution that cherishes bureaucracy (as every institution does!). The real contribution of these studies is in broadening our understanding of the influence of culture. Hiebert's observation that exegeting humans requires a system-to-systems approach has proven correct in my experience.[10]

It is worth the time it takes to consider the various systems at play in your context, even for veteran leaders. The systems that you are doubtless dealing with now—physical, social, and technological—will remain a source of concern even after you master the systemic intricacies. The ones that will quickly demand your attention are likely the social and cultural systems. As with learning in other areas, keeping a record of what you are observing for a comparative analysis will help to ground you (or refresh your thoughts) in the culture and society more quickly than a scattered approach. As leaders, even newly appointed ones, we are in a teaching role, with all the responsibilities and accountability that accompany our authority. Take time to understand and to ask questions. If it disturbs people with whom you work, pull out your

10. Paul G. Hiebert, *The Gospel in Human Contexts: Anthropological Explorations for Contemporary Missions* (Grand Rapids: Baker Academic, 2009), 133.

notes and share what you are learning. From my experience, it is amazing how much you can learn by this approach and how receptive others are to engage with you.

The reason I included some findings from the GLOBE project was to introduce you as leaders to an important and ongoing resource. The scholars working on the project, doubtless including many from your area, are working on the intersection of culture, leadership, and organizations. You should avail yourself of their work as soon as you are able. Additionally, begin to use the recognized categories in your reports and with your colleagues. We too often use leadership literature in an uncritical way that actually moves us away from the principles of contextualization. Remember that part of your job will inevitably impact the schemas of practice that are developed within your organization and likely in the churches as well. It is a real privilege to serve in an intercultural context.

As we come to the end of this book, it is important to acknowledge once again that in our roles as leaders, we are responsible for and accountable to our organization and its mission. We are entrusted by God's people to serve faithfully and to be reliable witnesses. But above all, we serve the mission of God not, fundamentally, as leaders, but as followers of Christ. We remember his words, "Peace be with you. As the Father has sent me, so I send you" (John 20:21). So we pray together for wisdom and discernment to the Triune God: Father, Son, and Holy Spirit.

Index